W9-BTP-453

Adobe
Photoshop CC
2019 release

CLASSROOM IN A BOOK®
The official training workbook from Adobe

Andrew Faulkner & Conrad Chavez

WHERE ARE THE LESSON FILES?

Purchase of this Classroom in a Book in any format gives you access to the lesson files you'll need to complete the exercises in the book.

You'll find the files you need on your **Account** page at peachpit.com on the **Registered Products** tab.

1   Go to www.peachpit.com/register.

2   Sign in or create a new account.

3   Enter the ISBN: 9780135261781

4   Answer the questions as proof of purchase.

5   The lesson files can be accessed through the Registered Products tab on your Account page.

6   Click the Access Bonus Content link below the title of your product to proceed to the download page. Click the lesson file links to download them to your computer.

CONTENTS

GETTING STARTED

Adobe® Photoshop® CC, the benchmark for digital imaging excellence, provides strong performance, powerful image editing features, and an intuitive interface. Adobe Camera Raw, included with Photoshop CC, offers flexibility and control as you work with raw images as well as TIFF and JPEG images. Photoshop CC gives you the digital editing tools you need to transform images more easily than ever before.

About Classroom in a Book

Adobe Photoshop CC Classroom in a Book® (2019 release) is part of the official training series for Adobe graphics and publishing software, developed with the support of Adobe product experts. The lessons are designed to let you learn at your own pace. If you're new to Adobe Photoshop, you'll learn the fundamental concepts and features you'll need to master the program. And if you've been using Adobe Photoshop for a while, you'll find that Classroom in a Book teaches many advanced features, including tips and techniques for using the latest version of the application and preparing images for the web.

Although each lesson provides step-by-step instructions for creating a specific project, there's room for exploration and experimentation. You can follow the book from start to finish, or do only the lessons that match your interests and needs. Each lesson concludes with a review section summarizing what you've covered.

What's new in this edition

This edition covers new features in Adobe Photoshop CC, such as removing objects with upgraded Content-Aware Fill, creating placeholders with the new Frame tool, designing reflected and radial art using Paint Symmetry, correcting mistakes with the updated Undo feature, saving time with simplified transformations (such as scaling and rotating layers), and using the redesigned Home screen.

This edition is also chock-full of extra information on Photoshop features and how to work effectively with this robust and professional application. You'll learn best practices for organizing, managing, and showcasing your photos, as well as how to optimize images for the web. And throughout this edition, look for tips and techniques from one of Adobe's own experts, Photoshop evangelist Julieanne Kost.

Prerequisites

Before you begin to use *Adobe Photoshop CC Classroom in a Book (2019 release)*, you should have a working knowledge of your computer and its operating system. Make sure that you know how to use the mouse and standard menus and commands, and also how to open, save, and close files. If you need to review these techniques, see the documentation for your Microsoft® Windows® PC or Apple® Mac® computer.

To complete the lessons in this book, you'll need to have both Adobe Photoshop CC (2019 release) and Adobe Bridge CC 2019 installed.

Installing Adobe Photoshop and Adobe Bridge

Before you begin using *Adobe Photoshop CC Classroom in a Book (2019 release)*, make sure that your system is set up correctly and that you've installed the required software and hardware. You must license the Adobe Photoshop CC software separately. For system requirements and complete instructions on installing the software, visit helpx.adobe.com/photoshop/system-requirements.html. Note that some Photoshop CC features, including all 3D features, require at least 512MB of VRAM (graphics memory), and in Windows a 64-bit operating system is required.

Many of the lessons in this book use Adobe Bridge. You must install Photoshop and Bridge on your computer using the Adobe Creative Cloud desktop application, available at adobe.com/creativecloud/desktop-app.html. Follow the onscreen instructions.

Starting Adobe Photoshop

You start Photoshop just as you do most software applications.

To start Adobe Photoshop in Windows: Click the Start button in the taskbar, and in the alphabetical list under A, click Adobe Photoshop CC 2019.

To start Adobe Photoshop in Mac: Click the Adobe Photoshop CC 2019 icon in the Launchpad or Dock.

If you don't see Adobe Photoshop CC, type **Photoshop** into the search box in the taskbar (Windows) or in Spotlight (Mac), and when the Adobe Photoshop CC 2019 application icon appears, select it, and press Enter or Return.

Online content

Your purchase of this Classroom in a Book includes online materials provided by way of your Account page on peachpit.com. These include:

Lesson Files

To work through the projects in this book, you will need to download the lesson files from peachpit.com. You can download the files for individual lessons, or it may be possible to download them all in a single file.

Web Edition

The Web Edition is an online interactive version of the book, providing an enhanced learning experience. Your Web Edition can be accessed from any device with a connection to the Internet, and it contains:

* The complete text of the book
* Hours of instructional video keyed to the text
* Interactive quizzes

In addition, the Web Edition may be updated when Adobe adds significant feature updates between major Creative Cloud releases. To accommodate the changes, sections of the online book may be updated or new sections may be added.

Accessing the Lesson Files and Web Edition

If you purchased an eBook from peachpit.com or adobepress.com, your Web Edition will automatically appear under the Digital Purchases tab on your Account page. Click the Launch link to access the product. Continue reading to learn how to register your product to get access to the lesson files.

If you purchased an eBook from a different vendor or you bought a print book, you must **register** your purchase on peachpit.com in order to access the online content:

1 Go to www.peachpit.com/register.
2 Sign in or create a new account.
3 Enter the ISBN: **9780135261781**.
4 Answer the questions as proof of purchase.
5 The **Web Edition** will appear under the Digital Purchases tab on your Account page. Click the **Launch** link to access the product.

The **Lesson Files** can be accessed through the Registered Products tab on your Account page. Click the Access Bonus Content link below the title of your product to proceed to the download page. Click the lesson file links to download them to your computer.

● **Note:** As you complete each lesson, you may want to keep your start files. In case you overwrite them, you can restore the original files by downloading the corresponding lesson files from your Account page at peachpit.com.

Restoring default preferences

The preferences file stores information about panel and command settings. Each time you quit Adobe Photoshop, the positions of the panels and certain command settings are recorded in the preferences file. Any selections you make in the Preferences dialog box are also saved in the preferences file.

To ensure that what you see onscreen matches the images and instructions in this book, you should restore the default preferences as you begin each lesson. If you prefer to preserve your preferences, be aware that the tools, panels, and other settings in Photoshop CC may not match those described in this book.

If you have customized your color settings, use the following procedure to save them as a preset before you start work in this book. When you want to restore your color settings, you can simply select the preset you created.

To save your current color settings:

1   Start Adobe Photoshop.

2   Choose Edit > Color Settings.

3   Note what is selected in the Settings menu:

   • If it is anything other than Custom, write down the name of the settings file, and click OK to close the dialog box. You do not need to perform steps 4–6 of this procedure.

   • If Custom is selected in the Settings menu, click Save (*not* OK).

The Save dialog box opens. The default location is the Settings folder, which is where you want to save your file. The default filename extension is .csf (color settings file).

4   In the File Name field (Windows) or Save As field (Mac), type a descriptive name for your color settings, preserving the .csf file extension. Then click Save.

5   In the Color Settings Comment dialog box, type any descriptive text that will help you identify the color settings later, such as the date, specific settings, or your workgroup.

6   Click OK to close the Color Settings Comment dialog box, and again to close the Color Settings dialog box.

To restore your color settings:

1   Start Adobe Photoshop.

2   Choose Edit > Color Settings.

3   From the Settings menu in the Color Settings dialog box, choose the settings file you noted or saved in the previous procedure, and click OK.

Additional resources

Adobe Photoshop CC Classroom in a Book (2019 release) is not meant to replace documentation that comes with the program or to be a comprehensive reference for every feature. Only the commands and options used in the lessons are explained in this book. For comprehensive information about program features and tutorials, refer to these resources:

Adobe Photoshop Help and Support: helpx.adobe.com/support/photoshop.html is where you can find and browse Help and Support content on Adobe.com. You can go there directly from Photoshop by choosing Help > Photoshop Help.

Home screen: In Photoshop, the Home screen contains a Learn link to featured tutorials on the web. You'll see the Learn link in the list along the left side.

Learn panel: Choose Window > Learn to open interactive tutorials that load sample files into Photoshop and lead you step by step through fundamental skills and features. (If Photoshop is displaying the Home screen, click the Ps icon in the top left corner to be able to open the Learn panel.)

Photoshop tutorials: helpx.adobe.com/photoshop/tutorials.html lists online tutorials for beginner and experienced users. You can go there directly from Photoshop by choosing Help > Tutorials.

Photoshop blog: theblog.adobe.com/creative-cloud/photoshop/ brings you tutorials, product news, and inspirational articles about using Photoshop.

Julieanne Kost's blog: blogs.adobe.com/jkost/ is where Adobe product evangelist Julieanne Kost posts useful tips and videos that introduce and provide valuable insights on the latest Photoshop features.

Adobe Forums: forums.adobe.com lets you tap into peer-to-peer discussions, questions, and answers on Adobe products.

Adobe Photoshop CC product home page: adobe.com/products/photoshop.html

Adobe Add-ons: www.adobeexchange.com/creativecloud.html is a central resource for finding tools, services, extensions, code samples, and more to supplement and extend your Adobe Creative Cloud tools.

Resources for educators: adobe.com/education and edex.adobe.com offer a treasure trove of information for instructors who teach classes on Adobe software. Find solutions for education at all levels, including free curricula that use an integrated approach to teaching Adobe software and can be used to prepare for the Adobe Certified Associate exams.

Adobe Authorized Training Centers

Adobe Authorized Training Centers offer instructor-led courses and training on Adobe products.

A directory of AATCs is available at training.adobe.com/training/partner-finder.html.

1 GETTING TO KNOW THE WORK AREA

Lesson overview

In this lesson, you'll learn how to do the following:

- Open image files in Adobe Photoshop.

- Select and use tools in the Tools panel.

- Set options for a selected tool using the options bar.

- Use various methods to zoom in to and out from an image.

- Select, rearrange, and use panels.

- Choose commands in panel and context menus.

- Open and use a panel in the panel dock.

- Undo actions to correct mistakes or to make different choices.

This lesson will take about an hour to complete. Please log in to your account on peachpit.com to download the lesson files for this chapter, or go to the Getting Started section at the beginning of this book and follow the instructions under "Accessing the Lesson Files and Web Edition."

As you work on this lesson, you'll preserve the start files. If you need to restore the start files, download them from your Account page.

PROJECT: BIRTHDAY CARD DESIGN

As you work with Adobe Photoshop, you'll discover that you can often accomplish the same task in several ways. To make the best use of the extensive editing capabilities in Photoshop, you must first learn to navigate the work area.

Starting to work in Adobe Photoshop

The Adobe Photoshop work area includes menus, toolbars, and panels that give you quick access to a variety of tools and options for editing and adding elements to your image. You can also add commands and filters to the menus by installing third-party software known as plug-ins.

In Photoshop, you primarily work with bitmapped digital images (continuous-tone images that have been converted into a series of small squares, or picture elements, called *pixels*). You can also work with vector graphics, which are drawings made of smooth lines that retain their crispness when scaled. You can create original artwork in Photoshop, or you can import images from many sources, such as:

- Photographs from a digital camera or mobile phone
- Stock photography, such as images from the Adobe Stock service
- Scans of photographs, transparencies, negatives, graphics, or other documents
- Captured video images
- Artwork created in drawing programs

Starting Photoshop and opening a file

● **Note:** Typically, you won't need to reset defaults when you're working on your own projects. However, you'll reset the preferences before working on most lessons in this book to ensure that what you see onscreen matches the descriptions in the lessons. For more information, see "Restoring Default Preferences" on page 5.

To begin, you'll start Adobe Photoshop and reset the default preferences.

1 Click the Adobe Photoshop CC 2019 icon in your Start menu (Windows) or the Launchpad or Dock (Mac), and then immediately hold down Ctrl+Alt+Shift (Windows) or Command+Option+Shift (Mac) to reset the default settings.

If you don't see Adobe Photoshop CC 2019, type **Photoshop** into the search box in the taskbar (Windows) or in Spotlight (Mac), and when the Adobe Photoshop CC 2019 application icon appears, select it, and press Enter or Return.

2 When prompted, click Yes to confirm that you want to delete the Adobe Photoshop Settings file.

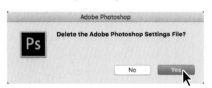

In Photoshop, the Home screen appears as shown in the following illustration.

A —
B —
C —
D —
E —
F —

G —
H —

A. *Exit to Photoshop*
B. *Home screen content*
C. *Learn in-app tutorials*
D. *Lightroom CC photos*
E. *Create new document*
F. *Open document*
G. *Search*
H. *Creative Cloud profile*

When you start Photoshop, it displays the Home screen, which gives you a number of ways to get started. If you already know what you want to do, you can click the Photoshop icon in the upper left corner to go straight to the Photoshop application workspace.

The Search icon in the upper right corner is useful in three ways: Click it to enter text which Photoshop will use to find content in your synced Lightroom CC photos, in Adobe Stock images, and in Learn tutorials about Photoshop.

To the left, you see a list of view options and buttons:

- **Home** presents informative content about the current version, including a tour. When you upgrade to a new version of Photoshop, this screen may include information about new features and changes. There is a drop zone in the bottom right corner where you can drag and drop a document to open it in Photoshop, but you can actually drop a document anywhere within the Home screen to open it. After you've opened at least one document, you'll see recently opened files in the Home screen.

- **Learn** presents links to a range of tutorials that open in Photoshop, where the Learn panel leads you through the steps for each lesson using actual Photoshop controls.

- **LR Photos** lists images synced to your Creative Cloud account's Lightroom CC online photo storage.

3 Choose File > Open, and navigate to the Lessons/Lesson01 folder that you copied to your hard drive from the peachpit.com website. (If you haven't downloaded the files, see "Accessing the Lesson Files and Web Edition" on page 4.)

4 Select the 01End.psd file, and click Open. Click OK if the Embedded Profile Mismatch dialog box appears, and click No if a message about updating text layers appears.

● **Note:** The Home screen may have a different appearance depending on the width of the Photoshop application window, or if you're using a trial version of Photoshop.

The 01End.psd file opens in its own window, in the default Photoshop workspace. The end files in this book show you what you are creating in each project. In this project, you'll create a birthday card.

A. *Menu bar*
B. *Options bar*
C. *Exit to home screen*
D. *Tools panel*
E. *In-app search*
F. *Share an Image button*
G. *Workspaces menu*
H. *Panels*

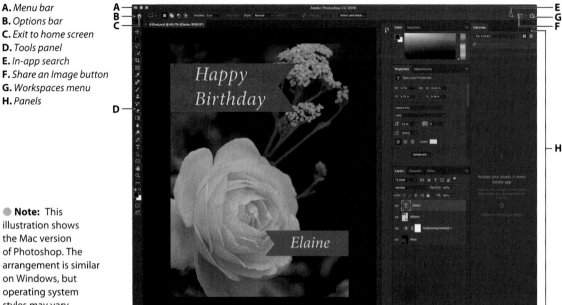

● **Note:** This illustration shows the Mac version of Photoshop. The arrangement is similar on Windows, but operating system styles may vary.

The default workspace in Photoshop consists of the menu bar and options bar at the top of the screen, the Tools panel on the left, and several open panels in the panel dock on the right. When you have documents open, one or more image windows also appear, and you can display them at the same time using the tabbed interface. The Photoshop user interface is very similar to the one in Adobe Illustrator® and Adobe InDesign®, so learning how to use the tools and panels in one application means that you'll be familiar with them when you work in the others.

There is one main difference between the Photoshop work area on Windows and that on the Mac: Windows always presents Photoshop in a contained window. On the Mac, you can choose whether to work with an application frame, which contains the Photoshop document windows and panels within a frame that is distinct from other applications you may have open; only the menu bar is outside the application frame. The application frame is enabled by default; to disable the application frame, choose Window > Application Frame, but note that the illustrations in this book are created with the application frame enabled.

5 Choose File > Close, or click the close button (the x next to the filename) on the title bar of the image window. (Do not close Photoshop.) Notice that the filename was added to the Recent Files list in the Start workspace.

Using the tools

Photoshop provides an integrated set of tools for producing sophisticated graphics for print, web, and mobile viewing. We could easily fill the entire book with details on the wealth of Photoshop tools and tool configurations. While that would certainly be a useful reference, it's not the goal of this book. Instead, you'll start gaining experience by configuring and using a few tools on a sample project. Every lesson will introduce you to more tools and ways to use them. By the time you finish all the lessons in this book, you'll have a solid foundation for further explorations of the Photoshop toolset.

Selecting and using a tool from the Tools panel

The Tools panel is the long, narrow panel on the far left side of the work area. It contains selection tools, painting and editing tools, foreground- and background-color selection boxes, and viewing tools.

● **Note:** For a complete list of the tools in the Tools panel, see the Appendix, "Tools panel overview."

You'll start by using the Zoom tool, which also appears in many other Adobe applications, including Illustrator, InDesign, and Acrobat.

1   Choose File > Open, navigate to the Lessons/Lesson01 folder, and double-click the 01Start.psd file to open it.

The 01Start.psd file contains the background image and a ribbon graphic that you'll use to create the birthday card that you viewed in the end file.

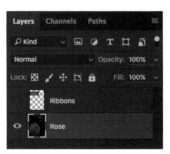

2   Click the double arrows just above the Tools panel to toggle to a double-column view. Click the double arrows again to return to a single-column Tools panel and use your screen space more efficiently.

▶ **Tip:** You can customize the Tools panel by arranging, removing, and adding tools. To do this, hold down the Edit Toolbar icon just below the Zoom tool, and choose Edit Toolbar.

3 Examine the status bar at the bottom of the work area (Windows) or image window (Mac), and notice the percentage that appears on the far left. This represents the current enlargement view of the image, or zoom level.

4 Move the pointer over the Tools panel, and hover it over the magnifying-glass icon until a tool tip appears. The tool tip displays the tool's name (Zoom tool) and keyboard shortcut (Z).

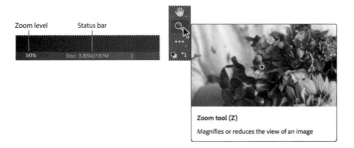

Zoom tool (Z)
Magnifies or reduces the view of an image

5 Click the Zoom tool icon (🔍) in the Tools panel, or press Z to select it.

6 Move the pointer over the image window. The pointer now looks like a tiny magnifying glass with a plus sign in the center of the glass (🔍).

7 Click anywhere in the image window.

The image enlarges to a preset percentage level, which replaces the previous value in the status bar. If you click again, the zoom advances to the next preset level, up to a maximum of 12800%.

8 Hold down the Alt key (Windows) or Option key (Mac) so that the Zoom tool pointer appears with a minus sign in the center of the magnifying glass (🔍), and then click anywhere in the image. Then release the Alt or Option key.

Now the view zooms out to a lower preset magnification, so that you can see more of the image, but in less detail.

Note: You can use other methods to zoom in and out. For example, when the Zoom tool is selected, you can select the Zoom In or Zoom Out mode on the options bar. You can choose View > Zoom In or View > Zoom Out. Or, you can type a new percentage in the status bar and press Enter or Return.

9   If Scrubby Zoom is selected in the options bar, click anywhere on the image and drag the Zoom tool to the right. The image enlarges. Drag the Zoom tool to the left to zoom out.

When Scrubby Zoom is selected, you can drag the Zoom tool across the image to zoom in and out.

10 Deselect Scrubby Zoom in the options bar if it's selected. Then, using the Zoom tool, drag a rectangle to enclose part of the rose blossom.

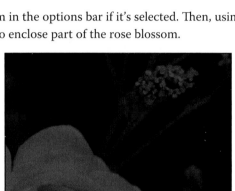

The image enlarges so that the area you enclosed in your rectangle now fills the entire image window.

11 Click Fit Screen in the options bar to see the entire image again.

You have used the Zoom tool in four different ways to change the magnification in the image window: clicking, holding down a keyboard modifier while clicking, dragging to zoom in and out, and dragging to define a magnification area. Many of the other tools in the Tools panel can be used with keyboard combinations and options as well. You'll have opportunities to use these techniques as you work through the lessons in this book.

Zooming and scrolling with the Navigator panel

The Navigator panel is another speedy way to make large changes in the zoom level, especially when the exact percentage of magnification is unimportant. It's also a great way to scroll around in an image, because the thumbnail shows you exactly what part of the image appears in the image window. To open the Navigator panel, choose Window > Navigator.

The slider under the image thumbnail in the Navigator panel enlarges the image when you drag to the right (toward the large mountain icon) and reduces it when you drag to the left.

The red rectangular outline represents the area of the image that appears in the image window. When you zoom in far enough that the image window shows only part of the image, you can drag the red outline around the thumbnail area to see other areas of the image. This is also an excellent way to verify which part of an image you're working on when you work at very high zoom levels.

Brightening an image

One of the most common edits you're likely to make is to brighten an image taken with a digital camera or phone. You'll brighten this image by changing its brightness and contrast values.

1   In the Layers panel, on the right side of the workspace, make sure the Rose layer is selected.

2 In the Adjustments panel, which is above the Layers panel in the panel dock, click the Brightness/Contrast icon to add a Brightness/Contrast adjustment layer. The Properties panel opens, displaying the Brightness/Contrast settings.

3 In the Properties panel, move the Brightness slider to **98** and the Contrast slider to **18**.

The image of the rose brightens.

In these lessons, we'll often instruct you to enter specific numbers in panels and dialog boxes to achieve particular effects. When you're working on your own projects, experiment with different values to see how they affect your image. There is no right or wrong setting; the values you should use depend on the results you want.

4 In the Layers panel, click the eye icon for the Brightness/Contrast adjustment layer to hide its effect, and then click the eye icon again to show the effect.

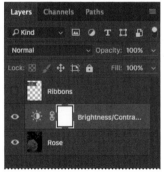

Adjustment layers let you make changes to your image, such as adjusting the brightness of the rose, without affecting the actual pixels. Because you've used an adjustment layer, you can always disable the edit by hiding or deleting the adjustment layer—and you can edit the adjustment layer at any time. You'll use adjustment layers in several lessons in this book.

Layering is one of the fundamental and most powerful features in Photoshop. Photoshop includes many kinds of layers, some of which contain images, text, or solid colors, and others that simply interact with layers below them. You'll learn more about layers in Lesson 4, "Layer Basics," and throughout the book.

5 Double-click the Properties panel tab to collapse it.

6 Choose File > Save As, name the file **01Working.psd**, and click OK or Save.

7 Click OK in the Photoshop Format Options dialog box.

Saving the file with a different name ensures that the original file (01Start.psd) remains unchanged. That way, you can return to it if you want to start over.

You've just completed your first task in Photoshop. Your image is bright and punchy and ready for a birthday card.

Sampling a color

● **Note:** When a layer mask is selected, the default foreground color is white and the default background color is black. You'll learn more about layer masks in Chapter 6.

By default, the foreground color in Photoshop is black and the background color is white. You can change the foreground and background colors in several ways. One way is to use the Eyedropper tool to sample a color from the image. You'll use the Eyedropper tool to sample the blue of one ribbon so that you can match that color when you create another ribbon.

First, you'll need to display the Ribbons layer so you can see the color you want to sample.

1 In the Layers panel, click the Visibility column for the Ribbons layer to make the layer visible. When a layer is visible, an eye icon (👁) appears in that column.

 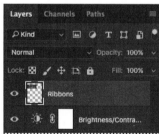

A ribbon with "Happy Birthday" written on it appears in the image window.

2 Select the Ribbons layer in the Layers panel so that it's the active layer.

3 Select the Eyedropper tool (🖋) in the Tools panel.

4 Click the blue area in the Happy Birthday ribbon to sample a blue color.

● **Note:** If you have trouble finding the Eyedropper tool, click the Search icon near the top right corner of the workspace, and type **eyedropper**. Click Eyedropper Tool in the search results; the tool will be selected in the Tools panel for you.

The foreground color changes in the Tools panel and the Color panel. Anything you draw will be this color until you change the foreground color again.

Working with tools and tool properties

When you selected the Zoom tool in the previous exercise, you saw that the options bar provided ways for you to change the view of the current image window. Now you'll learn more about setting tool properties using context menus, the options bar, panels, and panel menus. You'll use all of these methods as you work with tools to add the second ribbon to your birthday card.

Using context menus

Context menus are short menus that contain commands and options appropriate to specific elements in the work area. They are sometimes called "right-click" or "shortcut" menus. Usually, the commands on a context menu are also available in the menu bar or panel menus, but using the context menu can save time.

1 Select the Zoom tool (🔍), and zoom in so you can clearly see the lower third of the card.

2 Select the Rectangular Marquee tool (⬚) in the Tools panel.

The Rectangular Marquee tool selects rectangular areas. You'll learn more about selection tools in Lesson 3, "Working with Selections."

3   Drag the Rectangular Marquee tool to create a selection about ¾ inch tall and 2½ inches wide, ending at the right edge of the card. (See the illustration below.) As you drag the tool, Photoshop displays the width and height of the selected area. It's okay if the size of your selection is a little different from ours.

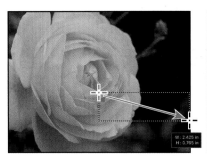 

Selection areas are shown by moving dotted lines, sometimes referred to as *marching ants*.

4   Select the Brush tool (✐) in the Tools panel.

5   In the image window, right-click (Windows) or Control-click (Mac) anywhere in the image to open the Brush tool context menu.

Context menus usually show a list of commands, but in this case, it's a pop-up panel with options for the Brush tool.

6   Click the arrow next to the General Brushes folder to expand it, select the first brush (Soft Round), and change the size to **65** pixels.

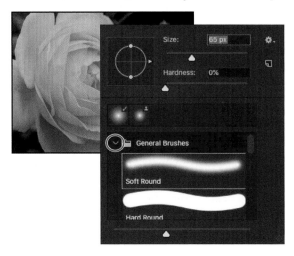

▶ **Tip:** You can also close a context menu by clicking outside it. Be careful when you click, so that you don't paint an unwanted stroke or accidentally change a setting or selection.

7   Press Enter or Return to close the context menu.

8 Drag the Brush tool across the selected area until it's fully painted blue. Don't worry about staying within the selection; you can't affect anything outside the selection as you paint.

9 When the bar is colored in, choose Select > Deselect so that nothing is selected.

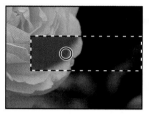 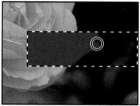 

The selection is gone, but the blue bar remains.

Selecting and using a hidden tool

The Tools panel arranges some of the tools in groups, with only one tool shown for each group. The other tools in the group are hidden behind that tool. A small triangle in the lower right corner of a button is your clue that other tools are available but hidden under that tool.

You'll use the Polygonal Lasso tool to remove a triangular notch from the color bar so that it matches the ribbon at the top of the card.

1 Position the pointer over the third tool from the top in the Tools panel until the tool tip appears. The tool tip identifies the Lasso tool (◯), with the keyboard shortcut L. Select the Lasso tool.

2 Select the Polygonal Lasso tool (◁), which is hidden behind the Lasso tool, using one of the following methods:

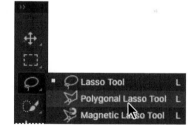

- Press and hold the mouse button over the Lasso tool to open the pop-up list of hidden tools, and select the Polygonal Lasso tool.

- Alt-click (Windows) or Option-click (Mac) the tool button in the Tools panel to cycle through the hidden lasso tools until the Polygonal Lasso tool is selected.

- Press Shift+L, which cycles between the Lasso, Polygonal Lasso, and Magnetic Lasso tools.

With the Lasso tool, you can draw free-form selections; the Polygonal Lasso tool makes it easier to draw straight-edged sections of a selection border. You'll learn more about selection tools, making selections, and adjusting the selection contents in Lesson 3, "Working with Selections."

3   Move the pointer over the left edge of the blue color bar that you just painted. Click just to the left of the upper left corner of the bar to start your selection. You should begin your selection just outside the colored area.

4   Move the cursor to the right a little more than ¼ inch, and click about halfway between the top and bottom of the bar. You're creating the first side of the triangle. It doesn't need to be perfect.

5   Click just to the left of the bottom left corner of the bar to create the second side of the triangle.

6   Click the point where you started to finish the triangle.

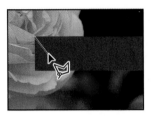

7   Press the Delete key on your keyboard to delete the selected area from the colored bar, creating a notch for your ribbon.

● **Note:** The Select menu contains Deselect and Deselect Layers commands; be mindful of which one you need to choose.

8   Choose Select > Deselect to deselect the area you deleted.

The ribbon is ready. Now you can add a name to your birthday card.

Setting tool properties in the options bar

Next, you'll use the options bar to select the text properties and then to type the name.

1   In the Tools panel, select the Horizontal Type tool (**T**).

The buttons and menus in the options bar now relate to the Type tool.

2   In the options bar, select a font you like from the first pop-up menu. (We used Minion Pro Italic, but you can use another font if you prefer.)

3   Specify **32 pt** for the font size.

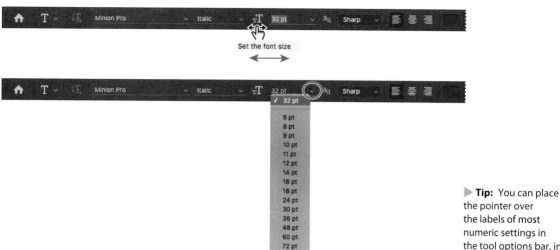

You can specify 32 points by typing directly in the font-size text box and pressing Enter or Return, or by *scrubbing* the font-size menu label (see the tip in the margin). You can also choose a standard font size from the font-size pop-up menu.

4   Click the Swatches tab to bring that panel forward, if it's not already visible, and select any light-colored swatch. (We chose Pastel Yellow.)

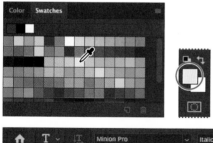

▶ **Tip:** You can place the pointer over the labels of most numeric settings in the tool options bar, in panels, and in dialog boxes in Photoshop to display a "scrubby slider." Dragging the pointing-finger slider to the right increases the value; dragging to the left decreases the value. Alt-dragging (Windows) or Option-dragging (Mac) changes the values in smaller increments; Shift-dragging changes them in larger increments.

The color you select appears in two places: as the Foreground Color in the Tools panel and in the text color swatch in the options bar. The Swatches panel is one easy way to select a color; later you'll learn other ways to select a color in Photoshop.

● **Note:** When you move the pointer over the swatches, it temporarily changes into an eyedropper. Set the tip of the eyedropper on the swatch you want, and click to select it.

5   Click the Horizontal Type Tool once anywhere on the left side of the colored bar. "Lorem Ipsum" placeholder text appears as a sample of the current type specifications. It's selected by default so that you can immediately type over it.

6   Type a name; we typed Elaine. It replaces the placeholder text. Don't worry if the text isn't positioned well; you'll correct that later.

7   Click the check mark icon in the options bar (✔) to commit the text.

While the pastel yellow looks OK, you'll now use a specific color that matches the text in the other ribbon. It's easier to find it if you change the Swatches panel display.

8   Click the menu button (≡) on the Swatches panel to open the panel menu, and choose Small List.

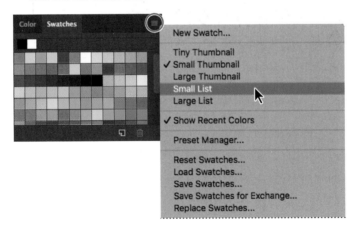

▶ **Tip:** If you want to select just some of the text in a layer, drag the Horizontal Type tool over a range of characters instead of double-clicking.

9   With the Type tool, double-click the text. The text becomes selected.

10 In the Swatches panel, scroll about halfway down the list to find the Light Yellow Orange swatch, and then select it.

11 Click the check mark button (✔) to commit and deselect the text.

Now the text appears in the orange color.

> **Tip:** You can also commit text edits by clicking outside the text layer.

Undoing actions in Photoshop

In a perfect world, you'd never make a mistake. You'd never click the wrong object. You'd always correctly anticipate how specific actions would bring your design ideas to life exactly as you imagined them. You'd never have to backtrack.

For the real world, Photoshop gives you the power to step back and undo actions so that you can try other options. You can experiment freely, knowing that you can reverse the process.

Even beginning computer users quickly come to appreciate the familiar Undo command. You'll use it to move back one step, and then step further backward. In this case, you'll go back to the light color that you originally chose for the name.

1 Choose Edit > Undo Edit Type Layer, or press Ctrl+Z (Windows) or Command+Z (Mac) to undo your last action.

The name returns to its previous color.

2 Choose Edit > Redo Edit Type Layer, or press Ctrl+Shift+Z (Windows) or Command+Shift+Z (Mac) to reapply the orange color to the name.

Undo reverses the last step.   Redo restores the undone step.

Tip: To see the steps you can undo and redo, look at the History panel (Window > History).

Each time you use the Undo command it reverses one more step, so if you want to undo five steps, you can apply the Undo command (or its keyboard shortcut) five times. The Redo command works the same way.

If you want to switch back and forth between the current and previous steps you did, choose Edit > Toggle Last State or press Ctrl+Alt+Z (Windows) or Command+Option+Z (Mac) to go back, and then choose the same command again to go forward. Applying Toggle Last State multiple times is a great way to see a before/after comparison of your last edit.

Tip: As you drag, magenta lines called *Smart Guides* may appear. They help align the edges of dragged content to other edges and guides. If they are getting in your way, you can disable them by deselecting the View > Show > Smart Guides command, or by holding down the Control key as you drag.

3 Once the name is back to the color you'd like it to be, use the Move tool (✛) to drag the name so it's centered in the blue bar.

4 Save the file. Your birthday card is done!

More about panels and panel locations

Photoshop panels are powerful and varied. Rarely would you need to see all panels simultaneously. That's why they're in panel groups, and why the default configurations leave many panels unopened.

The complete list of panels appears in the Window menu. Check marks appear next to the names of the panels that are open and active in their panel groups. You can open a closed panel or close an open one by selecting the panel name in the Window menu.

You can hide all panels at once—including the options bar and Tools panel—by pressing the Tab key. To reopen them, press Tab again.

You already used panels in the panel dock when you used the Layers and Swatches panels. You can drag panels to or from the panel dock. This is convenient for bulky panels or ones that you use only occasionally but want to keep handy.

You can arrange panels in other ways as well:

- To move an entire panel group, drag the title bar to another location in the work area.

- To move a panel to another group, drag the panel tab into that panel group so that a blue highlight appears inside the group, and then release the mouse button.

Note: When panels are hidden, a thin strip is visible at the edge of the document. Hover the pointer over the strip to temporarily reveal the panels docked along that edge.

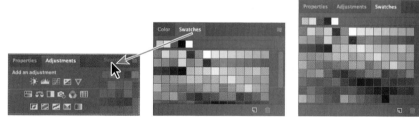

- To dock a panel or panel group, drag the title bar or panel tab onto the top of the dock.

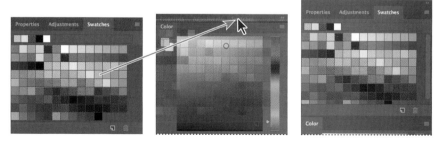

- To undock a panel or panel group so that it becomes a floating panel or panel group, drag its title bar or panel tab away from the dock.

Expanding and collapsing panels

You can resize panels to use screen space more efficiently and to see fewer or more panel options, either by dragging or clicking to toggle between preset sizes:

- To collapse open panels to icons, click the double arrow in the title bar of the dock or panel group. To expand a panel, click its icon or the double arrow.

- To change the height of a panel, drag its bottom edge.

- To change the width of a dock, position the pointer on the left edge of the dock until it becomes a double-headed arrow, and then drag to the left to widen the dock, or to the right to narrow it.

- To resize a floating panel, move the pointer over the right, left, or bottom edge of the panel until it becomes a double-headed arrow, and then drag the edge in or out. You can also pull the lower right corner in or out.

● **Note:** Some panels cannot be resized, such as the Character and Paragraph panels, but you can still collapse them.

- To collapse a panel group so that only the dock header bar and tabs are visible, double-click a panel tab or panel title bar. Double-click again to restore it to the expanded view. You can open the panel menu even when the panel is collapsed.

Notice that the tabs for the panels in the panel group and the button for the panel menu remain visible after you collapse a panel.

Special notes about the Tools panel and options bar

The Tools panel and the options bar share some characteristics with other panels:

- You can drag the Tools panel by its title bar to a different location in the work area. You can move the options bar to another location by dragging the grab bar at the far left end of the panel.

- You can hide the Tools panel and options bar.

However, some panel features are not available or don't apply to the Tools panel or options bar:

- You cannot group the Tools panel or options bar with other panels.

- You cannot resize the Tools panel or options bar.

- You cannot stack the Tools panel or options bar in the panel dock.

- The Tools panel and options bar do not have panel menus.

▶ **Tip:** To restore the default Essentials workspace, click the workspace icon at the top right corner of the application window, and choose Reset Essentials.

Changing interface settings

By default, the panels, dialog boxes, and background in Photoshop are dark. You can lighten the interface or make other changes in the Photoshop Preferences dialog box:

1   Choose Edit > Preferences > Interface (Windows) or Photoshop CC > Preferences > Interface (Mac).

2   Select a different color theme, or make other changes.

When you select a different theme, you can see the changes immediately. You can also select specific colors for different screen modes and change other interface settings in this dialog box.

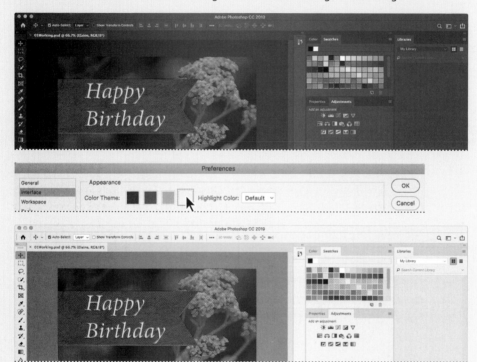

3   When you're satisfied with the changes, click OK.

Review questions

1 Describe at least two types of images you can open in Photoshop.

2 How do you select tools in Photoshop?

3 Describe two ways to zoom in to or out from an image.

Review answers

1 You can open a photograph from a digital camera. You can also open a scanned image of a photographic print, a transparency or negative film frame, or a graphic. You can open images downloaded from the Internet such as photography from Adobe Stock, or images uploaded to your Creative Cloud Files or your Lightroom CC photos.

2 To select a tool in Photoshop, click its icon in the Tools panel, or press the tool's keyboard shortcut. A selected tool remains active until you select a different tool. To select a hidden tool, either use a keyboard shortcut to toggle through the tools, or click and hold the tool in the Tools panel to open a pop-up menu of the hidden tools.

3 Choose commands from the View menu to zoom in on or out from an image, or to fit it onscreen, or use the zoom tools and click or drag over an image to enlarge or reduce the view. You can also use keyboard shortcuts or the Navigator panel to control the display of an image.

2 BASIC PHOTO CORRECTIONS

Lesson overview

In this lesson, you'll learn how to do the following:

- Understand image resolution and size.

- View and access files in Adobe Bridge.

- Straighten and crop an image.

- Adjust the tonal range of an image.

- Use the Spot Healing Brush tool to repair part of an image.

- Use the content-aware Patch tool to remove or replace objects.

- Use the Clone Stamp tool to touch up areas.

- Remove digital artifacts from an image.

- Apply the Smart Sharpen filter to finish retouching photos.

 This lesson will take about an hour to complete. Please log in to your account on peachpit.com to download the lesson files for this chapter, or go to the Getting Started section at the beginning of this book and follow the instructions under "Accessing the Lesson Files and Web Edition."

As you work on this lesson, you'll preserve the start files. If you need to restore the start files, download them from your Account page.

PROJECT: VINTAGE PHOTOGRAPH RESTORATION

Photoshop includes a variety of tools and commands for improving the quality of a photographic image. This lesson steps you through the process of acquiring, resizing, and retouching a vintage photograph.

Strategy for retouching

● **Note:** In this lesson, you retouch an image using Photoshop. For some images, such as those saved in camera raw format, it may be more efficient to work in Adobe Camera Raw, which is installed with Photoshop. You'll learn about the tools Camera Raw has to offer in Lesson 12, "Working with Camera Raw."

How much retouching you do depends on the image you're working on and your goals for it. For many images, you may need only to change the resolution, lighten the image, or repair a minor blemish. For others, you may need to perform several tasks and employ more advanced tools and techniques.

Organizing an efficient sequence of tasks

Most retouching procedures follow these general steps, though not every task may be necessary for all projects:

- Duplicating the original image; working in a copy of the image file makes it easy to recover the original later if necessary

- Ensuring that the resolution is appropriate for the way you'll use the image

- Cropping the image to its final size and orientation

- Removing any color casts

- Adjusting the overall contrast or tonal range of the image

- Repairing flaws in scans of damaged photographs (such as rips, dust, or stains)

- Adjusting the color and tone in specific parts of the image to bring out highlights, midtones, shadows, and desaturated colors

- Sharpening the image

The order of the tasks may vary depending on the project, though you should always start by duplicating the image and adjusting its resolution. Sharpening should usually be your final step. For the other tasks, consider your project and plan accordingly, so that the results of one process do not cause unintended changes to other aspects of the image, making it necessary for you to redo some of your work.

Adjusting your process for different intended uses

The retouching decisions you make for an image depend in part on how you'll use the image. For example, if an image is intended for black-and-white publication on newsprint, you might make different cropping and sharpening choices than if the image is intended for a full-color web page. Photoshop supports RGB color mode for web and mobile device authoring and desktop photo printing, CMYK color mode for preparing an image for printing using process colors, Grayscale mode for black-and-white printing, and other color modes for more specialized purposes.

Resolution and image size

When you edit an image in Photoshop for a specific use, you need to make sure the image contains an appropriate number of *pixels*, the small squares that describe an image and establish the degree of detail it contains. You can work this out from the *pixel dimensions*, or the number of pixels along an image's width and height.

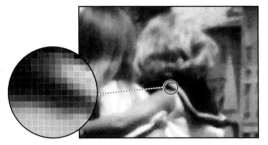

Pixels in a photographic image

When you multiply an image's width by its height in pixels, you find out how many pixels are in the image. For example, a 1000 × 1000 pixel image has 1,000,000 pixels (one megapixel), and a 2000 × 2000 pixel image has 4,000,000 pixels (four megapixels). Pixel dimensions affect file size and upload/download time.

In Photoshop, *resolution* means the number of pixels per unit of physical length, such as pixels per inch (ppi).

Does changing resolution affect file size? Only when the pixel dimensions change. For example, a 7 × 7 inch image at 300 ppi is 2100 × 2100 pixels; if you change either the size in inches or the ppi value (resolution) while keeping the pixel dimensions at 2100 × 2100 pixels, the file size does not change. But if you change the size in inches without changing the ppi value (or vice versa), the pixel dimensions must change, and so will the file size. For example, if the image in the above example is changed to 72 ppi while maintaining 7 × 7 inches, the pixel dimensions must change to 504 × 504 pixels, and the file size decreases accordingly.

Resolution requirements vary depending on the intended output. An image might be considered *low resolution* when its ppi value is below 150 to 200 ppi. An image with a ppi value above 200 ppi is generally considered *high resolution* because it can contain enough detail to take advantage of the device resolution offered by commercial or fine art printers and high-resolution (Retina/HiDPI) device displays.

Factors such as viewing distance and output technology influence the resolution our eyes actually perceive, and this affects resolution requirements too. A 220-ppi laptop display may appear to have the same high resolution as a 360-ppi smartphone, because the laptop is viewed farther away. But 220 ppi might not be enough resolution for a high-end printing press or fine art inkjet printer, which might reproduce the most detail at 300 ppi and up. At the same time, a 50-ppi image can appear perfectly sharp on a highway billboard because it's seen from hundreds of feet away.

Note: In Photoshop, the 100% view does not preview the image's ppi value (resolution); the image is shown at the ppi value of your display. In other words, at 100% zoom, each display pixel shows one image pixel. This means 100% may appear smaller on a very high resolution display.

Note: For computer displays and televisions, the term *resolution* often describes only the pixel dimensions (such as 1920 × 1080 pixels) instead of a pixel density ratio (300 pixels per inch). In Photoshop, resolution is the pixels per inch value, not the pixel dimensions.

Note: To determine the resolution needed for an image you'll print on a press, follow this industry guideline: Edit the image to a ppi value that is 1.5 to 2 times the halftone screen frequency (in lines per inch, or lpi) used by the printer. For example, if the image will be printed using a screen frequency of 133 lpi, the image should be 200 ppi (133 × 1.5).

Because of the way display and output technologies work, your images may not need to match the device resolution of high-resolution printers. For example, while some commercial printing platesetters and photo-quality inkjet printers may have a device resolution of 2400 dots per inch (dpi) or more, the appropriate image resolution to send to those devices may be only 200 to 360 ppi for photos. This is because the device dots are grouped into larger halftone cells or inkjet dot patterns that build tones and colors. Similarly, a 500-ppi smartphone display may not necessarily require 500-ppi images. Whatever your medium, you should verify the appropriate image resolution of your final images by consulting with your production team or output service provider.

Opening a file with Adobe Bridge

In this book, you'll work with different start files in each lesson. You may make copies of these files and save them under different names or locations, or you may work from the original start files and then download them from the peachpit.com website again if you want a fresh start.

In this lesson, you'll retouch a scan of a damaged and discolored vintage photograph so it can be shared or printed. The final image size will be 7 × 7 inches.

In Lesson 1, you used the Open command to open a file. You'll start this lesson by comparing the original scan to the finished image in Adobe Bridge, a visual file browser that helps take the guesswork out of finding the image file that you need.

● **Note:** If Bridge isn't installed, you'll need to install it from Adobe Creative Cloud. For more information, see page 3.

● **Note:** If Bridge asks you if you want to import preferences from a previous version of Bridge, select Don't Show Again, and click No.

1 Start Photoshop, and then immediately hold down Ctrl+Alt+Shift (Windows) or Command+Option+Shift (Mac) to reset the default settings.

2 When prompted, click Yes to confirm that you want to delete the Adobe Photoshop Settings file.

3 Choose File > Browse In Bridge. If you're prompted to enable the Photoshop extension in Bridge, click Yes or OK.

Adobe Bridge opens, displaying a collection of panels, menus, and buttons.

4 Select the Folders tab in the upper left corner, and then browse to the Lessons folder you downloaded onto your hard disk, so that the lessons in the Lessons folder appear in the Content panel.

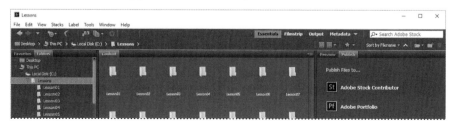

5   With the Lessons folder still selected in the Folders panel, choose File > Add To Favorites.

Adding files, folders, application icons, and other assets that you use often to the Favorites panel lets you access them quickly.

6   Select the Favorites tab to open the panel, and click the Lessons folder to open it. Then, in the Content panel, double-click the Lesson02 folder.

Thumbnail previews of the folder contents appear in the Content panel.

7   Compare the 02Start.tif and 02End.psd files. To enlarge the thumbnails in the Content panel, drag the thumbnail slider at the bottom of the Bridge window to the right.

▶ **Tip:** In Bridge, you can see a larger preview of a selected item in the Preview panel. Click the Preview tab to see the panel; if it's closed, choose Window > Preview Panel.

In the 02Start.tif file, notice that the image is crooked, the colors are relatively dull, and the image has a green color cast and a distracting crease. You'll fix all of these problems in this lesson, and a few others. You'll start by cropping and straightening the image.

8   Double-click the 02Start.tif thumbnail to open the file in Photoshop. Click OK if you see the Embedded Profile Mismatch dialog box.

9   In Photoshop, choose File > Save As. Choose Photoshop from the Format menu, and name the file **02Working.psd**. Then click Save.

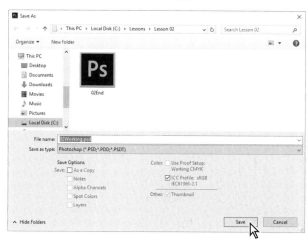

Straightening and cropping the image in Photoshop

▶ **Tip:** Deselect the Delete Cropped Pixels option if you want to crop nondestructively, so that you can revise the crop later.

You'll use the Crop tool to straighten, trim, and scale the photograph. By default, cropping deletes cropped pixels.

1   In the Tools panel, select the Crop tool (⌐⊐.).

Crop handles appear, and a *crop shield* covers the area outside the cropping region, to help focus your attention on the cropped area.

2   In the options bar, choose W × H × Resolution from the Select a Preset Aspect Ratio or Crop Size menu. (Ratio is the default value.) A crop overlay appears.

3   In the options bar, type **7 in** for the width, **7 in** for the height, and **200** px/in for the resolution.

First, you'll straighten the image.

4   Click the Straighten icon in the options bar. The pointer changes to the Straighten tool.

5   Click at the top left corner of the photo, press the mouse button as you drag a straight line across the top edge of the photo, and then release.

Photoshop straightens the image so that the line you drew is parallel with the top of the image area. You drew a line across the top of the photo, but any line that defines either the vertical or horizontal axis of the image will work.

Now, you'll trim the white border and scale the image.

6   Drag the corners of the crop grid inward to the corners of the photo itself to crop out the white border. If you need to adjust the position of the photo, click and drag it within the crop grid.

7   Press Enter or Return to accept the crop.

▶ **Tip:** If you need to adjust the crop, choose Edit > Undo, and try again.

The image is now cropped, and the cropped image fills the image window, straightened, sized, and positioned according to your specifications.

▶ **Tip:** To quickly straighten a photo and crop out the scanned background, choose File > Automate > Crop And Straighten Photos. It can also automatically separate multiple photos scanned in one image.

8   To see the image dimensions, choose Document Dimensions from the pop-up menu at the bottom of the application window.

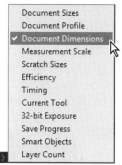

9   Choose File > Save to save your work. Click OK if you see the Photoshop Format Options dialog box.

Adjusting the color and tone

You'll use Curves and Levels adjustment layers to remove the color cast and adjust the color and tone in the image. The Curves or Levels options may look complex, but don't be intimidated. You'll work with them more in later lessons; for now, you'll take advantage of their tools to quickly brighten and adjust the tone of the image.

1 Click Curves in the Adjustments panel to add a Curves adjustment layer.

2 Select the White Point tool on the left side of the Properties panel.

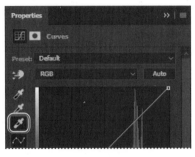

▶ **Tip:** If the Libraries panel is open and taking up a lot of screen space, go ahead and collapse or close it, because it won't be used in this lesson.

The White Point tool defines what color value should be made a neutral white. Once defined, all other colors and tones shift accordingly. When done correctly, this is a quick way to remove a color cast and correct image brightness. To set an accurate white point, click an area of the image that should be the brightest neutral area of the image that contains detail.

3 Click a white stripe on the girl's dress.

The white stripe has a warm color cast that affects the entire image, and it's darker than it should be. Clicking it removes the color cast and lightens it, dramatically improving image contrast and color. Try clicking different white areas, such as the child's sailor dress, a stripe on the woman's dress, or the girl's sock, to see how the color values at each location change the result.

Now you'll use a Levels adjustment layer to fine-tune the tonal range of the image.

4   Click the Levels icon () in the Adjustments panel to add a Levels adjustment layer.

The Levels histogram in the Properties panel displays the range of dark and light values in the image. You'll learn more about working with levels in later lessons. Right now, you just need to know that the left triangle represents the black point (the point Photoshop defines as the darkest in the image), the right triangle represents the white point (the lightest in the image), and the middle triangle represents the midtones.

5   Drag the left triangle (black point) under the histogram to the right, where significant shadow tones start to appear. Our value was **15**.

6   Drag the middle triangle a little to the right to adjust the midtones. Our value was **.90**.

● **Note:** The color and tone edits in this section are relatively basic; it's possible to do them all using only Levels or Curves. Typically, Curves is used for edits that are more specialized or complex.

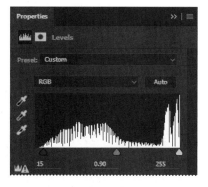

Now that you've adjusted the color, you'll flatten the image so it's easier to work with while you touch it up. Flattening an image merges all of its layers into the Background layer, which reduces the file size; you can still make changes to the entire image. But only flatten if you no longer need the flexibility of adjusting the edits you previously made using separate layers.

7   Choose Layer > Flatten Image.

The adjustment layers merge with the Background layer.

As owner of Gawain Weaver Art Conservation, Gawain Weaver has conserved and restored original works by artists ranging from Eadweard Muybridge to Man Ray, and from Ansel Adams to Cindy Sherman. He teaches workshops internationally as well as online on the care and identification of photographs.

Find out more at gawainweaver.com.

Real-world photo restoration

The tools in Photoshop make restoration of old or damaged photographs seem like magic, giving virtually anyone the power to scan, retouch, print, and frame their photo collections.

However, when dealing with works by famous artists, museums, galleries, and collectors need to preserve original objects to the greatest degree possible despite deterioration or accidental damage. Professional art conservators are called upon to clean dust and soiling from print surfaces, remove discoloration and staining, repair tears, stabilize prints to prevent future damage, and even paint in missing areas of a work.

Carleton E. Watkins, Nevada Fall, 700 FT, Yosemite Valley, CA, mammoth albumen print, 15⅝" × 20¾".
This print was removed from its mount to remove the stains and then remounted.

"Photograph conservation is both a science and an art," says Weaver. "We must apply what we know about the chemistry of the photograph, its mount, and any varnishes or other coatings in order to safely clean, preserve, and enhance the image. Since we cannot quickly 'undo' a step in a conservation treatment, we must always proceed with great caution and a healthy respect for the fragility of the photographic object, whether it's a 160-year-old salt print of Notre Dame or gelatin silver print of Half Dome from the 1970s."

Many of the manual tools of an art conservator have analogous digital versions in Photoshop:

 An art conservator might wash a photograph to remove the discolored components of the paper, or even use a mild bleaching process known as light-bleaching to oxidize and remove the colored components of a stain or overall discoloration. In Photoshop, you can use a Curves adjustment layer to remove the color cast from an image.

 A conservator working on a fine-art photograph might use special paints and fine brushes to manually "in-paint" damaged areas of a photograph. Likewise, you can use the Spot Healing Brush in Photoshop to spot out specks of dust or dirt on a scanned image.

 A conservator might use Japanese papers and wheat-starch paste to carefully repair and rebuild torn paper before finalizing the repair with some skillful in-painting. In Photoshop, you can remove a crease or repair a tear in a scanned image with a few clicks of the Clone Stamp tool.

A fixative was applied to the artist's signature with a small brush to protect it when the mount was washed.

"Although our work has always been first and foremost about the preservation and restoration of the original photographic object, there are instances, especially with family photographs, where the use of Photoshop is more appropriate," says Weaver. "More dramatic results can be achieved in far less time. After digitization, the original print can be safely stored away, while the digital version can be copied or printed for many family members. Often, we first clean or unfold family photographs to safely reveal as much of the original image as possible, and then we repair the remaining discoloration, stains, and tears on the computer after digitization."

Using the Spot Healing Brush tool

● **Note:** The Healing Brush tool works similarly to the Spot Healing Brush tool, except that it requires you to sample source pixels before retouching an area.

The next task is to remove the crease in the photo. You'll use the Spot Healing Brush to erase the crease. While you're at it, you'll use it to address a few other issues.

The Spot Healing Brush tool quickly removes blemishes and other imperfections. It samples pixels around the retouched area and matches the texture, lighting, transparency, and shading of the sampled pixels to the pixels being healed.

The Spot Healing Brush is excellent for retouching blemishes in portraits, but also works nicely wherever there's a uniform appearance near the areas you want to retouch.

1 Zoom in to see the crease clearly.

2 In the Tools panel, select the Spot Healing Brush tool (🖌).

3 In the options bar, open the Brush pop-up panel, and specify a brush with a Size of about **25** px and **100%** Hardness. Make sure Content-Aware is selected in the options bar.

▶ **Tip:** To avoid creating obvious new seams or patterns, paint the Spot Healing Brush closely around the area you're repairing. Don't cover more area than necessary.

4 In the image window, drag the Spot Healing Brush down from the top of the crease. You can probably repair the entire crease with four to six neat downward strokes. As you drag, the stroke at first appears black, but when you release the mouse, the painted area is "healed."

5 Zoom in to see the white hair in the upper right area of the image. Then use the Spot Healing Brush to paint over the hair.

6 Zoom out, if necessary, to see the full sky. Then click the Spot Healing Brush wherever there are unwanted spots you want to heal.

7 Save your work so far.

Applying a content-aware patch

Use the Patch tool to remove larger unwanted elements from an image. You'll use a content-aware patch to remove an unrelated person from the right side of the photo. In Content-Aware mode, the Patch tool creates nearly seamless blending with the nearby content.

1 In the Tools panel, select the Patch tool (⬚), hidden under the Spot Healing Brush tool (⬚).

2 In the options bar, choose Content-Aware from the Patch menu. Type **4** into the Structure slider.

The Structure menu determines how closely the patch reflects the existing image patterns. You can choose from 1 to 7, with 1 allowing the loosest adherence to the source structure and 7 requiring the strictest.

3 Drag the Patch tool around the boy and his shadow, as closely as possible. You may want to zoom in to see him more clearly.

4 Click within the area you've just selected, and drag it to the left. Photoshop displays a preview of the content that will replace the boy. Keep dragging to the left until the preview area no longer overlaps the area occupied by the boy, but without overlapping the woman or the girl she's holding. Release the mouse button when the patch is positioned where you want it.

The selection changes to match the area around it. The boy is gone, and where he stood is a section of the bridge wall and of a building.

5   Choose Select > Deselect.

The effect was pretty impressive, but not quite perfect. You'll touch up the results next.

Repairing areas with the Clone Stamp tool

The Clone Stamp tool uses pixels from one area of an image to replace the pixels in another part of the image. Using this tool, you can not only remove unwanted objects from your images, but you can also fill in missing areas in photographs you scan from damaged originals.

You'll use the Clone Stamp tool to smooth out some irregularities in the height of the bridge wall and the windows on the building.

▶ **Tip:** You may need to set a larger brush size when editing higher resolution images.

1   Select the Clone Stamp tool (👤) in the Tools panel, and select a **60**-px brush with **30**% Hardness. Make sure that the Aligned option is selected.

2   Move the Clone Stamp tool to an area where the top of the bridge wall is smooth. That's the area you want to copy to smooth out the area that was patched.

3   Alt-click (Windows) or Option-click (Mac) to sample that part of the image as a source point. (When you press Alt or Option, the pointer appears as target cross-hairs.)

4   Drag the Clone Stamp tool across the top of the bridge wall in the patched area to even it out, and then release the mouse button.

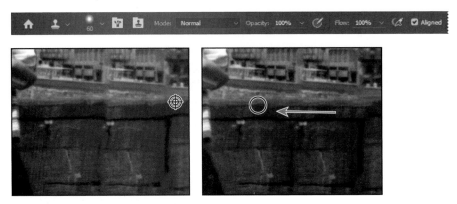

Each time you click the Clone Stamp tool, it begins again with a new source point, in the same relationship to the tool as the first stroke you made. That is, if you begin painting further right, it samples from stone that is further right than the original source point. That's because Aligned is selected in the options bar. Deselect Aligned if you want to start from the same source point each time.

5   Select a source point where the bottom of the bridge wall is even, and then drag
    the Clone Stamp tool across the bottom of the wall where you patched it.

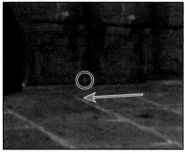

6   Select a smaller brush size, and deselect Aligned. Then select a source point
    over the rightmost windows in the lowest row on the building you patched.
    Click across to create accurate windows there.

7   Repeat step 6 to make any adjustments you want to apply to the lowest area
    of the building and the wall that runs in front of it.

8   If you like, you can use a smaller brush
    size to touch up the stones in the
    patched portion of the wall.

9   Save your work.

Sharpening the image

The last task you might want to do when retouching a photo is to sharpen the image. There are several ways to sharpen an image in Photoshop, but the Smart Sharpen filter gives you the most control. Because sharpening can emphasize artifacts, you'll remove those first.

1 Zoom in to about **400**% to see the boy's shirt clearly. The colored dots you see are artifacts of the scanning process.

2 Choose Filter > Noise > Dust & Scratches.

3 In the Dust & Scratches dialog box, leave the default settings with a Radius of **1** pixel and Threshold at **0**, and click OK.

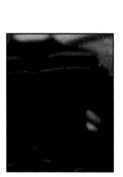 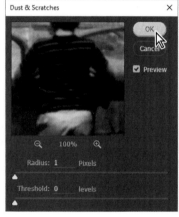 

The Threshold value determines how dissimilar the pixels should be before they are eliminated. The Radius value determines the size of the area searched for dissimilar pixels. The default values are great for tiny dots of color like the ones in this image.

Now that the artifacts are gone, you can sharpen the image.

4 Choose Filter > Sharpen > Smart Sharpen.

5 In the Smart Sharpen dialog box, make sure that Preview is selected, so you can see the effect of settings you adjust in the image window.

You can drag inside the preview window in the dialog box to see different parts of the image, or use the magnification buttons below the thumbnail to zoom in and out.

6   Make sure Lens Blur is chosen in the Remove menu.

You can choose to remove Lens Blur, Gaussian Blur, or Motion Blur in the Smart Sharpen dialog box. Lens Blur provides finer sharpening of detail and reduced sharpening halos. Gaussian Blur increases contrast along the edges in an image. Motion Blur reduces the effects of blur that resulted from the camera or the subject moving when the photo was taken.

7   Drag the Amount slider to about **60**% to sharpen the image.

8   Drag the Radius slider to about **1.5**.

The Radius value determines the number of pixels surrounding the edge pixels that affect the sharpening. The higher the resolution, the higher the Radius setting should usually be.

9   When you're satisfied with the results, click OK to apply the Smart Sharpen filter.

10 Choose File > Save, and then close the project file.

Your image is ready to share or print!

Extra credit

Converting a color image to black and white

You can get great results converting a color image to black and white (with or without a tint) in Photoshop.

1   Choose File > Open, and navigate to the bike.tif file in the Lesson02 folder. Click Open.

2   In the Adjustments panel, click the Black & White button to add a Black & White adjustment layer.

3   Adjust the color sliders to change the saturation of color channels. You can also experiment with options from the preset menu, such as Darker or Infrared. Or, select the targeted adjustment tool (✋) in the upper left corner of the Properties panel, position it over a color you want to adjust, and drag horizontally. The tool moves the sliders associated with the original color of the pixels where you started dragging; for example, dragging on the red bike frame adjusts the lightness of all red areas. We darkened the bike and made the background areas lighter.

4   If you want to colorize the entire photo with a single hue, select Tint in the Properties panel. Then, click the color swatch, and select a tint color (we used R=227, G=209, B=198).

Review questions

1 What does *resolution* mean?

2 What does the Crop tool do?

3 How can you adjust the tone and color of an image in Photoshop?

4 What tools can you use to remove blemishes in an image?

5 How can you remove artifacts such as colored pixels and scanned dust from an image?

Review answers

1 The term *resolution* refers to the number of pixels per unit of physical length in an image, expressed in pixels per inch (ppi). Printer resolution may be expressed in dots per inch (dpi), because device dots do not always correspond to image pixels.

2 You can use the Crop tool to trim, scale, or straighten an image.

3 You can adjust the tone and color of an image in Photoshop using the Curves and Levels adjustment layers, such as applying the White Point tool.

4 The Healing Brush, Spot Healing Brush, Patch, and Clone Stamp tools let you replace unwanted portions of an image with other areas of the image. The Clone Stamp tool copies the source area exactly; the Healing Brush and Spot Healing Brush tools blend the area with the surrounding pixels. The Spot Healing Brush tool doesn't require a source area; it "heals" areas to match the surrounding pixels. In Content-Aware mode, the Patch tool replaces a selection with content that matches the surrounding area.

5 The Dust & Scratches filter removes artifacts from an image.

3 WORKING WITH SELECTIONS

Lesson overview

In this lesson, you'll learn how to do the following:

- Make specific areas of an image active using selection tools.

- Reposition a selection marquee.

- Move and duplicate the contents of a selection.

- Use keyboard-mouse combinations that save time and hand motions.

- Deselect a selection.

- Constrain the movement of a selected area.

- Adjust the position of a selected area using the arrow keys.

- Add to and subtract from a selection.

- Rotate a selection.

- Use multiple selection tools to make a complex selection.

This lesson will take about an hour to complete. Please log in to your account on peachpit.com to download the lesson files for this chapter, or go to the Getting Started section at the beginning of this book and follow the instructions under "Accessing the Lesson Files and Web Edition."

As you work on this lesson, you'll preserve the start files. If you need to restore the start files, download them from your Account page.

PROJECT: SHADOWBOX COLLAGE

Learning how to select areas of an image is of primary
importance—you must first select what you want to
affect. As long as a selection is active, only the area
within the selection can be edited.

About selecting and selection tools

● **Note:** You'll learn how to select vector areas using the pen tools in Lesson 8, "Vector Drawing Techniques."

Making changes to an area within an image in Photoshop is a two-step process. You first use one of the selection tools to select the part of an image you want to change. Then you use another tool, filter, or other feature to make changes, such as moving the selected pixels to another location or applying a filter to the selected area. You can make selections based on size, shape, and color. When a selection is active, changes you make apply only to the selected area; other areas are unaffected.

The best selection tool for a specific area often depends on the characteristics of that area, such as shape or color. There are four primary types of selections:

Geometric selections The Rectangular Marquee tool (⬚) selects a rectangular area in an image. The Elliptical Marquee tool (◯), which is hidden under the Rectangular Marquee tool, selects elliptical areas. The Single Row Marquee tool (▭) and Single Column Marquee tool (▯) select either a 1-pixel-high row or a 1-pixel-wide column, respectively.

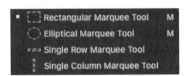

Freehand selections The Lasso tool (◯) traces a freehand selection around an area. The Polygonal Lasso tool (⬨) sets anchor points in straight-line segments around an area. The Magnetic Lasso tool (⬨) works something like a combination of the other two lasso tools, and gives the best results when good contrast exists between the area you want to select and its surroundings.

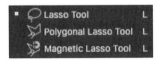

Edge-based selections The Quick Selection tool (⬤) quickly "paints" a selection by automatically finding and following defined edges in the image.

Color-based selections The Magic Wand tool (🪄) selects parts of an image based on the similarity in pixel color. It is useful for selecting odd-shaped areas that share a specific range of colors.

Getting started

First, you'll look at the image you will create as you explore the selection tools in Photoshop.

1   Start Photoshop, and then immediately hold down Ctrl+Alt+Shift (Windows) or Command+Option+Shift (Mac) to restore the default preferences. (See "Restoring Default Preferences" on page 5.)

2   When prompted, click Yes to confirm that you want to delete the Adobe Photoshop Settings file.

3   Choose File > Browse In Bridge to open Adobe Bridge.

4   In the Favorites panel, click the Lessons folder. Then double-click the Lesson03 folder in the Content panel to see its contents.

5   Study the 03End.psd file. Move the thumbnail slider to the right if you want to see the image in more detail.

● **Note:** If Bridge isn't installed, you'll be prompted to install it when you choose Browse In Bridge. For more information, see page 3.

The project is a shadowbox that includes a piece of coral, a sand dollar, a mussel, a nautilus, and a plate of small shells. The challenge in this lesson is to arrange these elements, which were scanned together on the single page you see in the 03Start.psd file.

● **Note:** If Bridge asks you if you want to import preferences from a previous version of Bridge, click No.

6   Double-click the 03Start.psd thumbnail to open the image file in Photoshop.

7   Choose File > Save As, rename the file **03Working.psd**, and click Save.

By saving another version of the start file, you don't have to worry about overwriting the original.

Using the Quick Selection tool

The Quick Selection tool provides one of the easiest ways to make a selection. You simply paint an area of an image, and the tool automatically finds the edges. You can add or subtract areas of the selection until you have exactly the area you want.

The image of the sand dollar in the 03Working.psd file has clearly defined edges, making it an ideal candidate for the Quick Selection tool. You'll select just the sand dollar, not the background behind it.

1 Select the Zoom tool in the Tools panel, and then zoom in so that you can see the sand dollar well.

2 Select the Quick Selection tool (🖌) in the Tools panel.

3 Select Auto-Enhance in the options bar.

When Auto-Enhance is selected, the Quick Selection tool creates better quality selections, with edges that are truer to the object. The selection process is a little slower than using the Quick Selection tool without Auto-Enhance, but the results are superior.

4 Click on an off-white area near the outside edge of the sand dollar.

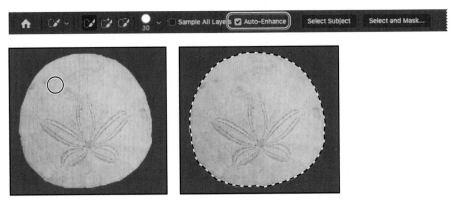

The Quick Selection tool finds the full edge automatically, selecting the entire sand dollar. Leave the selection active so that you can use it in the next exercise.

Moving a selected area

Once you've made a selection, any changes you make apply exclusively to the pixels within the selection. The rest of the image is not affected by those changes.

To move the selected area to another part of the composition, you use the Move tool. This image has only one layer, so the pixels you move will replace the pixels beneath them. This change is not permanent until you deselect the moved pixels, so you can try different locations for the selection you're moving before you make a commitment.

▶ **Tip:** If you deselect an area by accident, you may be able to restore the selection by choosing Edit > Undo or Select > Reselect.

1 If the sand dollar is not still selected, repeat the previous exercise to select it.

2 Zoom out so you can see both the shadowbox and the sand dollar.

3 Select the Move tool (✛). Notice that the sand dollar remains selected.

4 Drag the selected area (the sand dollar) up to the upper left area of the frame, which is labeled "A." Position it over the silhouette in the frame, leaving the lower left part of the silhouette showing as a shadow.

5 Choose Select > Deselect, and then choose File > Save.

In Photoshop, it's not easy to lose a selection. Unless a selection tool is active, clicking elsewhere in the image will not deselect the active area. To deliberately deselect a selection, you can choose Select > Deselect, press Ctrl+D (Windows) or Command+D (Mac), or click outside the selection with any selection tool.

Julieanne Kost is an official Adobe Photoshop evangelist.

Tool tips from the Photoshop evangelist

Move tool tip

If you're moving objects in a multilayer file with the Move tool and you need to select one of the layers, try this: With the Move tool selected, position the pointer over any area of an image, and right-click (Windows) or Control-click (Mac). The context menu that appears lists all layers where content exists under the pointer, so that you can select a different layer.

Manipulating selections

You can move selections, reposition them as you create them, and even duplicate them. In this section, you'll learn several ways to manipulate selections. Most of these methods work with any selection; you'll use them here with the Elliptical Marquee tool, which lets you select ovals or perfect circles.

One of the most useful things you may find in this section is the introduction of keyboard shortcuts that can save you time and arm motions.

Repositioning a selection marquee while creating it

Selecting ovals and circles can be tricky. It's not always obvious where you should start dragging, so sometimes the selection will be off-center, or the ratio of width to height won't match what you need. In this exercise, you'll learn techniques for managing those problems, including two important keyboard-mouse combinations that can make your Photoshop work much easier.

As you perform this exercise, be very careful to follow the directions about keeping the mouse button or specific keys pressed. If you accidentally release the mouse button at the wrong time, simply start the exercise again from step 1.

1 Select the Zoom tool (Q), and click the plate of shells at the bottom of the image window to zoom in to at least 100% view (use 200% view if the entire plate of shells will still fit in the image window on your screen).

2 Select the Elliptical Marquee tool (◯), hidden under the Rectangular Marquee tool (▢).

3 Move the pointer over the plate of shells, and drag diagonally across the oval plate to create a selection, but *do not release the mouse button*. It's OK if your selection does not match the plate shape yet.

If you accidentally release the mouse button, draw the selection again. In most cases—including this one—the new selection replaces the previous one.

4 Still holding down the mouse button, press the spacebar, and continue to drag the selection. Instead of resizing the selection, now you're moving it. Position it so that it more closely aligns with the plate.

● **Note:** You don't have to include every pixel in the plate of shells, but the selection should be the shape of the plate, and should contain the shells comfortably.

5 Carefully release the spacebar (but not the mouse button) and continue to drag, trying to make the size and shape of the selection match the oval plate of shells as closely as possible. If necessary, hold down the spacebar again and drag to move the selection marquee into position around the plate of shells.

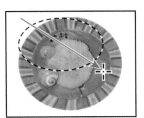 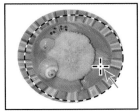 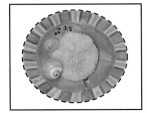

Begin dragging a selection.   *Press the spacebar to move it.*   *Complete the selection.*

6 When the selection border is positioned appropriately, release the mouse button.

7 Choose View > Fit On Screen or use the slider in the Navigator panel to reduce the zoom view so that you can see all of the objects in the image window.

Leave the Elliptical Marquee tool and the selection active for the next exercise.

Moving selected pixels with a keyboard shortcut

Now you'll use a keyboard shortcut to move the selected pixels onto the shadow-box. The shortcut temporarily switches the active tool to the Move tool, so you don't need to select it from the Tools panel.

1 If the plate of shells is not still selected, repeat the previous exercise to select it.

2 With the Elliptical Marquee tool (⬭) selected in the Tools panel, press Ctrl (Windows) or Command (Mac), and move the pointer within the selection.

The pointer icon now includes a pair of scissors (▸✂) indicating that the selection will be cut from its current location.

3 Drag the plate of shells onto the area of the shadowbox labeled "B." (You'll use another technique to nudge the oval plate into the exact position in a minute.)

4 Release the mouse button, but don't deselect the plate of shells.

● **Note:** If you try to move the pixels but Photoshop displays an alert saying "Could not use the Move tool because the layer is locked," make sure you start dragging by positioning the pointer inside the selection.

● **Note:** You can release the Ctrl or Command key after you start dragging, and the Move tool remains active. Photoshop reverts to the previously selected tool when you deselect, whether you click outside the selection or use the Deselect command.

Moving a selection with the arrow keys

You can make minor adjustments to the position of selected pixels by using the arrow keys. You can nudge the selection in increments of either one pixel or ten pixels.

When a selection tool is active in the Tools panel, the arrow keys nudge the selection border, but not the contents. When the Move tool is active, the arrow keys move both the selection border and its contents.

You'll use the arrow keys to nudge the plate of shells. Before you begin, make sure that the plate of shells is still selected in the image window.

1 Press the Up Arrow key (⬆) on your keyboard a few times to move the oval upward.

Notice that each time you press the arrow key, the plate of shells moves one pixel. Experiment by pressing the other arrow keys to see how they affect the selection.

2   Hold down the Shift key as you press an arrow key.

When you hold down the Shift key, the selection moves ten pixels every time you press an arrow key.

Sometimes the border around a selected area can distract you as you make adjustments. You can hide the edges of a selection temporarily without actually deselecting, and then display the selection border once you've completed the adjustments.

▶ **Tip:** Selection edges, guidelines, and other visible items that aren't actual objects are called *extras*, so another way to hide the selection edges is to deselect the View > Extras command.

3   Choose View > Show > Selection Edges to deselect the command, hiding the selection border around the plate of shells.

4   Use the arrow keys to nudge the plate of shells until it's positioned over the silhouette, so that there's a shadow on the left and bottom of the plate. Then choose View > Show > Selection Edges to reveal the selection border again.

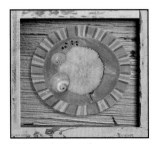   

Hidden selection edges   *Visible selection edges*

5   Choose Select > Deselect, or press Ctrl+D (Windows) or Command+D (Mac).

6   Choose File > Save to save your work so far.

Using the Magic Wand tool

The Magic Wand tool selects all the pixels of a particular color or color range. It's most useful for selecting an area of similar colors surrounded by areas of very different colors. As with many of the selection tools, after you make the initial selection, you can add or subtract areas of the selection.

The Tolerance option sets the sensitivity of the Magic Wand tool. This value limits or extends the range of pixel similarity. The default tolerance value of 32 selects the color you click plus 32 lighter and 32 darker tones of that color. You may need to adjust the tolerance level up or down depending on the color ranges and variations in the image.

If a multicolored area that you want to select is set against a background of a different color, it can be much easier to select the background than the area itself. In this procedure, you'll use the Rectangular Marquee tool to select a larger area, and then use the Magic Wand tool to subtract the background from the selection.

1　Select the Rectangular Marquee tool (⬚), hidden under the Elliptical Marquee tool (◯).

2　Drag a selection around the piece of coral. Make sure that your selection is large enough so that a margin of white appears between the coral and the edges of the marquee.

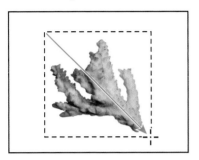

At this point, the coral and the white background area are selected. You'll subtract the white area from the selection so that only the coral remains in the selection.

3　Select the Magic Wand tool (🪄), hidden under the Quick Selection tool (✒).

4　In the options bar, confirm that the Tolerance value is **32**. This value determines the range of colors the wand selects.

5　Click the Subtract From Selection button (▣) in the options bar.

A minus sign appears next to the wand in the pointer icon. Anything you select now will be subtracted from the initial selection.

6　Click in the white background area within the selection marquee.

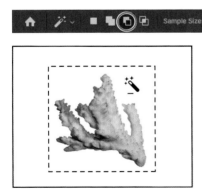

The Magic Wand tool selects the entire background, subtracting it from the selection. Now all the white pixels are deselected, leaving the coral perfectly selected.

7   Select the Move tool (✛), and drag the coral to the area of the shadowbox labeled "C," positioning it so that a shadow appears to the left of and below the coral.

8   Choose Select > Deselect, and then save your work.

Softening the edges of a selection

To smooth the hard edges of a selection, you can apply anti-aliasing or feathering, or use the Select and Mask option.

Anti-aliasing smooths the jagged edges of a selection by softening the color transition between edge pixels and background pixels. Since only the edge pixels change, no detail is lost. Anti-aliasing is useful when cutting, copying, and pasting selections to create composite images.

Anti-aliasing is available for the Lasso, Polygonal Lasso, Magnetic Lasso, Elliptical Marquee, and Magic Wand tools. (Select the tool to display its options in the options bar.) To apply anti-aliasing, you must select the option before making the selection. Once a selection is made, you cannot add anti-aliasing to it.

Feathering blurs edges by building a transition boundary between the selection and its surrounding pixels. This blurring can cause some loss of detail at the edge of the selection.

You can define feathering for the marquee and lasso tools as you use them, or you can add feathering to an existing selection. Feathering effects become apparent when you move, cut, or copy the selection.

- To use the Select and Mask option, first make a selection, and then click Select and Mask in the options bar to open its dialog box. You can use the Select and Mask option to smooth the outline, feather it, or contract or expand it.

- To use anti-aliasing, select a lasso tool, or the Elliptical Marquee or Magic Wand tool, and select Anti-alias in the options bar.

- To define a feathered edge for a selection tool, select any of the lasso or marquee tools. Enter a Feather value in the options bar. This value defines the width of the feathered edge and can range from 1 to 250 pixels.

- To define a feathered edge for an existing selection, choose Select > Modify > Feather. Enter a value for the Feather Radius, and click OK.

Selecting with the lasso tools

As we mentioned earlier, Photoshop includes three lasso tools: the Lasso tool, the Polygonal Lasso tool, and the Magnetic Lasso tool. You can use the Lasso tool to make selections that require both freehand and straight lines, using keyboard short-cuts to move back and forth between the Lasso tool and the Polygonal Lasso tool. You'll use the Lasso tool to select the mussel. It takes a bit of practice to alternate between straight-line and freehand selections—if you make a mistake while you're selecting the mussel, simply deselect and start again.

1   If the window magnification is below 100%, select the Zoom tool (⌕) and click the nautilus to zoom in to at least 100%.

2   Select the Lasso tool (◯). Starting at the lower left section of the mussel, drag around the rounded end of the mussel, tracing the shape as accurately as possible. *Do not release the mouse button.*

3   When you reach a corner or straight part of the edge, press the Alt (Windows) or Option (Mac) key, and then release the mouse button so that the lasso pointer changes to the polygonal lasso shape (⧖). *Do not release the Alt or Option key.*

4   Begin clicking along the end of the mussel to place anchor points, following the contours of the mussel. Be sure to hold down the Alt or Option key throughout this process. This lets you create perfectly straight segments along the selection.

▶ **Tip:** Go slowly until you become comfortable with the Lasso tool. If you make a mistake or accidentally release the mouse button during steps 2–8, choose Edit > Undo and start again at step 2.

Drag with the Lasso tool.

Click with the Polygonal Lasso tool.

The selection border automatically stretches like a rubber band between anchor points.

5   When you reach the tip of the mussel, hold down the mouse button as you release the Alt or Option key. The pointer again appears as the lasso icon.

6   Carefully drag around the tip of the mussel, holding down the mouse button.

7   When you finish tracing the tip and reach the straight segments along the lower side of the mussel, first press Alt or Option again, and then release the mouse button. Click along the straight segments of the lower side of the mussel as needed. Continue to trace the straight and curved mussel edges until you arrive back at the starting point of your selection at the left end of the mussel.

8 Click the starting point of the selection, and then release Alt or Option. The mussel is now entirely selected. Leave the mussel selected for the next exercise.

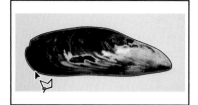 

Rotating a selection

Now you'll rotate the mussel.

Before you begin, make sure that the mussel is still selected.

1 Choose View > Fit On Screen to resize the image window to fit on your screen.

2 Press Ctrl (Windows) or Command (Mac) as you drag the selected mussel to the section of the shadowbox labeled "D."

The pointer changes to the Move tool icon when you press Ctrl or Command.

3 Choose Edit > Transform > Rotate.

The mussel and selection marquee are enclosed in a bounding box.

4 Move the pointer outside the bounding box so that it becomes a curved, two-headed arrow (↱). Drag to rotate the mussel to a 90-degree angle. You can verify the angle in the transformation values display next to the pointer, or in the Rotate box in the options bar. Press Enter or Return to commit the transformation.

5 If necessary, select the Move tool (✛), and drag to reposition the mussel, leaving a shadow to match the others. When you're satisfied, choose Select > Deselect.

6 Choose File > Save.

Selecting with the Magnetic Lasso tool

You can use the Magnetic Lasso tool to make freehand selections of areas with high-contrast edges. When you draw with the Magnetic Lasso tool, the selection border automatically snaps to the edge between areas of contrast. You can also control the selection path by occasionally clicking the mouse to place anchor points in the selection border.

You'll use the Magnetic Lasso tool to select the nautilus so that you can move it to the shadowbox.

1   Select the Zoom tool (🔍), and click the nautilus to zoom in to at least 100%.

2   Select the Magnetic Lasso tool (🪢), hidden under the Lasso tool (🪢).

3   Click once along the left edge of the nautilus, and then move the Magnetic Lasso tool along the edge to trace its outline.

▶ **Tip:** In low-contrast areas, you may want to click to place your own fastening points. You can add as many as you need. To remove the most recent fastening point, press Delete, and then move the mouse back to the remaining fastening point and continue selecting.

Even though you're not holding down the mouse button, the tool snaps to the edge of the nautilus and automatically adds fastening points.

4   When you reach the left side of the nautilus again, double-click to return the Magnetic Lasso tool to the starting point, closing the selection. Or you can move the Magnetic Lasso tool over the starting point and click once.

5   Double-click the Hand tool (✋) to fit the entire image in the window.

6 Select the Move tool (✛), and drag the nautilus onto its silhouette in the section of the frame labeled "E," leaving a shadow below it and on the left side.

7 Choose Select > Deselect, and then choose File > Save.

Selecting from a center point

In some cases, it's easier to make elliptical or rectangular selections by drawing a selection from an object's center point. You'll use this technique to select the head of the screw for the shadowbox corners.

1 Select the Zoom tool (🔍), and zoom in on the screw to a magnification of about 300%. Make sure that you can see the entire screw head in your image window.

2 Select the Elliptical Marquee tool (◯) in the Tools panel.

3 Move the pointer to the approximate center of the screw.

4 Click and begin dragging. Then, without releasing the mouse button, press Alt (Windows) or Option (Mac) as you continue dragging the selection to the outer edge of the screw.

The selection is centered over its starting point.

▶ **Tip:** To select a perfect circle, press Shift as you drag. Hold down Shift while dragging the Rectangular Marquee tool to select a perfect square.

5 When you have the entire screw head selected, release the mouse button first, and then release Alt or Option (and the Shift key if you used it). Do not deselect, because you'll use this selection in the next exercise.

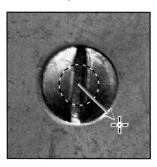
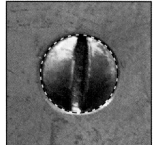

6 If necessary, reposition the selection border using one of the methods you learned earlier. If you accidentally released the Alt or Option key before you released the mouse button, select the screw again.

Resizing and copying a selection

Now you'll move the screw to the lower right corner of the wooden shadowbox, and then duplicate it for the other corners.

Resizing the contents of a selection

You'll start by moving the screw, but it's too large for the space. You'll need to resize it as well.

Before you begin, make sure that the screw is still selected. If it's not, reselect it by completing the previous exercise.

1   Choose View > Fit On Screen so that the entire image fits within the image window.

2   Select the Move tool (⊕) in the Tools panel.

3   Position the pointer within the screw selection.

The pointer becomes an arrow with a pair of scissors (➤✂), indicating that dragging the selection will cut it from its current location and move it to the new location.

4   Drag the screw onto the lower right corner of the shadowbox.

5   Choose Edit > Transform > Scale. A bounding box appears around the selection.

6   Drag one of the corner points inward to reduce the screw to about 40% of its original size, or until it is small enough to sit on the shadowbox frame.

As you resize the object, the selection marquee resizes, too. Both resize proportionally by default.

7   Press Enter or Return to commit the change and remove the transformation bounding box.

8   Use the Move tool to reposition the screw after resizing it, so that it is centered in the corner of the shadowbox frame.

► **Tip:** If the screw won't move or resize smoothly, as if it gets "stuck," hold down the Control key to temporarily disable snapping to magenta Smart Guides as you drag. Or permanently disable them by deselecting the View > Show > Smart Guides command.

► **Tip:** If you don't want to maintain original proportions while resizing, press the Shift key as you drag a corner handle of a transformation bounding box.

9   Leaving the screw selected, choose File > Save to save your work.

Moving and duplicating a selection simultaneously

You can move and duplicate a selection at the same time. You'll copy the screw for the other three corners of the frame. If the screw is no longer selected, reselect it now, using the techniques you learned earlier.

1 With the Move tool (✛) selected, press Alt (Windows) or Option (Mac) as you position the pointer inside the screw selection.

The pointer changes, displaying the usual black arrow and an additional white arrow, which indicates that a duplicate will be made when you move the selection.

2 Continue holding down the Alt or Option key as you drag a duplicate of the screw straight up to the top right corner of the frame. Release the mouse button and the Alt or Option key, but don't deselect the duplicate image.

3 Hold down Alt+Shift (Windows) or Option+Shift (Mac), and drag a new copy of the screw straight left to the upper left corner of the frame.

Pressing the Shift key as you move a selection constrains the movement horizontally or vertically in 45-degree increments.

4 Repeat step 3 to drag a fourth screw to the lower left corner of the frame.

5 When you're satisfied with the position of the fourth screw, choose Select > Deselect, and then choose File > Save.

Copying selections

You can use the Move tool to copy selections as you drag them within or between images, or you can copy and move selections using commands on the Edit menu. The Move tool uses less memory, because it doesn't use the clipboard.

Photoshop has several copy and paste commands:

- **Copy** takes the selected area on the active layer and puts it on the clipboard.
- **Copy Merged** creates a merged copy of all the visible layers in the selected area.
- **Paste** inserts the clipboard contents at the center of the image. If you paste into another image, the pasted content becomes a new layer.

On the Edit > Paste Special submenu, Photoshop also provides specialized pasting commands to give you more options in certain situations:

- **Paste in Place** pastes clipboard content at the location it had in the original image, instead of at the center of the document.
- **Paste Into** pastes clipboard content inside the active selection in the same or a different image. The source selection is pasted onto a new layer, and the area outside the selection is converted into a layer mask.
- **Paste Outside** is the same as Paste Into except that Photoshop pastes the content outside the active selection and converts the area inside the selection to a layer mask.

If two documents have different pixel dimensions, the content you paste between them may appear to change size. This is because the content maintains its pixel dimensions as it is pasted into a document with different pixel dimensions. You can resize a pasted selection, but the image quality of the selection may decrease if it's enlarged.

Cropping an image

Now that your composition is in place, you'll crop the image to a final size. You can use either the Crop tool or the Crop command to crop an image.

1   Select the Crop tool (⌐□), or press C to switch from the current tool to the Crop tool. Photoshop displays a crop boundary around the entire image.

2   In the options bar, make sure Ratio is selected in the Preset pop-up menu and that there are no ratio values specified. Then confirm that Delete Cropped Pixels is selected.

When Ratio is selected but no ratio values are specified, you can crop the image with any proportions.

▶ **Tip:** To crop an image with its original proportions intact, choose Original Ratio from the Preset pop-up menu in the options bar.

3   Drag the crop handles so that the shadowbox is in the highlighted area, omitting the backgrounds from the original objects at the bottom of the image. Crop the frame so that there's an even area of white around it.

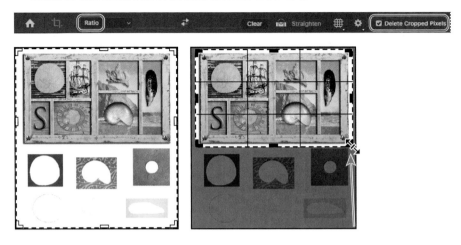

4   When you're satisfied with the position of the crop area, click the Commit Current Crop Operation button (✓) in the options bar.

5   Choose File > Save to save your work.

You've used several different selection tools to move all the seashells into place. The shadowbox is complete!

Review questions

1 Once you've made a selection, what area of the image can be edited?

2 How do you add to and subtract from a selection?

3 How can you move a selection while you're creating it?

4 What does the Quick Selection tool do?

5 How does the Magic Wand tool determine which areas of an image to select? What is tolerance, and how does it affect a selection?

Review answers

1 Only the area within an active selection can be edited.

2 To add to a selection, click the Add To Selection button in the options bar, and then click the area you want to add. To subtract from a selection, click the Subtract From Selection button in the options bar, and then click the area you want to subtract. You can also add to a selection by pressing Shift as you drag or click; to subtract, press Alt (Windows) or Option (Mac) as you drag or click.

3 To reposition a selection as you're creating it, continue to press the mouse button as you hold down the spacebar and drag.

4 The Quick Selection tool expands outward from where you click to automatically find and follow defined edges in the image.

5 The Magic Wand tool selects adjacent pixels based on their similarity in color. The Tolerance value determines how many color tones the Magic Wand tool will select. The higher the tolerance setting, the more tones are selected.

4   LAYER BASICS

Lesson overview

In this lesson, you'll learn how to do the following:

- Organize artwork on layers.

- Create, view, hide, and select layers.

- Rearrange layers to change the stacking order of artwork.

- Apply blending modes to layers.

- Resize and rotate layers.

- Apply a gradient to a layer.

- Apply a filter to a layer.

- Add text and layer effects to a layer.

- Add an adjustment layer.

- Save a copy of the file with the layers flattened.

This lesson will take less than an hour to complete. Please log in to your account on peachpit.com to download the lesson files for this chapter, or go to the Getting Started section at the beginning of this book and follow the instructions under "Accessing the Lesson Files and Web Edition."

As you work on this lesson, you'll preserve the start files. If you need to restore the start files, download them from your Account page.

PROJECT: TRAVEL POSTCARD

Pineapple and flower photography © Image Source, www.imagesource.com

In Photoshop, you can isolate different parts of an image on layers. Each layer can then be edited as discrete artwork, giving you tremendous flexibility as you compose and revise an image.

About layers

Every Photoshop file contains one or more *layers*. New files are generally created with a *background layer,* which contains a color or an image that shows through the transparent areas of subsequent layers. All new layers in an image are transparent until you add text or artwork.

Working with layers is analogous to placing portions of a drawing on clear sheets of film, such as those viewed with an overhead projector: Individual sheets may be edited, repositioned, and deleted without affecting the other sheets. When the sheets are stacked, the entire composition is visible.

Getting started

You'll start the lesson by viewing an image of the final composition.

1 Start Photoshop, and then immediately hold down Ctrl+Alt+Shift (Windows) or Command+Option+Shift (Mac) to restore the default preferences. (See "Restoring Default Preferences" on page 5.)

2 When prompted, click Yes to delete the Adobe Photoshop Settings file.

3 Choose File > Browse In Bridge to open Adobe Bridge.

4 In the Favorites panel, click the Lessons folder. Then double-click the Lesson04 folder in the Content panel to see its contents.

● **Note:** If Bridge isn't installed, you'll be prompted to install it. For more information, see page 3.

5 Study the 04End.psd file. Move the thumbnail slider to the right if you want to see the image in more detail.

This layered composite represents a postcard. You will create it in this lesson as you learn how to create, edit, and manage layers.

6 Double-click the 04Start.psd file to open it in Photoshop.

7 Choose File > Save As, rename the file **04Working.psd**, and click Save. Click OK if you see the Photoshop Format Options dialog box.

Saving another version of the start file frees you to make changes without worrying about overwriting the original.

Using the Layers panel

The Layers panel lists all the layers in an image, displaying the layer names and thumbnails of the content on each layer. You can use the Layers panel to hide, view, reposition, delete, rename, and merge layers. The layer thumbnails are automatically updated as you edit the layers.

1   If the Layers panel is not visible in the work area, choose Window > Layers.

The Layers panel lists five layers for the 04Working.psd file (from top to bottom): Postage, HAWAII, Flower, Pineapple, and Background.

2   Select the Background layer to make it active (if it's not already selected). Notice the layer thumbnail and the icons shown for the Background layer:

- The lock icon (🔒) indicates that the layer is protected.

- The eye icon (👁) indicates that the layer is visible in the image window. If you click the eye, the image window no longer displays that layer.

Tip: Use the context menu to hide or resize the layer thumbnail. Right-click (Windows) or Control-click (Mac) a thumbnail in the Layers panel to open the context menu, and then choose a thumbnail size.

The first task for this project is to add a photo of the beach to the postcard. First, you'll open the beach image in Photoshop.

3　In Photoshop, choose File > Open, navigate to the Lesson04 folder, and then double-click the Beach.psd file to open it.

The Layers panel changes to display the layer information for the active Beach.psd file. Notice that only one layer appears in the Beach.psd image: Layer 1, not Background. (For more information, see the sidebar "About the background layer.")

About the background layer

When you create a new image with a white or colored background, the bottom layer in the Layers panel is named Background, and is always opaque. An image can have only one background layer. You cannot change the stacking order of a background layer, its blending mode, or its opacity. You can, however, convert a background layer to a regular layer.

When you create a new image with transparent content, the image doesn't have a background layer. The bottom layer isn't constrained like the background layer; you can move it anywhere in the Layers panel, and change its opacity and blending mode.

To convert a background layer into a regular layer:

1　Click the lock icon next to the layer name. The layer name changes to a numbered default layer name.

2　Rename the layer.

To convert a regular layer into a background layer:

1　Select a layer in the Layers panel.

2　Choose Layer > New > Background From Layer.

Renaming and copying a layer

To add content to an image and simultaneously create a new layer for it, drag an object or layer from one file into the image window of another file. Whether you drag from the image window of the original file or from its Layers panel, only the active layer is reproduced in the destination file.

You'll drag the Beach.psd image onto the 04Working.psd file. Before you begin, make sure that both the 04Working.psd and Beach.psd files are open, and that the Beach.psd file is selected.

First, you'll give Layer 1 a more descriptive name.

1   In the Layers panel, double-click the name Layer 1, type **Beach**, and then press Enter or Return. Keep the layer selected.

● **Note:** When you rename a layer, make sure you double-click the layer name text. If you double-click outside the name, other layer options may appear instead.

2   Choose Window > Arrange > 2-Up Vertical. Photoshop displays both of the open image files. Select the Beach.psd image so that it is the active file.

3   Select the Move tool (✛), and use it to drag the Beach.psd image onto the 04Working.psd image window.

▶ **Tip:** If you hold down Shift as you drag an image from one file into another, the dragged image automatically centers itself in the target image window.

▶ **Tip:** You can also transfer layers between documents by copying and pasting: Select layers in the Layers panel, choose Edit > Copy, switch to another document, and choose Edit > Paste.

▶ **Tip:** Need images for a project like this one? In Photoshop, choose File > Search Adobe Stock to download low-resolution placeholder images from the Adobe Stock online photo library. If you purchase the images, Photoshop replaces the placeholders with high-resolution images.

The Beach layer now appears in the 04Working.psd file image window and its Layers panel, between the Background and Pineapple layers. Photoshop always adds new layers directly above the selected layer; you selected the Background layer earlier.

4   Close the Beach.psd file without saving changes to it.

Viewing individual layers

▶ **Tip:** If you need to center the Beach layer, select the Beach layer in the Layers panel, choose Select > All, and then choose Layer > Align > Horizontal Centers or Vertical Centers.

The 04Working.psd file now contains six layers. Some of the layers are visible and some are hidden. The eye icon (👁) next to a layer thumbnail in the Layers panel indicates that the layer is visible.

1   Click the eye icon (👁) next to the Pineapple layer to hide the image of the pineapple.

You can hide or show a layer by clicking this icon or clicking in its column, also called the Show/Hide Visibility column.

2 Click again in the Show/Hide Visibility column to display the pineapple.

Adding a border to a layer

Now you'll add a white border around the Beach layer to create the impression that it's an old photograph.

1 Select the Beach layer. (To select the layer, click the layer name in the Layers panel.)

The layer is highlighted, indicating that it is active. Changes you make in the image window affect the active layer.

2 To make the opaque areas on this layer more obvious, hide all layers except the Beach layer: Press Alt (Windows) or Option (Mac) as you click the eye icon (👁) next to the Beach layer.

The white background and other objects in the image disappear, leaving only the beach image against a checkerboard background. The checkerboard indicates transparent areas of the active layer.

3 Choose Layer > Layer Style > Stroke.

The Layer Style dialog box opens. Now you'll select the options for the white stroke around the beach image.

4 Specify the following settings:

- Size: **5** px

- Position: Inside

- Blend Mode: Normal

- Opacity: **100**%

- Color: White (Click the Color box, and select white in the Color Picker.)

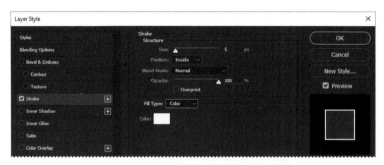

5 Click OK. A white border appears around the beach photo.

Rearranging layers

The order in which the layers of an image are organized is called the *stacking order.* The stacking order determines how the image is viewed—you can change the order to make certain parts of the image appear in front of or behind other layers.

You'll rearrange the layers so that the beach image is in front of another image that is currently hidden in the file.

1 Make the Postage, HAWAII, Flower, Pineapple, and Background layers visible by clicking the Show/Hide Visibility column next to their layer names.

The beach image is almost entirely blocked by images on other layers.

2 In the Layers panel, drag the Beach layer up so that it is positioned between the Pineapple and Flower layers—when you've positioned it correctly, you'll see a double blue line between the layers in the panel—and then release the mouse button.

The Beach layer moves up one level in the stacking order, and the beach image appears on top of the pineapple and background images but under the postmark, flower, and the word "HAWAII."

▶ **Tip:** You can also control the stacking order of layered images by selecting them in the Layers panel and choosing Layer > Arrange, and then choosing Bring To Front, Bring Forward, Send Backward, or Send To Back.

Changing the opacity of a layer

You can reduce the opacity of any layer to reveal the layers below it. In this case, the postmark is too dark on the flower. You'll edit the opacity of the Postage layer to let the flower and other images show through.

1   Select the Postage layer, and then click the arrow next to the Opacity field to display the Opacity slider. Drag the slider to 25%. You can also type **25** in the Opacity box or scrub the Opacity label.

The Postage layer becomes partially transparent, so you can better see the layers underneath. Notice that the change in opacity affects only the image area of the Postage layer. The Pineapple, Beach, Flower, and HAWAII layers remain opaque.

2   Choose File > Save to save your work.

Duplicating a layer and changing the blending mode

You can apply different blending modes to a layer. *Blending modes* affect how the color pixels on one layer blend with pixels on the layers underneath. First you'll use blending modes to increase the intensity of the image on the Pineapple layer so that it doesn't look so dull. Then you'll change the blending mode on the Postage layer. (Currently, the blending mode for both layers is Normal.)

1   Click the eye icons next to the HAWAII, Flower, and Beach layers to hide them.

2   Right-click or Control-click the Pineapple layer, and choose Duplicate Layer from the context menu. (Make sure you click the layer name, not its thumbnail, or you'll see the wrong context menu.) Click OK in the Duplicate Layer dialog box.

A layer called "Pineapple copy" appears above the Pineapple layer in the Layers panel.

3 With the Pineapple copy layer selected, choose Overlay from the Blending Modes menu in the Layers panel.

▶ **Tip:** Notice that the image changes as you move the mouse over the options in the Blending Modes menu. This is a quick way to preview the effect of each blending mode.

The Overlay blending mode blends the Pineapple copy layer with the Pineapple layer beneath it to create a vibrant, more colorful pineapple with deeper shadows and brighter highlights.

4 Select the Postage layer, and choose Multiply from the Blending Modes menu.

The Multiply blending mode multiplies the colors in the underlying layers with the color in the top layer. In this case, the postmark becomes a little stronger.

5 Choose File > Save to save your work.

Resizing and rotating layers

You can resize and transform layers.

1 Click the Visibility column on the Beach layer to make the layer visible.

2 Select the Beach layer in the Layers panel, and choose Edit > Free Transform.

A Transform bounding box appears around the beach image. The bounding box has handles on each corner and each side.

First, you'll resize and angle the layer.

3 Drag a corner handle inward to scale the beach photo down by about 50%. (Watch the Width and Height percentages in the options bar.)

4 With the bounding box still active, position the pointer just outside one of the corner handles until it becomes a curved double arrow. Drag clockwise to rotate the beach image approximately 15 degrees. You can also enter **15** in the Set Rotation box in the options bar.

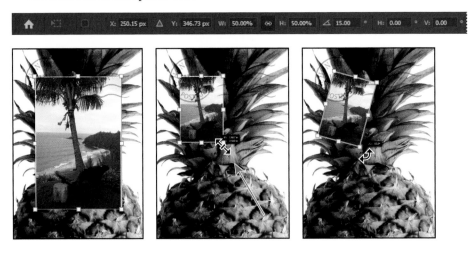

▶ **Tip:** You can also commit a transformation by clicking outside the transform bounding box. Just make sure you aren't clicking somewhere that will alter a setting or layer accidentally.

5 Click the Commit Transform button (✔) in the options bar.

6 Make the Flower layer visible. Then, select the Move tool (✛), and drag the beach photo so that its corner is tucked neatly beneath the flower, as in the illustration.

7 Choose File > Save.

Using a filter to create artwork

Next, you'll create a new layer with no artwork on it. (Adding empty layers to a file is comparable to adding blank sheets of film to a stack of images.) You'll use this layer to add realistic-looking clouds to the sky with a Photoshop filter.

1 In the Layers panel, select the Background layer to make it active, and then click the Create A New Layer button (▣) at the bottom of the Layers panel.

A new layer, named Layer 1, appears between the Background and Pineapple layers. The layer has no content, so it has no effect on the image.

● **Note:** You can also create a new layer by choosing Layer > New > Layer, or by choosing New Layer from the Layers panel menu.

2 Double-click the name Layer 1, type **Clouds**, and press Enter or Return to rename the layer.

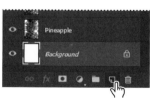 

Tip: If you expect to use a certain color frequently in multiple documents, add it to your Creative Cloud Libraries. Create a swatch of the color in the Swatches panel, and then drag the swatch to a library in the Libraries panel. Now that color is available to any Photoshop document that you open.

3 In the Tools panel, click the foreground color swatch, select a sky blue color from the Color Picker, and click OK. We selected a color with the following values: R=48, G=138, B=174. The Background Color remains white.

4 With the Clouds layer still active, choose Filter > Render > Clouds.

Realistic-looking clouds appear behind the image.

5 Choose File > Save.

Dragging to add a new layer

Tip: If you're adding artwork from a Creative Cloud library, you can simply drag and drop it from the Libraries panel into a Photoshop document. You can also do this with Adobe Stock images stored in your Creative Cloud Libraries.

You can add a layer to an image by dragging an image file from Bridge, or from the desktop in Explorer (Windows) or the Finder (Mac). You'll add another flower to the postcard now.

1 If Photoshop fills your monitor, reduce the size of the Photoshop window:

- On Windows, click the Restore button ( ) in the upper right corner, and then drag the lower right corner of the Photoshop window to make it smaller.

- On a Mac, click the green Maximize/Restore button ( ) in the upper left corner of the image window, or drag the lower right corner of the Photoshop window to make it smaller.

2 In Photoshop, select the Pineapple copy layer in the Layers panel to make it the active layer.

Blending modes

Blending modes affect how the color pixels on one layer blend with pixels on the layers beneath them. The default blending mode, Normal, hides pixels beneath the top layer unless the top layer is partially or completely transparent. Each of the other blending modes lets you control the way the pixels in the layers interact with each other.

Often, the best way to see how a blending mode affects your image is simply to try it. You can easily experiment with different blending modes in the Layers panel, watching the image change as you move the mouse over different options in the Blending Modes menu. As you experiment, keep in mind how different groups of blending modes affect an image. Generally, if you want to:

- Darken your image, try Darken, Multiply, Color Burn, Linear Burn, or Darker Color.

- Lighten your image, try Lighten, Screen, Color Dodge, Linear Dodge, or Lighter Color.

- Increase the contrast in the image, try Overlay, Soft Light, Hard Light, Vivid Light, Linear Light, Pin Light, or Hard Mix.

- Change the actual color values of the image, try Hue, Saturation, Color, or Luminosity.

- Create an inversion effect, try Difference or Exclusion.

The following blending modes often come in handy, and can be good places to start your experimentation:

- **Multiply** does just what the name implies: It multiplies the color in the underlying layers with the color in the top layer.

- **Lighten** replaces pixels in the underlying layers with those in the top layer whenever the pixels in the top layer are lighter.

- **Overlay** multiplies either the colors or the inverse of the colors, depending on the underlying layers. Patterns or colors overlay the existing pixels while preserving the highlights and shadows of the underlying layers.

Multiply

Lighten

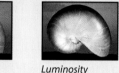

Overlay

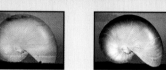

Luminosity

Difference

- **Luminosity** replaces only the luminance of the underlying colors with that of the top layer.

- **Difference** subtracts darker colors from lighter ones.

3 In Explorer (Windows) or the Finder (Mac), navigate to the Lessons folder you downloaded from the peachpit.com website. Then navigate to the Lesson04 folder.

4 Select Flower2.psd, and drag it from Explorer or the Finder onto your image.

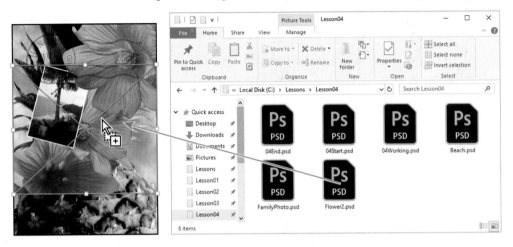

Tip: You can drag images from a Bridge window to Photoshop as easily as you can drag from the Windows or Mac desktop.

The Flower2 layer appears in the Layers panel, directly above the Pineapple copy layer. Photoshop places the image as a Smart Object, which is a layer you can edit without making permanent changes. You'll work more extensively with Smart Objects in Lesson 5.

5 Position the Flower2 layer in the lower left corner of the postcard, so that about half of the top flower is visible.

Tip: You can also commit a transformation by pressing Enter or Return.

6 Click the Commit Transform button (✓) in the options bar to accept the layer.

Adding text

Now you're ready to create some type using the Horizontal Type tool, which places the text on its own type layer. You'll then edit the text and apply a special effect.

1 Make the HAWAII layer visible. You'll add text just below this layer, and apply special effects to both layers.

2 Choose Select > Deselect Layers, so that no layers are selected.

3 In the Tools panel, select the Horizontal Type tool (**T**). Then, choose Window > Character to open the Character panel. Do the following in the Character panel:

*   Select a serif font (we used Birch Std; if you use a different font, adjust other settings accordingly).

*   Select a font style (we used Regular).

*   Select a large font size (we used 36 points).

*   Select a large tracking value () (we used 250).

*   Click the color swatch, select a shade of grassy green in the Color Picker, and click OK to close the Color Picker.

*   Click the Faux Bold button (**T**).

*   Click the All Caps button (**TT**).

*   Select Crisp from the Anti-aliasing menu (ᵃa).

4 Click just below the "H" in the word "HAWAII," and type **Island Paradise**, replacing the selected placeholder text that appears. Then click the Commit Any Current Edits button (✓) in the options bar.

● **Note:** If you make a mistake when you click to set the type, simply click away from the type and repeat step 4.

The Layers panel now includes a layer named Island Paradise with a "T" thumbnail, indicating that it is a type layer. This layer is at the top of the layer stack because no layers were selected when it was created.

The text appears where you clicked, which probably isn't exactly where you want it to be positioned.

5 Select the Move tool (✣), and drag the "Island Paradise" text so that it is centered below "HAWAII."

Applying a gradient to a layer

You can apply a color gradient to all or part of a layer. In this example, you'll apply a gradient to the word "HAWAII" to make it more colorful. First you'll select the letters, and then you'll apply the gradient.

1 Select the HAWAII layer in the Layers panel to make it active.

2 Right-click or Control-click the thumbnail in the HAWAII layer, and choose Select Pixels.

● **Note:** Make sure you click the thumbnail, rather than the layer name, or you'll see the wrong context menu.

Everything on the HAWAII layer (the white lettering) is selected. Now that you've selected the area to fill, you'll apply a gradient.

3   In the Tools panel, select the Gradient tool (▣).

4   Click the Foreground Color swatch in the Tools panel, select a bright shade of orange in the Color Picker, and click OK. The Background Color should still be white.

5   In the options bar, make sure that Linear Gradient (▣) is selected.

6   In the options bar, click the arrow next to the Gradient Editor box to open the Gradient Picker. Select the Foreground To Background swatch (it's the first one), and then click anywhere outside the gradient picker to close it.

Note: Though the layer contains the word "HAWAII," it is not an editable type layer. The text has been rasterized (converted to pixels).

Tip: To list the gradient options by name rather than by sample, click the menu button in the gradient picker, and choose either Small List or Large List. Or, hover the pointer over a thumbnail until a tool tip appears, showing the gradient name.

7   With the selection still active, drag the Gradient tool from the bottom to the top of the letters. If you want to be sure you drag straight up, press the Shift key as you drag. When the pointer reaches the top of the letters, release the mouse button.

The gradient extends across the type, starting with orange at the bottom and gradually blending to white at the top.

8   Choose Select > Deselect to deselect the HAWAII type.

9   Save the work you've done so far.

Applying a layer style

You can enhance a layer by adding a shadow, stroke, satin sheen, or other special effect from a collection of automated and editable layer styles. These styles are easy to apply, and they link directly to the layer you specify.

Like layers, layer styles can be hidden by clicking their eye icons (👁) in the Layers panel. Layer styles are nondestructive, so you can edit or remove them at any time. You can apply a copy of a layer style to a different layer by dragging the effect onto the destination layer.

Earlier, you used a layer style to add a stroke to the beach photo. Now, you'll add drop shadows to the text to make it stand out.

▶ **Tip:** You can also open the Layer Style dialog box by clicking the Add A Layer Style button at the bottom of the Layers panel and then choosing a layer style, such as Bevel & Emboss, from the pop-up menu.

1 Select the Island Paradise layer, and then choose Layer > Layer Style > Drop Shadow.

2 In the Layer Style dialog box, make sure that the Preview option is selected, and then, if necessary, move the dialog box so that you can see the Island Paradise text in the image window.

3 In the Structure area, select Use Global Light, and then specify the following settings:

- Blend Mode: Multiply
- Opacity: **75%**
- Angle: **78** degrees
- Distance: **5** px
- Spread: **30%**
- Size: **10** px

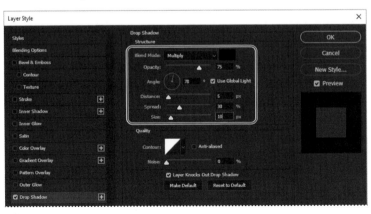

▶ **Tip:** To change the Global Light settings, choose Layer > Layer Style > Global Light.

When Use Global Light is selected, one "master" lighting angle is available in all the layer effects that use shading. If you set a lighting angle in one of these effects, every other effect with Use Global Light selected inherits the same angle setting.

Angle determines the lighting angle at which the effect is applied to the layer. Distance determines the offset distance for a shadow or satin effect. Spread determines how gradually the shadow fades toward the edges. Size determines how far the shadow extends.

Photoshop adds a drop shadow to the "Island Paradise" text in the image.

4   Click OK to accept the settings and close the Layer Style dialog box.

 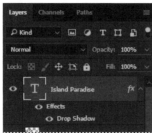

In the Layers panel, the layer style appears nested in the Island Paradise layer. An Effects heading is listed first, and under that, the layer styles applied to the layer. An eye icon (👁) appears next to the effect category and next to each effect. To turn off an effect, click its eye icon. Click the visibility column again to restore the effect. To hide all layer styles, click the eye icon next to Effects. To collapse the list of effects, click the arrow next to the layer.

5   Make sure that eye icons appear for both items nested in the Island Paradise layer.

6   Press Alt (Windows) or Option (Mac), and in the Layers panel, drag the Effects listing or the fx symbol (*fx*) for the Island Paradise layer onto the HAWAII layer.

▶ **Tip:** If you expect to use a layer style frequently in multiple documents, add it to your Creative Cloud Libraries. Select a layer using the style, click the Add Content button at the bottom of the Libraries panel, make sure Layer Style is selected, and then click Add. Now that style is available to any open Photoshop document.

The Drop Shadow layer style is applied to the HAWAII layer, copying the settings you applied to the Island Paradise layer. Now you'll add a green stroke around the word HAWAII.

7   Select the HAWAII layer in the Layers panel, click the Add A Layer Style button (*fx*) at the bottom of the panel, and then choose Stroke from the pop-up menu.

8   In the Structure area of the Layer Style dialog box, specify the following settings:

- Size: **4** px

- Position: Outside

- Blend Mode: Normal

- Opacity: **100**%

- Color: Green (Select a shade that goes well with the one you used for the "Island Paradise" text.)

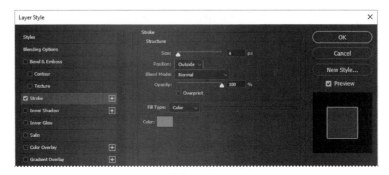

9   Click OK to apply the stroke.

Now you'll add a drop shadow and a satin sheen to the flower.

Julieanne Kost is an official Adobe Photoshop evangelist.

Tool tips from the Photoshop evangelist

Blending effects

Blending layers in a different order or on different groups changes the effect. You can apply a blending mode to an entire layer group and get a very different result than if you apply the same blending mode to each of the layers individually. When a blending mode is applied to a group, Photoshop treats the group as a single merged object. Experiment with blending modes to get the effect you want.

10 Select the Flower layer, and choose Layer > Layer Style > Drop Shadow. Then change the following settings in the Structure area:

- Opacity: **60**%

- Distance: **13** px

- Spread: **9**%

- Make sure Use Global Light is selected, and that the Blend Mode is Multiply. Do not click OK.

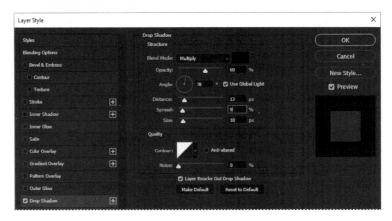

● **Note:** Be sure to click the word Satin. If you click only the check box, Photoshop applies the layer style with its default settings, but you won't see the options.

11 With the Layer Style dialog box still open, click the word Satin on the left to select it and display its options. Then make sure Invert is selected, and apply the following settings:

- Color (next to Blend Mode): Choose a color that enhances the flower color, such as a fuschia hue

- Opacity: **20**%

- Distance: **22** px

The Satin layer effect applies interior shading to create a satiny finish. The contour controls the shape of the effect; Invert flips the contour curve.

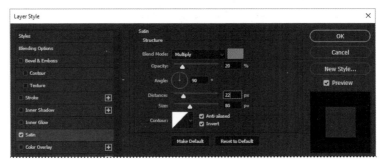

12 Click OK to apply both layer styles.

Before applying layer styles

The flower with the drop shadow and satin layer styles applied

Adding an adjustment layer

You can add adjustment layers to an image to apply color and tonal adjustments without permanently changing the pixel values in the image. For example, if you add a Color Balance adjustment layer to an image, you can experiment with different colors repeatedly, because the change occurs only on the adjustment layer. If you decide to return to the original pixel values, you can hide or delete the adjustment layer.

You've used adjustment layers in other lessons. Here, you'll add a Hue/Saturation adjustment layer to change the color of the purple flower. An adjustment layer affects all layers below it in the image's stacking order unless a selection is active when you create it or you create a clipping mask.

1 Select the Flower2 layer in the Layers panel.

2 Click the Hue/Saturation icon in the Adjustments panel to add a Hue/Saturation adjustment layer.

3 In the Properties panel, apply the following settings:

- Hue: **43**

- Saturation: **19**

- Lightness: **0**

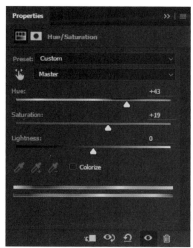

The changes affect the Flower2, Pineapple Copy, Pineapple, Clouds, and Background layers. The effect is interesting, but you want to change only the Flower2 layer.

● **Note:** Be sure to click the layer name, not the thumbnail, to see the appropriate context menu.

4 Right-click (Windows) or Control-click (Mac) the layer name on the Hue/Saturation adjustment layer, and choose Create Clipping Mask.

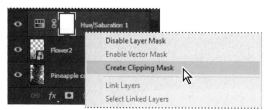

An arrow appears in the Layers panel, indicating that the adjustment layer applies only to the Flower2 layer. You'll learn more about clipping masks in Lessons 6 and 7.

Extra credit

Using an effect more than once in a layer style

A great way to add visual impact to a design element is to apply multiple instances of effects such as strokes, glows, or shadows. You don't have to duplicate layers to do this, because you can apply multiple instances of an effect inside the Layer Style dialog box.

1   Open 04End.psd in your Lesson04 folder.

2   In the Layers panel, double-click the Drop Shadow effect applied to the HAWAII layer.

3   In the effects list on the left side of the Layer Style dialog box, click the + button to the right of the Drop Shadow effect, and select the second Drop Shadow effect.

Now for the fun part! You can adjust your second drop shadow to change options such as color, size, and opacity.

4   In the Drop Shadow options area, click the color swatch, move the pointer outside the Layer Style dialog box so that the pointer changes into an eyedropper, and click the bottom flower to sample its purplish color. Then match the Drop Shadow settings as shown below, and click OK.

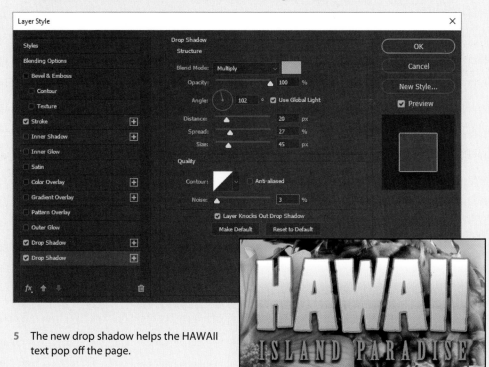

5   The new drop shadow helps the HAWAII text pop off the page.

Updating layer effects

Layer effects are automatically updated when you make changes to a layer. You can edit the text and watch how the layer effect tracks the change.

Tip: You can search for layers in the Layers panel by layer type, layer name, effect, mode, attribute, and color. You can also display only the selected layers: Choose Select > Isolate Layers, or choose Selected from the Kind menu in the Layers panel to enter Isolation Mode.

1 Select the Island Paradise layer in the Layers panel.

2 In the Tools panel, select the Horizontal Type tool (**T**).

3 In the options bar, set the font size to **32** points, and press Enter or Return.

You were able to change the settings for the entire type layer, even though you didn't select the text by highlighting the characters (as you would have to do in a word processing program). This worked because in Photoshop, you can change settings for an entire type layer by selecting it in the Layers panel, as long as a type tool is selected. "Island Paradise" now appears in 32-point type.

4 Using the Horizontal Type tool, click between "Island" and "Paradise," and type **of**.

As you edit the text, the layer styles are applied to the new text.

5 You don't actually need the word "of," so delete it.

6 Select the Move tool (✛), and drag "Island Paradise" to center it beneath the word "HAWAII."

Note: You don't have to click the Commit Any Current Edits button after making the text edits, because selecting the Move tool has the same effect.

When you add text, layer effects are automatically applied.

Center the text beneath the word "HAWAII."

7 Choose File > Save.

Adding a border

The Hawaii postcard is nearly done. The elements are almost all arranged correctly in the composition. You'll finish up by positioning the postmark and then adding a white postcard border.

Note: The Auto-Select option can save time by letting you select a layer by clicking it with the Move tool, instead of having to select it in the Layers panel. But in documents where many layers overlap, if the wrong layer is selected when you click, try turning off Auto-Select.

1 Select the Move tool, and in the options bar, make sure Auto-Select is disabled.

2 Select the Postage layer, and then use the Move tool (✛) to drag it to the middle right of the image, as in the illustration.

3 Select the Island Paradise layer in the Layers panel, and then click the Create A New Layer button (◻) at the bottom of the panel.

4 Choose Select > All.

5 Choose Select > Modify > Border. In the Border Selection dialog box, type **10** pixels for the Width, and click OK.

A 10-pixel border is selected around the entire image. Now, you'll fill it with white.

6 Select white for the Foreground Color, and then choose Edit > Fill.

7 In the Fill dialog box, choose Foreground Color from the Contents menu, and click OK.

 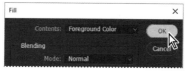

8 Choose Select > Deselect.

9 Double-click the Layer 1 name in the Layers panel, and rename the layer **Border.**

Flattening and saving files

When you finish editing all the layers in your image, you can merge or *flatten* layers to reduce the file size. Flattening combines all the layers into a single background layer. However, you cannot edit layers once you've flattened them, so you shouldn't flatten an image until you are certain that you're satisfied with all your design decisions. Rather than flattening your original PSD files, it's a good idea to save a copy of the file with its layers intact, in case you need to edit a layer later.

● **Note:** If the sizes do not appear in the status bar, click the status bar pop-up menu arrow, and choose Document Sizes.

To appreciate what flattening does, notice the two numbers for the file size in the status bar at the bottom of the image window. The first number represents what the file size would be if you flattened the image. The second number represents the file size without flattening. This lesson file, if flattened, would be 2–3MB, but the current file is much larger. So flattening is well worth it in this case.

1 Select any tool but the Type tool (**T**), to be sure that you're not in text-editing mode. Then choose File > Save (if it is available) to be sure that all your changes have been saved in the file.

2 Choose Image > Duplicate.

3 In the Duplicate Image dialog box, name the file **04Flat.psd**, and click OK.

4 Leave the 04Flat.psd file open, but close the 04Working.psd file.

▶ **Tip:** The Flatten Image command is also on the Layer menu, and on the context menu when you right-click/Ctrl-click a layer name.

5 Choose Flatten Image from the Layers panel menu.

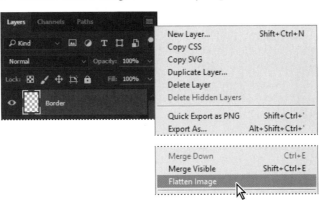

Only one layer, named Background, remains in the Layers panel.

6 Choose File > Save. Even though you chose Save rather than Save As, the Save As dialog box appears.

7 Make sure the location is the Lessons/Lesson04 folder, and then click Save to accept the default settings and save the flattened file.

You have saved two versions of the file: a one-layer, flattened copy as well as the original file, in which all the layers remain intact.

You've created a colorful, attractive postcard. This lesson only begins to explore the vast possibilities and the flexibility you gain when you master the art of using Photoshop layers. You'll get more experience and try out different techniques for layers in almost every chapter as you move forward in this book.

▶ **Tip:** If you want to flatten only some of the layers in a file, click the eye icons to hide the layers you don't want to flatten, and then choose Merge Visible from the Layers panel menu.

Use layer comps to store and switch among design ideas

The Layer Comps panel (choose Window > Layer Comps) provides one-click flexibility in switching between different views of a multilayered image file. A layer comp is simply a definition of the settings in the Layers panel. Whenever you want to preserve a specific combination of layer properties, create a new layer comp. Then, by switching from one layer comp to another, you can quickly review the two designs. The beauty of layer comps becomes apparent when you want to demonstrate a number of possible design arrangements. When you've created a few layer comps, you can review the design variations without having to tediously select and deselect eye icons or change settings in the Layers panel.

Say, for example, that you are designing a brochure, and you're producing a version in English as well as in French. You might have the French text on one layer, and the English text on another in the same image file. To create two different layer comps, you would simply turn on visibility for the French layer and turn off visibility for the English layer, and then click the Create New Layer Comp button in the Layer Comps panel. Then you'd do the inverse—turn on visibility for the English layer and turn off visibility for the French layer, and click the Create New Layer Comp button—to create an English layer comp. To view the different layer comps, click the Layer Comp box for each comp in the Layer Comps panel in turn.

Layer comps can be an especially valuable feature when the design is in flux or when you need to create multiple versions of the same image file. If some aspects need to stay consistent among layer comps, you can change the visibility, position, or appearance of one layer in a layer comp and then sync it to see that change reflected in all the other layer comps.

Extra credit

Exploring design options with Adobe Stock

Visualizing different ideas for a design project is easier when you can experiment with images. The Libraries panel in Photoshop gives you direct access to millions of Adobe Stock images. We'll add a stock image of a ukulele to this lesson's composition.

1   In the Lesson04 folder, open 04End.psd. Save it as 04End_Working.

2   In the Layers panel, select the Beach layer.

3   In the Libraries panel, make sure the search field is set to Search Adobe Stock, type **ukulele** into the field, and locate a vertical image of a ukulele on a white background with no shadow.

4   Drag the ukulele image into the document. Drag a corner handle to proportionally scale the image to about 25% of its original size. Apply the changes to finish importing the image.

5   Choose Current Library from the search field menu (⌄). The image is now in your library. Click the ⊗ to clear the search.

6   Now remove the background. With the ukulele layer selected, choose the Magic Wand tool in the Tools panel, and click anywhere within the white background. If the image you picked has an ID number in a corner, Shift-drag around the numbers with the Rectangular Marquee tool to include them, in the selection. Alt/Option-click the Add Layer Mask button (◻) at the bottom of the Layers panel.

7   With the Move tool, drag the ukulele to the upper left corner so that it partially overlaps with the small photo of the beach view. You've just added an Adobe Stock photo to your postcard image!

Adobe Stock search results

Stock image in document

Licensing an image

Until it's licensed, the ukulele image is a low-resolution version with an Adobe Stock watermark. You don't have to license the ukulele image used here, but you must license images used in a final project. With the ukulele layer selected, click License Asset in the Properties panel and follow the prompts. After licensing, the image is automatically replaced with a high-resolution version without a watermark. If you plan to license many images, consider an Adobe Stock monthly plan or a pack of credits.

You've added a new element to your postcard using Adobe Stock!

Review questions

1 What is the advantage of using layers?

2 When you create a new layer, where does it appear in the Layers panel stack?

3 How can you make artwork on one layer appear in front of artwork on another layer?

4 How can you apply a layer style?

5 When you've completed your artwork, what can you do to minimize the file size without changing the quality, dimensions, or compression?

Review answers

1 Layers let you move and edit different parts of an image as discrete objects. You can also hide individual layers as you work on other layers.

2 A new layer always appears immediately above the active layer.

3 You can make artwork on one layer appear in front of artwork on another layer by dragging layers up or down the stacking order in the Layers panel or by using the Layer > Arrange commands—Bring To Front, Bring Forward, Send Backward, and Send To Back. However, you can't change the layer position of a background layer.

4 To apply a layer style, select the layer, and then click the Add A Layer Style button in the Layers panel, or choose Layer > Layer Style > [style].

5 To minimize file size, you can flatten the image, which merges all the layers onto a single background. It's a good idea to duplicate image files with layers intact before you flatten them, in case you have to make changes to a layer later.

5 QUICK FIXES

Lesson overview

In this lesson, you'll learn how to do the following:

- Remove red eye.

- Brighten an image.

- Adjust the features of a face.

- Combine images to create a panorama.

- Crop and straighten an image and fill in any resulting empty areas.

- Blur the background of an image using Iris Blur.

- Merge two images to extend depth of field.

- Apply optical lens correction to a distorted image.

- Remove an object and seamlessly fill the empty space.

- Adjust the perspective of an image to match another image.

 This lesson will take about an hour to complete. Please log in to your account on peachpit.com to download the lesson files for this chapter, or go to the Getting Started section at the beginning of this book and follow the instructions under "Accessing the Lesson Files and Web Edition."

As you work on this lesson, you'll preserve the start files. If you need to restore the start files, download them from your Account page.

PROJECT: RED EYE REDUCTION

PROJECT: CORRECTING
IMAGE DISTORTION

PROJECT: PANORAMA FROM MULTIPLE IMAGES

Sometimes just one or two clicks in Photoshop can
turn an image from so-so (or worse) to awesome.
Quick fixes get you the results you want without a lot
of fuss.

Getting started

Not every image requires a complicated makeover using advanced features in Photoshop. In fact, once you're familiar with Photoshop, you can often improve an image quickly. The trick is to know what's possible and how to find what you need.

In this lesson, you'll make quick fixes to several images using a variety of tools and techniques. You can use these techniques individually, or team them up when you're working with an image that needs just a little more help.

1   Start Photoshop, and then immediately hold down Ctrl+Alt+Shift (Windows) or Command+Option+Shift (Mac) to restore the default preferences. (See "Restoring Default Preferences" on page 5.)

2   When prompted, click Yes to delete the Adobe Photoshop Settings file.

Improving a snapshot

If you're sharing a snapshot with family and friends, you may not need it to look professional. But you probably don't want glowing eyes, and it would be good if the picture isn't too dark to show important detail. Photoshop gives you the tools to make quick changes to a snapshot.

Correcting red eye

Red eye occurs when the retina of a subject's eye is reflected by the camera flash. It commonly occurs in photographs taken in a dark room, because the subject's irises are wide open. Fortunately, red eye is easy to fix in Photoshop. In this exercise, you will remove the red eye from the woman's eyes in the portrait.

You'll start by viewing the before and after images in Adobe Bridge.

1   Choose File > Browse In Bridge to open Adobe Bridge.

2   In the Favorites panel in Bridge, click the Lessons folder. Then, in the Content panel, double-click the Lesson05 folder to open it.

3   Adjust the thumbnail slider, if necessary, so that you can see the thumbnail previews clearly. Then look at the RedEye_Start.jpg and RedEye_End.psd files.

● Note: If you haven't installed Bridge, you'll be prompted to do so when you choose Browse In Bridge. For more information, see page 3.

● Note: If Bridge asks you if you want to import preferences from a previous version of Bridge, click No.

RedEye_Start.jpg   RedEye_End.psd

Not only does red eye make an ordinary person or animal appear unusual, but it can distract from the subject of the image. It's easy to correct red eye in Photoshop, and you'll quickly lighten this image too.

4   Double-click the RedEye_Start.jpg file to open it in Photoshop.

5   Choose File > Save As, choose Photoshop for the Format, name the file **RedEye_Working.psd**, and click Save.

6   Select the Zoom tool (🔍), and then drag to zoom in to see the woman's eyes. If Scrubby Zoom isn't selected, drag a marquee around the eyes to zoom in.

7   Select the Red Eye tool (⁺◉), hidden under the Spot Healing Brush tool (🩹).

8   In the options bar, reduce the Pupil Size to **23%** and the Darken Amount to **62%**.

The Darken Amount specifies how dark the pupil should be.

9   Click the pupil in the woman's left eye. The red reflection disappears.

10 Click the pupil in the woman's right eye to remove the red reflection there, too.

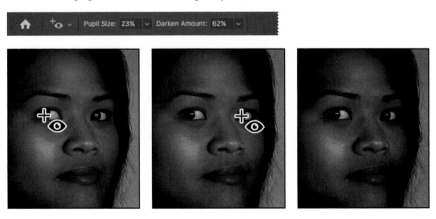

If the red reflection is directly over the pupil, clicking the pupil removes it. However, if the red reflection is slightly off the pupil, try clicking the highlight in the eye first. You may need to try a few different spots, but it's easy to undo and try again.

11 Choose View > Fit On Screen to see the entire image.

12 Choose File > Save.

Brightening an image

The woman's eyes no longer glow red, but the overall image is a bit dark. You can brighten an image in several different ways, as you've already seen. You can try adding adjustment layers for Brightness/Contrast, Levels, and Curves, depending on the degree of adjustment you want to make. For a quick fix or a good starting point, try the Auto button or the presets, which are available in both the Levels and Curves adjustments. Let's try a Curves adjustment layer for this image.

1 Click Curves in the Adjustments panel.

2 Click Auto to apply an automatic correction. The image brightens.

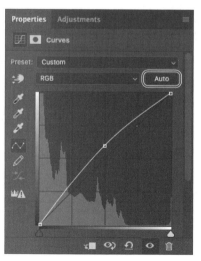

3   Choose Lighter from the Preset menu. The curve changes slightly. The difference between the two curves is that a preset applies the same curve to every image, while Auto customizes the curve after analyzing an individual image.

4   Click the Reset to Adjustment Defaults button (⟳) at the bottom of the Properties panel to revert back to the unadjusted image.

5   Select the on-image adjustment tool (🖐) in the Curves panel, and then click the center of the forehead and drag upwards. That brightens the image nicely, and also improves the contrast.

▶ **Tip:** If you want to use the Auto button or the white point or black point samplers (eyedropper icons) in the Curves or Levels adjustments, use them before applying manual adjustments. Like presets, adjustments by those tools replace manual adjustments.

▶ **Tip:** To see how much you've brightened the image, hide the Curves layer, and then show it again.

6   Choose Layer > Flatten Image.

7   Save the file.

Adjusting facial features with Liquify

The Liquify filter is useful when you want to distort only part of an image. It includes Face-Aware Liquify options that can automatically recognize faces in images, and then lets you easily adjust facial features such as the eyes, nose, and mouth. For example, you can adjust the size of or distance between the eyes. Being able to adjust facial features can be useful for photos used in advertising and fashion, when portraying a certain look or expression may be more important than faithfully representing a specific person.

1 With RedEye_Working.psd still open, choose Filter > Liquify.

2 In the Properties panel, expand the Face-Aware Liquify options.

▶ **Tip:** When the Face tool (👤) is selected in the Liquify toolbar, handles appear as you hover the pointer over different parts of the face. You can drag those handles to adjust different parts of the face directly, as an alternative to dragging the Face-Aware Liquify sliders.

3   Make sure the Eyes section is expanded and that the link icon is selected for both Eye Size and Eye Height; then enter **32** for Eye Size and **10** for Eye Height.

When the link icon is not selected for an Eyes option, you can set different values for the left and right eyes.

4   Make sure the Mouth section is expanded, and then enter **5** for Smile and **9** for Mouth Height.

5   Make sure the Face Shape section is expanded, and then enter **40** for Jawline and **50** for Face Width.

6   Deselect and reselect the Preview option to compare the image before and after your changes.

Before Face-Aware Liquify   *After Face-Aware Liquify*

▶ **Tip:** The Face-Aware Liquify options have a limited range because they're designed for subtle, believable distortions. If you want to exaggerate faces into caricatures or extreme expressions, you may want to use the more advanced manual tools along the left side of the Liquify dialog box.

Feel free to experiment with any of the Face-Aware Liquify options to get a better sense of the possibilities for quick, easy alterations.

7   Click OK to exit Liquify. Close the document and save your changes.

The Face-Aware Liquify features are available only when Photoshop recognizes a face in an image. It may not recognize a face that is turned too far away from the camera or when a face is partially covered by hair, sunglasses, or a hat shadow.

Blurring a background

The interactive blurs in the Blur Gallery let you customize a blur as you preview it on your image. You'll use an iris blur to blur the background in an image, focusing the viewer's attention on the main attraction—in this case, the egret. You'll apply the blur as a Smart Filter so that you can modify it later if you want to.

You'll start by looking at the start and end files in Bridge.

1   Choose File > Browse In Bridge to open Adobe Bridge.

2   In the Favorites panel in Bridge, click the Lessons folder. Then, in the Content panel, double-click the Lesson05 folder to open it.

3   Compare the Egret_Start.jpg and Egret_End.psd thumbnail previews.

Egret_Start.jpg   *Egret_End.psd*

In the final image, the egret appears sharper, as its reflection and the grass around it have been blurred. Iris Blur, one of the interactive blurs in the Blur Gallery, makes the task an easy one—no masking required.

4   Choose File > Return To Adobe Photoshop, and choose File > Open As Smart Object.

5   Select the Egret_Start.jpg file in the Lesson05 folder, and click OK or Open.

Photoshop opens the image. There is one layer in the Layers panel, and it's a Smart Object, as indicated by the badge on the layer thumbnail icon.

6   Choose File > Save As, choose Photoshop for the Format, name the file **Egret_Working.psd**, and click Save. Click OK in the Photoshop Format Options dialog box.

7 Choose Filter > Blur Gallery > Iris Blur.

A blur ellipse is centered on your image. You can adjust the location and scope of the blur by moving the center pin, feather handles, and ellipse handles. At the top right corner of the Blur Gallery task space, you also see the expandable Field Blur, Tilt-Shift Blur, Path Blur, and Spin Blur panels.

8 Drag the center pin so that it's at the bottom of the bird's body.

9 Click the ellipse, and drag inward to tighten the focus around the bird.

▶ Tip: If you have an iPhone camera that produces an HEIF depth map, such as an iPhone Plus or iPhone X, you can create a more realistic background blur effect by loading the depth map into the Lens Blur filter (Filter > Blur > Lens Blur).

A   B   C   D

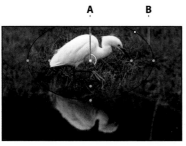 

A. *Center* **B.** *Ellipse* **C.** *Feather handle* **D.** *Blur*

10 Press Alt (Windows) or Option (Mac) as you click and drag the feather handles to match those in the first image below. Pressing Alt or Option lets you drag each handle separately.

11 Click and drag on the Blur ring to reduce the amount of blur to **5** px, creating a gradual but noticeable blur. You can also change the same value by moving the Blur slider in the Iris Blur area of the Blur Tools panel.

12 Click OK in the options bar to apply the blur.

The blur may be a little too subtle. You'll edit the blur to increase it slightly.

13 Double-click the Blur Gallery in the Egret layer in the Layers panel to open it again. Adjust the blur to **6** px, and click OK in the options bar to apply it.

The egret is accentuated by blurring the rest of the image. Because you applied the filter to a Smart Object, you can hide or edit the effect without altering the original image.

14 Save the file, and then close it.

Blur Gallery

The Blur Gallery includes five interactive blurs: Field Blur, Iris Blur, Tilt-Shift, Path Blur, and Spin Blur. Each gives you on-image selective motion blur tools, with an initial blur pin. You can create additional blur pins by clicking on the image. You can apply a single blur or a combination of blurs, and you can create a strobe effect for path and spin blurs.

Before *After*

Field Blur applies a gradient blur to areas of the image, defined by pins you create and settings you specify for each. When you first apply Field Blur, a pin is placed in the center of the image. You can adjust the blur relative to that point by dragging the blur handle or specifying a value in the Blur Tools panel; you can also drag the pin to a different location.

Before *After*

Iris Blur simulates a shallow depth-of-field effect, gradually blurring everything outside the focus ring. Adjust the ellipse handles, feather handles, and blur amount to customize the iris blur.

Before *After*

Tilt-Shift simulates an image taken with a tilt-shift lens. This blur defines areas of sharpness and then fades to a blur at the edges. You can use this effect to simulate photos of miniature objects.

Before *After*

Spin Blur is a radial-style blur measured in degrees. You can change the size and shape of the ellipse, re-center the rotation point by pressing Alt or Option as you click and drag, and adjust the blur angle. You can also specify the blur angle in the Blur Tools panel. Multiple spin blurs can overlap.

Before   *After*

Before   *After*

Path Blur creates motion blurs along paths you draw. You control the shape and amount of the blur.

When you first apply a Path Blur, a default path appears. Drag the end point to reposition it. Click the center point and drag to change the curve. Click to add additional curve points. The arrow on the path indicates the blur's direction.

You can also create a multiple-point path or a shape. Blur shapes describe the local motion blurs, similar to camera shake (see "Camera Shake Reduction" on page 140). The Speed slider in the Blur Tools panel determines the speed for all the path blurs. The Centered Blur option ensures that the blur shape for any pixel is centered on that pixel, resulting in more stable-feeling motion blurs; to make the motion appear more fluid, deselect this option.

In the **Effects** tab, you specify the bokeh parameters to control the appearance of blurred areas. Light Bokeh brightens the blurred areas; Bokeh Color adds more vivid colors to lightened areas that aren't blown out to white; Light Range determines the range of tones that the settings affect.

You can add a **strobe effect** to spin and path blurs. Select the **Motion Effects** tab to bring its panel forward. The Strobe Strength slider determines how much blur shows between flash exposures (0% gives no strobe effect; 100% gives full strobe effect with little blur between exposures). Strobe Flashes determines the number of exposures.

Before   *After*

Applying a blur will smooth out visible digital image noise or film grain that's in the original image, and this mismatch between the original and blurred areas can make the blur appear artificial. You can use the **Noise** tab to restore noise or grain so that blurred areas match up with unblurred areas. Start with the Amount slider, and then use the other Noise options to match the character of the original grain. Increase the Color value if the original has visible color noise, and lower the Highlights value if you need to balance the noise level in the highlights compared to the shadows.

Creating a panorama

Sometimes a vista is just too large for a single shot. Photoshop makes it easy to combine multiple images into a panorama so that your viewers can get the full effect.

Once again, you'll take a look at the end file first, to see where you're going.

1 Choose File > Browse In Bridge.

2 Navigate to the Lesson05 folder, if you're not there already. Then, look at the Skyline_End.psd thumbnail preview.

Tip: In Bridge, you can preview a selected image in full screen mode by pressing the spacebar. This is useful for previewing detailed or large images such as a panorama. Press the spacebar again to close the preview.

Skyline_End.psd

You'll combine four shots of the Seattle skyline into a single wide panorama image so that viewers get a sense of the whole scene. Creating a panorama from multiple images requires only a few clicks. Photoshop does the rest.

Tip: You can also open selected images from Bridge directly into Photomerge by choosing Tools > Photoshop > Photomerge.

3 Return to Photoshop.

4 With no files open in Photoshop, choose File > Automate > Photomerge.

5 In the Source Files area, click Browse, and navigate to the Lesson05/Files For Panorama folder.

6 Shift-select all the images in the folder, and click OK or Open.

7 In the Layout area of the Photomerge dialog box, select Perspective.

The best option for merging photos isn't always Perspective; it depends on how the originals were photographed. If you're not completely happy with the result of a particular merge, you can always try again with a different Layout option. If you're not sure which one to use, you can simply click Auto.

8 At the bottom of the Photomerge dialog box, select Blend Images Together, Vignette Removal, Geometric Distortion Correction, and Content Aware Fill Transparent Areas. Then click OK.

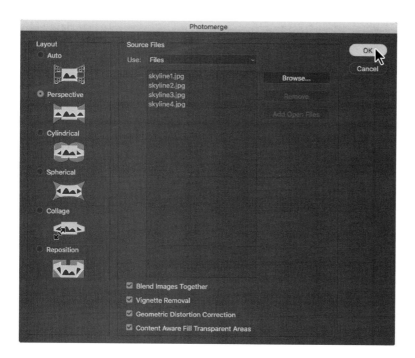

Blend Images Together blends images based on the optimal borders between them, instead of just creating a simple rectangular blend. Vignette Removal performs exposure compensation in images with darkened edges. Geometric Distortion Correction compensates for barrel, pincushion, or fisheye distortion. Content Aware Fill Transparent Areas automatically patches the empty areas between the merged image edges and the sides of the canvas.

Photoshop creates the panorama image. It's a complex process, so you may have to wait a few moments while Photoshop works. When it's finished, you'll see the full vista in the image window with five layers in the Layers panel. The bottom four layers are the original four images you selected. Photoshop identified the overlapping areas of the images and matched them, correcting any angular discrepancies. The top layer, containing "(merged)" in the layer name, is a single panorama image blended from all of the images you selected, combined with formerly empty areas filled in by Content Aware Fill. Those areas are indicated by the selection.

● **Note:** Photomerge will require more time when you merge more images, or images with large pixel dimensions. Photomerge works faster on computers that are newer or that have more RAM.

▶ **Tip:** If you want to see how the panorama looks without the areas created by Content Aware Fill, hide the top layer.

Getting the best results with Photomerge

If you know you're going to create a panorama when you take your shots, keep the following guidelines in mind to get the best result.

Overlap images by 15% to 40% Sufficient overlap helps Photomerge blend edges seamlessly. Over 50% overlap won't help and creates too many images.

Use a consistent focal length If you use a zoom lens, keep the focal length the same for all the pictures in the panorama.

Use a tripod if possible You'll get the best results if the camera is at the same level when you take each of the shots. A tripod with a rotating head makes that easier.

Take the photos from the same position If you're not using a tripod with a rotating head, try to stay in the same position as you take the photos, so that they are taken from the same viewpoint.

Avoid lenses that produce creative distortion They can interfere with Photomerge. (The Auto option does adjust for images you take with fisheye lenses.)

Use the same exposure The images will blend more gracefully if they all have the same exposure. For example, either use flash for all the images or for none of them.

Try different layout options If you don't like the results you get when you create the panorama, try again using a different layout option. Often, Auto selects the appropriate option, but sometimes you'll get a better image with one of the other options.

9 Choose Select > Deselect.

10 Choose Layer > Flatten Image.

11 Choose File > Save As. Choose Photoshop for the Format, and name the file **Skyline_Working.psd**. Save the file in the Lesson05 folder. Click Save.

The panorama looks great, but it's a little dark. You'll add a Levels adjustment layer to brighten it a little bit.

12 Click the Levels icon in the Adjustments panel to add a Levels adjustment layer.

13 Select the White Point eyedropper in the Properties panel, and then click on a white area of the clouds.

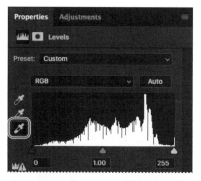

The sky gets bluer, and the entire image brightens.

14 Save your work. Click OK in the Photoshop Format Options dialog box.

It's that easy to create a panorama!

● **Note:** In this case, the Photoshop Format Options alert may appear because a layer was added. The Photoshop Format Options dialog box usually won't appear for Photoshop documents containing only a Background layer.

Filling empty areas when cropping

The panorama image looks great except for two things: The horizon is slightly tilted, and the lower handrail is incomplete where the rocks on the right descend into the water. If you were to rotate the image, empty areas might appear at the corners, requiring a tighter crop and losing parts of the image. Fortunately, the same Content-Aware technology that filled in empty areas resulting from the panorama merge can also fill in empty areas that can result from straightening and cropping.

1   Make sure **Skyline_Working.psd** is open, and make sure the Background layer is selected in the Layers panel.

2   Choose Layer > Flatten Image.

3   In the Tools panel, select the Crop tool. The crop rectangle and its handles appear around the image.

4   In the options bar, select the Straighten button (⬚), and make sure Content-Aware is selected.

5   Position the Straighten pointer on the horizon at the left edge of the image, and drag to the right to create a Straighten line that's aligned with the horizon; release the mouse button when you reach the end of the horizon at the right edge of the image.

Notice there is now white space that needs to be filled near the corners.

6   With the crop rectangle still active, drag the image down until the incomplete part of the lower guardrail is outside the crop rectangle.

7   Click the Commit button in the options bar (✔) to apply the current crop settings. Content-Aware Crop fills in the empty areas at the top and sides of the image.

8   Save your changes, and close the document.

Correcting image distortion

The Lens Correction filter fixes common camera lens flaws, such as barrel and pincushion distortion, chromatic aberration, and vignetting. *Barrel distortion* is a lens defect that causes straight lines to bow out toward the edges of the image. *Pincushion distortion* is the opposite effect, causing straight lines to bend inward. *Chromatic aberration* appears as a color fringe along the edges of image objects. *Vignetting* occurs when the edges of an image, especially the corners, are darker than the center.

Some lenses exhibit these defects depending on the focal length or the f-stop used. The Lens Correction filter can apply settings based on the camera, lens, and focal length that were used to make the image. The filter can also rotate an image or fix image perspective caused by tilting a camera vertically or horizontally. The filter's image grid makes it easier and more accurate to make these adjustments than using the Transform command.

1   Choose File > Browse In Bridge.

2   Navigate to the Lesson05 folder if you're not already there, and then look at the Columns_Start.psd and Columns_End.psd thumbnail previews.

Columns_Start.psd   *Columns_End.psd*

In this case, the original image of a Greek temple is distorted, with the columns appearing to be bowed. This photo was shot at a range that was too close with a wide-angle lens. You'll quickly correct the lens barrel distortion.

3   Double-click the Columns_Start.psd file to open it in Photoshop.

4   Choose File > Save As. In the Save As dialog box, name the file **Columns_Working.psd**, and save it in the Lesson05 folder. Click OK if the Photoshop Format Options dialog box appears.

▶ **Tip:** If the crop rectangle from the previous exercise is still visible and distracting, switch to a tool such as the Hand tool.

5 Choose Filter > Lens Correction. The Lens Correction dialog box opens.

6 Select Show Grid at the bottom of the dialog box, if it's not already selected.

An alignment grid overlays the image. To the right are options for automatic corrections based on lens profiles. In the Custom tab are manual controls for correcting distortion, chromatic aberration, and perspective.

The Lens Correction dialog box includes auto-correction options. You'll adjust one setting in the Auto Correction tab and then customize the settings.

7 In the Correction area of the Auto Correction tab, make sure Auto Scale Image is selected, and that Transparency is selected from the Edge menu.

8 Select the Custom tab.

9 In the Custom tab, drag the Remove Distortion slider to about **+52.00** to remove the barrel distortion in the image. Alternatively, you could select the Remove Distortion tool (⊞) and drag in the image preview area until the columns are straight. The adjustment causes the image borders to bow inward. However, because you selected Auto Scale Image, the Lens Correction filter automatically scales the image to adjust the borders.

▶ **Tip:** Watch the alignment grid as you make these changes so that you can see when the vertical columns are straightened in the image.

10 Click OK to apply your changes and close the Lens Correction dialog box.

The curving distortion caused by the wide-angle lens and low shooting angle is eliminated.

11 (Optional) To compare the image before and after the last change, press Ctrl+Z (Windows) or Command+Z (Mac) to undo the filter, and then press Ctrl+Shift+Z (Windows) or Command+Shift+Z (Mac) to redo the filter.

12 Choose File > Save to save your changes, click OK if the Photoshop Format Options dialog box appears, and then close the image.

The temple looks much more stable now!

Extending depth of field

When you're shooting a photo, you often have to choose to focus on either the background or the foreground. If you want the entire image to be in focus, you can take two photos—one with the background in focus and one with the foreground in focus—and then merge the two in Photoshop.

Because you'll need to align the images exactly, it's helpful to use a tripod to keep the camera steady. However, you may be able to get good results with a handheld camera if you pay attention to framing and alignment. In this exercise, you'll add depth of field to an image of a wine glass in front of a beach.

1 Choose File > Browse In Bridge.

2 Navigate to the Lesson05 folder, if you're not there already, and then look at the Glass_Start.psd and Glass_End.psd thumbnail previews.

Glass_Start.psd   Glass_End.psd

The first image has two layers. Depending on which layer is visible, either the glass in the foreground or the beach in the background is in focus. You'll extend the depth of field to make both clear.

3 Double-click the Glass_Start.psd file to open it.

4 Choose File > Save As. Name the file **Glass_Working.psd**, and save it in the Lesson05 folder. Click OK if the Photoshop Format Options dialog box appears.

5   In the Layers panel, hide the Beach layer, so that only the Glass layer is visible. The glass is in focus, but the background is blurred. Then, show the Beach layer again. Now the beach is in focus, but the glass is blurred.

You'll merge the layers, using the part of each layer that is in focus. First, you need to align the layers.

6   Shift-click to select both of the layers.

7 Choose Edit > Auto-Align Layers.

Because these images were shot from the same angle, Auto will work just fine.

8 Select Auto, if it isn't already selected. Make sure neither Vignette Removal nor Geometric Distortion is selected. Then click OK to align the layers.

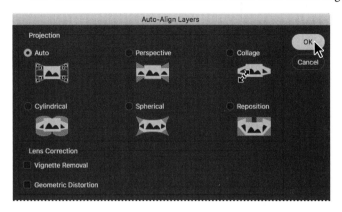

Tip: When aligning layers that are not involved in a panorama, Reposition is often the best alignment option to use. In this exercise, Reposition is the projection that the Auto option chose.

Now that the layers are perfectly aligned, you're ready to blend them.

9 Make sure both layers are still selected in the Layers panel. Then choose Edit > Auto-Blend Layers.

10 Select Stack Images and Seamless Tones And Colors, if they aren't already selected. Make sure Content Aware Fill Transparent Areas is not selected, and then click OK.

Tip: The technique in this exercise, called *focus stacking*, is useful for macro photography, where depth of field is typically very shallow. Multiple images with shallow depth of field are shot at different focus distances, and then merged.

Both the wine glass and the beach behind it are in focus.

11 Save your work, and close the file.

Removing objects using Content-Aware Fill

You've used the content-aware features in some pretty impressive ways in earlier lessons, and to fill in the sky in the panorama project in this lesson. Now you'll use Content-Aware Fill to remove an unwanted object and have Photoshop convincingly fill in the area instead of leaving a blank space.

1   Choose File > Browse In Bridge.

2   Navigate to the Lesson05 folder, if you're not there already, and then look at the JapaneseGarden_Start.jpg and Japanese Garden_End.jpg thumbnail previews.

JapaneseGarden_Start.jpg   Japanese Garden_End.jpg

You'll use the Content-Aware Fill tool to remove a rock and its reflection.

3   Double-click the JapaneseGarden_Start.jpg file to open it in Photoshop.

4   Choose File > Save As, choose Photoshop for the format type, and name the new file **JapaneseGarden_Working.psd**. Click Save. Click OK if the Photoshop Format Options dialog box appears.

5   Select the Lasso tool, and in the options bar, set Feather to 25px.

6 Drag a selection marquee around the rock on the left and the rock's reflection below it, including some of the water around it. The selection can be approximate.

7 Choose Edit > Content-Aware Fill.

*A. Sampling Brush tool **B.** Sampling area **C.** Content-Aware Fill options **D.** Preview zoom **E.** Reset*

The left side of the Content-Aware Fill dialog box displays the image and the selection you made. The colored area (displayed in green by default) indicates areas you want Content-Aware Fill to sample (use as a source) for filling the removed area.

The right side previews the results of the sampling area combined with the settings in the Content-Aware Fill options panel.

With the current sampling area and settings, the rock is successfully removed, but some of the tree leaves from the sampling area may be filling in the water, and that isn't desirable.

> **Tip:** Preview is a panel. You can drag the divider between the image and the Preview panel. You can drag the Preview panel tab to undock it, making Preview a floating panel. This Preview panel is available only when using Content-Aware Fill.

8 Press the] key to enlarge the Sampling Brush tool until the options bar indicates that the brush size is around 700 pixels. The Sampling Brush tool is selected by default when you open the Content-Aware Fill dialog box.

Notice that a minus sign (−) appears in the Sampling Brush pointer. This is because the tool is set to Subtract mode, which is indicated in the options bar.

9 Paint over foliage to exclude it from the sampling area. Areas you exclude are no longer green. As you do this, the fill is recalculated, and you can see the updated results in the Preview panel.

10 As soon as the fill looks like it consists only of water, you can stop painting.

It may take some trial and error for the results to be successful. You may be able to improve the results using the following technique:

- Use the Sampling Brush in Subtract mode to exclude more areas, to stop them from contributing incorrect content to the fill. For example, it might help to also exclude the lantern and all the areas that are not water.

- Use the Lasso tool to change the original selection. For example, try using the Lasso tool in Subtract mode to trim the selection where unwanted foliage is included, while still including all of the rock.

- Adjust the Fill Settings. For this exercise, adjusting the Color Adaptation setting should be the most useful. You probably won't use the other options, although they are useful in other situations. Rotation Adaptation is useful for re-creating missing areas of content that's radial (such as a flower) or along an arc. Scale helps adapt a fill for patterned content. The Mirror option can be useful for symmetrical content.

11 When you're satisfied with the result, click OK, and then choose Select > Deselect.

In the Layers panel, notice that by default, the fill is created as a new layer named Background Copy. If you hide the new layer, you can see the entire original image in the Background layer.

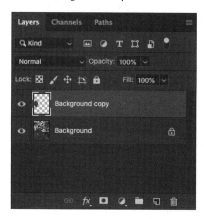

12 Save your work as a Photoshop document, and then close it.

Tip: To quickly switch the Lasso tool between the Add and Subtract modes, press the E key.

Tip: Content-Aware Fill randomizes results to make fixes look more natural, but if you want more consistent results, select the Enable Repeatability option. This will cause the preview to take longer to calculate and display.

Tip: If you don't want Content-Aware Fill to create the fill as a new layer, before closing Content-Aware Fill, change the Output To option in Output Settings.

Using the Content-Aware Move tool

The Content-Aware Move tool is very impressive when you're working with some images, and less impressive with others. For best results, use it when the background is consistent enough that Photoshop will be able to recognize and replicate a pattern, such as meadows, solid-colored walls, sky, wood grains, or water.

The Extend mode of the Content-Aware tool can be useful with architectural subjects, especially when they're shot on a plane parallel to the camera; it's less effective for subjects shot at an angle.

If you're working with an image that has multiple layers, select Sample All Layers in the options bar to include them all in the selection.

The Structure and Color options define how closely the results reflect the existing image patterns. In the Structure settings, 1 is the loosest and 5 the strictest. The Color settings range from 0 (no color adaptation) to 10 (matching the color as closely as possible). Experiment with the options while the object is still selected to see which give you the best results in a particular image. You may want to hide the selection edges (choose View > Show > Selection Edges or View > Extras) to see how the object integrates into its new position.

Adjusting perspective in an image

The Perspective Warp feature lets you adjust the way objects in your image relate to the scene. You can correct distortions, change the angle from which an object appears to be viewed, or shift the perspective of an object so that it merges smoothly with a new background.

Using the Perspective Warp feature is a two-step process: defining the planes and adjusting them. You start in Layout mode, drawing *quads* to define two or more planes; it's a good idea to align the edges of the quads so that they are parallel with the lines of the original object. Then you switch to Warp mode, and manipulate the planes you defined.

You'll use Perspective Warp to merge images with different perspectives.

1   Choose File > Browse In Bridge.

2   Navigate to the Lesson05 folder, if you're not there already, and then look at the Bridge_Start.psd and Bridge_End.psd thumbnail previews.

Extra credit

Transformations with the Content-Aware Move tool

With the Content-Aware Move tool, you need only a few quick steps to duplicate a thistle so that it combines seamlessly with the background, and is also different enough that it doesn't look like an exact copy of the original.

1. Open Thistle.psd in your Lesson05/Extra Credit folder.

2. Select the Content-Aware Move tool (✕) (grouped with the healing brush and Red Eye tools).

3. In the options bar, choose Extend from the Mode menu. Choosing Extend duplicates the thistle; if you just want to reposition the single thistle, you would choose Move.

4. With the Content-Aware Move tool, draw a selection marquee around the thistle, with a margin large enough to include a little of the grass around it.

5. Drag the selection to the left, and drop it in the empty area of grass.

6. Right-click (Windows) or Control-click (Mac) the dragged thistle, and choose Flip Horizontal.

7. Drag the top left transformation handle to make the thistle smaller. If you think the copy of the thistle should be farther from the original, position the pointer inside the transformation rectangle and drag the thistle copy slightly to the left.

8. Press Enter or Return to make the transformations permanent, leaving the content selected so you can adjust the Structure and Color options to improve how the new thistle blends with the background.

9. Choose Select > Deselect, and save your changes.

Bridge_Start.psd   *Bridge_End.psd*

In the Bridge_Start.psd file, the image of the train has been combined with the image of a trestle bridge, but their perspectives don't match. If you're illustrating a story about a flying train that is making a landing on a trestle bridge, this might be perfect. But if you want a more realistic image, you'll need to adjust the perspective of the train to put it firmly on the tracks. You'll use Perspective Warp to do just that.

3   Double-click the Bridge_Start.psd file to open it in Photoshop

4   Choose File > Save As, and rename the file **Bridge_Working.psd**. Click OK in the Photoshop Format Options dialog box.

5   Select the Train layer.

● **Note:** Perspective Warp can work faster on a computer that qualifies for graphics acceleration. To see if your computer qualifies, see the Getting Started chapter for a link to the Photoshop system requirements.

The tracks are on the Background layer. The train is on the Train layer. Because the Train layer is a Smart Object, you can apply Perspective Warp and then modify the results if you're not satisfied.

6   Choose Edit > Perspective Warp.

A small animated tutorial appears, showing you how to draw a quad, which defines a plane.

7   Watch the animation, and then close it.

Now you'll create quads to define the planes of the train image.

8 Draw the quad for the side of the train: Click above the top of the smokestack, drag down to the railroad tie below the front wheel, and then drag across to the end of the caboose. The plane is currently a rectangle.

9 Drag a second quad for the front of the train, dragging across the cowcatcher at the bottom and into the trees at the top. Drag it to the right until it attaches to the left edge of the first quad.

10 Drag the corners of the planes to match the angles of the train. The bottom line of the side plane should run along the bottom of the train wheels; the top edge should border the top of the caboose. The front plane should mirror the lines of the cowcatcher and the top of the light.

Now that the quads are drawn, you're ready for the second step in the process: warping.

11 Click Warp in the options bar. Close the tutorial box that shows you how to warp the plane.

12 Click the Automatically Straighten Near Vertical Lines button, next to Warp in the options bar.

This makes the train appear properly vertical, making it easier to adjust the perspective accurately.

13 Drag the handles to manipulate the planes, moving the back end of the train down and into perspective with the tracks. Exaggerate the perspective toward the caboose for a more dramatic result.

14 Warp other parts of the train as needed. You may need to adjust the front of the train. Pay attention to the wheels; make sure you don't distort them as you warp the perspective.

While there are precise ways to adjust perspective, in many cases you may need to trust your eyes to tell you when it looks right. Remember that you can return to tweak it again later, because you're applying Perspective Warp as a Smart Filter.

15 When you're satisfied with the perspective, click the Commit Perspective Warp button (✔) in the options bar.

16 To compare the changed image with the original, hide the Perspective Warp filter in the Layers panel. Then show the filter again.

If you want to make further adjustments, double-click the Perspective Warp filter in the Layers panel. You can continue to adjust the existing planes, or click Layout in the options bar to reshape them. Remember to click the Commit Perspective Warp button to apply your changes.

17 Save your work, and close the file.

Changing the perspective of a building

In the exercise, you applied Perspective Warp to one layer to change its relationship with another. But you can also use Perspective Warp to change the perspective of an object in relationship to others in the same layer. For example, you can shift the angle from which you view a building.

In this case, you apply Perspective Warp the same way: In Layout mode, draw the planes of the object you want to affect. In Warp mode, manipulate those planes. Of course, because you're shifting angles within a layer, other objects on the layer will move too, so you need to watch for any irregularities.

In this image, as the perspective of the building shifted, so did the perspective of the trees surrounding it.

Camera Shake Reduction

Even with a steady hand, unintended camera motion can occur with slow shutter speeds or long focal lengths. The Camera Shake Reduction filter reduces the resulting camera shake, giving you a sharper image.

Before applying the Camera Shake Reduction filter

You'll get the best results if you apply the filter to a particular part of an image, rather than the entire image. It can be especially useful if text has become illegible due to camera shake.

To use the Camera Shake Reduction filter, open the image, and choose Filter > Sharpen > Shake Reduction. The filter automatically analyzes the image, selects a region of interest, and corrects the blur. Use the Detail loupe to examine the preview. That may be all you need to do. If so, click OK to close the Shake Reduction dialog box and apply the filter.

After applying the Camera Shake Reduction filter

You can adjust how Photoshop interprets the Blur Trace, which is the shape and size of the camera shake that Photoshop identified. You can change the region of interest or adjust its size, adjust the Smoothing and Artifact Suppression values, and more. For full information about the Camera Shake Reduction filter, see Photoshop Help.

Review questions

1 What is red eye, and how do you correct it in Photoshop?

2 How can you create a panorama from multiple images?

3 Describe how to fix common camera lens flaws in Photoshop. What causes these defects?

4 What conditions provide the best results when using the Content-Aware Move tool?

Review answers

1 Red eye occurs when a camera flash is reflected in the retinas of a subject's eyes. To correct red eye in Photoshop, zoom in to the subject's eyes, select the Red Eye tool, and then click each eye.

2 To blend multiple images into a panorama, choose File > Automate > Photomerge, select the files you want to combine, and click OK.

3 The Lens Correction filter fixes common camera lens flaws, such as barrel and pincushion distortion, in which straight lines bow out towards the edges of the image (barrel) or bend inward (pincushion); chromatic aberration, where a color fringe appears along the edges of image objects; and vignetting at the edges of an image, especially corners, that are darker than the center. Defects can occur from incorrectly setting the lens focal length or f-stop, or by tilting the camera vertically or horizontally.

4 The Content-Aware Move tool works best in images that have consistent backgrounds so that Photoshop can seamlessly replicate the patterns.

6 MASKS AND CHANNELS

Lesson overview

In this lesson, you'll learn how to do the following:

- Create a mask to remove a subject from a background.

- Refine a mask to include complex edges.

- Create a quick mask to make changes to a selected area.

- Edit a mask using the Properties panel.

- Manipulate an image using Puppet Warp.

- Save a selection as an alpha channel.

- View a mask using the Channels panel.

- Load a channel as a selection.

 This lesson will take about an hour to complete. Please log in to your account on peachpit.com to download the lesson files for this chapter, or go to the Getting Started section at the beginning of this book and follow the instructions under "Accessing the Lesson Files and Web Edition."

As you work on this lesson, you'll preserve the start files. If you need to restore the start files, download them from your Account page.

PROJECT: MAGAZINE COVER IMAGE

Use masks to isolate and manipulate specific parts of an image. The cutout portion of a mask can be altered, but the area surrounding the cutout is protected from change. You can create a temporary mask to use once, or you can save masks for repeated use.

Working with masks and channels

▶ **Tip:** Masks are essential for removing backgrounds from images, and for combining multiple images into a single composite image.

In Photoshop, masks isolate and protect parts of an image, just as masking tape protects window panes or trim from paint when a house is painted. When you create a mask based on a selection, the area you haven't selected is *masked,* or protected from editing. With masks, you can create and save time-consuming selections and use them again. In addition, you can use masks for other complex editing tasks—for example, to apply color changes or filter effects to an image.

In Photoshop, you can make temporary masks, called *quick masks,* or you can create permanent masks and store them as special grayscale channels called *alpha channels.* Photoshop also uses channels to store an image's color information. Unlike layers, alpha channels do not print. You use the Channels panel to view and work with alpha channels.

A key concept in masking is that black hides and white reveals. As in life, rarely is anything black and white. Shades of gray partially hide, depending on the gray levels.

Getting started

First, you'll view the image that you'll create using masks and channels.

1   Start Photoshop, and then immediately hold down Ctrl+Alt+Shift (Windows) or Command+Option+Shift (Mac) to restore the default preferences. (See "Restoring Default Preferences" on page 5.)

2   When prompted, click Yes to delete the Adobe Photoshop Settings file.

3   Choose File > Browse In Bridge to open Adobe Bridge.

● **Note:** If Bridge isn't installed, you'll be prompted to install it when you choose Browse In Bridge. For more information, see page 3.

4   Click the Favorites tab on the left side of the Bridge window. Select the Lessons folder, and then double-click the Lesson06 folder in the Content panel.

5   Study the 06End.psd file. To enlarge the thumbnail so that you can see it more clearly, move the thumbnail slider at the bottom of the Bridge window to the right.

In this lesson, you'll create a magazine cover. The model for the cover was photo-graphed in front of a different background, and the background isn't a single color, so it may be a challenge to mask. You'll use Select and Mask to quickly isolate the model over the final background.

6   Double-click the 06Start.psd thumbnail to open it in Photoshop. Click OK if you see an Embedded Profile Mismatch dialog box.

7   Choose File > Save As, rename the file **06Working.psd**, and click Save. Click OK if the Photoshop Format Options dialog box appears.

Saving a working version of the file lets you return to the original if you need it.

About masks and masking

Alpha channels, channel masks, clipping masks, layer masks, vector masks—
what's the difference? In some cases, they're interchangeable: A channel mask can
be converted to a layer mask, a layer mask can be converted to a vector mask, and
vice versa.

What they have in common is that they all store selections, and they all let you edit an
image nondestructively, so you can return at any time to your original. Here's a brief
description to help you keep them all straight.

- An **alpha channel** is an extra channel added to an image; it stores a selection as
  a grayscale image. You can use alpha channels to store masks independently of
  any layer, and you can convert alpha channels back to selections.

- A **layer mask** is an alpha channel attached to a specific layer. A layer mask
  controls which part of a layer is revealed or hidden. It appears as a blank
  thumbnail next to the layer thumbnail in the Layers panel until you add content
  to it; a black outline indicates that it's selected.

- A **vector mask** is a layer mask made of resolution-independent vector objects,
  not pixels. Vector masks have crisp edges and are created with the pen or shape
  tools. Their thumbnails appear the same as layer mask thumbnails.

- A **clipping mask** is formed when one layer masks another layer. You can use a
  clipping mask to confine an effect to a specific layer, rather than to everything
  below the layer in the layer stack. Using a clipping mask clips layers to a
  base layer; only that base layer is affected. Thumbnails of a clipped layer are
  indented, with a right-angle arrow pointing to the layer below. The name of the
  clipped base layer is underlined.

- A **channel mask** restricts editing to a specific channel (for example, a Cyan
  channel in a CMYK image). Channel masks are useful for making intricate,
  fringed, or wispy-edged selections. You can create a channel mask based on
  a dominant color in an image or a pronounced contrast in an isolated channel,
  for example, between the subject and the background.

Using Select and Mask and Select Subject

Photoshop provides a set of tools focused on creating and refining masks, collected
in a task space called Select and Mask. Inside Select and Mask, you'll use the Select
Subject tool to get a fast head start on the mask that will separate the model from
the background. Then you'll refine the mask using other Select and Mask tools,
such as the Quick Selection tool.

▶ **Tip:** When any
selection tool is active,
the Select and Mask
button is available in
the options bar. When
the Select and Mask
button is not available,
you can still use the
Select > Select and
Mask command.

1　In the Layers panel, make sure both layers are visible and the Model layer
　　is selected.

2　Choose Select > Select and Mask.

Select and Mask opens with the image. A semitransparent "onion skin" overlay indicates masked areas, which are represented by a checkerboard pattern. For now, the checkerboard pattern covers the entire image, because you haven't yet identified the areas to unmask.

Tip: For more help making selections, refer to Lesson 3, "Working with Selections."

3 In the Options bar, click the Select Subject button (or choose Select > Subject).

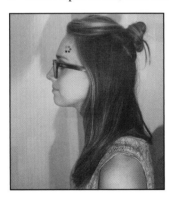 

Tip: You don't have to be in the Select and Mask dialog box to use the Select > Subject command. It's available even when a selection tool is not active. In addition, the Select Subject button appears in the options bar when some selection tools are active.

Using advanced machine learning technology, the Select Subject feature is trained to identify typical subjects of a photo, including people, animals, and objects, and then create a selection for them. The selection may not be perfect, but it's often close enough for you to refine easily and rapidly with other selection tools such as the Quick Selection tool. First, get a clear idea of the precision of the selection by using a different way to see the selection.

4 Click the View menu in the View Mode section, and choose Overlay. The masked area is now shown as a semitransparent red color instead of the onion skin checkerboard.

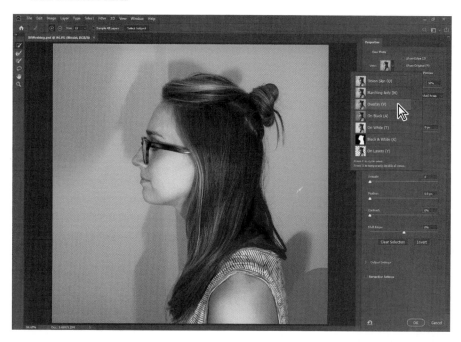

> **Tip:** When a selection tool is active, you can enter Select and Mask by clicking the Select and Mask button in the options bar instead of having to find the command in the menus.

The different View Modes are provided so that you can see the mask more easily over various backgrounds. In this case, the red overlay makes it easier to see missed areas and edges where loose hair isn't properly masked.

Notice that there are a few areas over the chest that were missed by Select Subject. You can easily add them to the selection using the Quick Selection tool.

5 Make sure the Quick Selection tool ( ) is selected. In the options bar, set up a brush with a size of **15** px.

6 Drag the Quick Selection tool over the missed areas (without extending into the background) to add the missed areas to the selection. Notice that the Quick Selection tool fills in the selection as it detects content edges, so you don't have to be exact. It's OK if you release the mouse button and drag more than once.

> **Tip:** Quickly cycle through the View Modes by pressing the F key. Viewing different modes helps you spot selection mistakes that might not be obvious in other modes.

> **Tip:** When creating a selection, increase the magnification if it helps you see missed areas.

Where you drag teaches the Quick Selection tool which areas should be revealed and not part of the mask. Do not drag the Quick Selection tool over or past the model's edge to the background, because this teaches the Quick Selection tool to include part of the background, and you don't want that. If you accidentally add unwanted areas to the mask, either choose Edit > Undo, or reverse the edit by painting over it with the Quick Selection tool in Subtract mode. To enable Subtract Mode for the Quick Selection tool, click the Subtract From Selection icon (⊖) in the options bar.

As you drag the Quick Selection tool over the model, the overlay disappears from the areas that you are marking to be revealed. Don't worry about total perfection at this stage.

▶ **Tip:** You can adjust the opacity of the onion skin by dragging the Transparency slider under the View Mode options.

7 Click the View menu in the View Mode section again, and choose On Layers. This shows you how the current Select and Mask settings look over any layers that are behind this layer. In this case, you're previewing how the current settings will mask the Model layer over the Magazine Background layer.

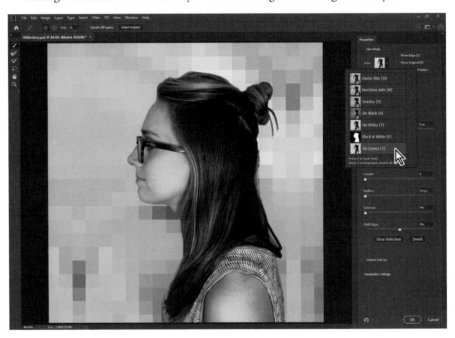

Inspect the edges around the model at a high magnification, such as 400%. Some of the original light background may still show between the model's edge and the magazine background, but overall the Select Subject and Quick Selection tools should have created clean edges for the shirt and face. Don't be concerned about edge gaps or imperfect hair edges, because you'll take care of those next.

Getting better and faster results with Select and Mask

When using Select and Mask, it's important to use different tools for image areas that should be fully revealed, areas that should be fully masked, and for partially masked edges (such as fuzzy dog hair). Try these recommendations:

- The Select Subject button can be a fast way to create an initial selection.

- The Quick Selection tool is useful for rapidly touching up a selection produced by Select Subject or for creating an initial selection. As you drag it, it uses edge detection technology to find mask edges automatically. Don't drag it on or over a mask edge; keep it fully inside (in Add mode) or outside (in Subtract mode) the areas that should be revealed.

- To paint or draw solid mask edges manually (without using any automatic edge detection), use the Brush, Lasso, or Polygonal Lasso tool. These also have an Add mode for marking revealed areas and a Subtract mode for marking masked areas.

- Instead of having to switch between Add and Subtract modes with the toolbar, you can leave a tool in Add mode, and when you want to temporarily use the tool in Subtract mode, hold down the Alt (Windows) or Option (Mac) key.

- To improve the mask along edges containing complex transitions such as hair, drag the Refine Edge Brush along those edges. Do not drag the Refine Edge brush over areas that should be fully revealed or fully masked.

- You don't have to do all of your selecting inside Select and Mask. For example, if you've already created a selection with another tool such as Color Range, leave that selection active, and then click Select > Select and Mask in the options bar to clean up the mask.

▶ **Tip:** In Select and Mask, the Polygonal Lasso tool is grouped with the Lasso tool.

Refining a mask

The mask is pretty good so far, but the Quick Selection tool couldn't quite capture all of the model's hair, such as the strands coming off of the bun on the back of the model's head. In Select and Mask, the Refine Edge Brush tool is designed to mask edges with challenging details.

1 At a magnification of 300% or higher, inspect the hair edges at the back of the model's head.

2 Select the Refine Edge Brush tool
   (). In the options bar, set up
   a brush with a size of **20** px and
   Hardness of **100**%.

3 Choose Overlay from the View menu
   in the View Mode section, so that the
   missing hair is visible.

4 Drag the Refine Edge Brush tool
   between the hair bun and the ends of
   the hair, where the selection needs to
   be improved. As you drag the Refine
   Edge Brush tool over the complex
   hair edge, you should see that the
   hair strands falling from the bun are
   now included in the visible areas.

5 Scroll down to the loop of hair that falls over the back of the shirt.

The original image background shows inside the loop. That background needs to be
replaced with the magazine background, so you'll use the Refine Edge Brush to add
that loop interior to the mask.

6 In the options bar, set up a Refine Edge brush with a size of **15** px, with
   Hardness of **100**%.

7 Drag the Refine Edge Brush tool over any obscured hairs to reveal them. You should see two things happen: Gaps in the mask within the loop of hair should become masked, while fine hairs are added to the visible areas.

8 Click the View option, and choose Black & White. This is another good way to check your mask. Inspect the mask at different magnifications, and when you're done, choose View > Fit on Screen.

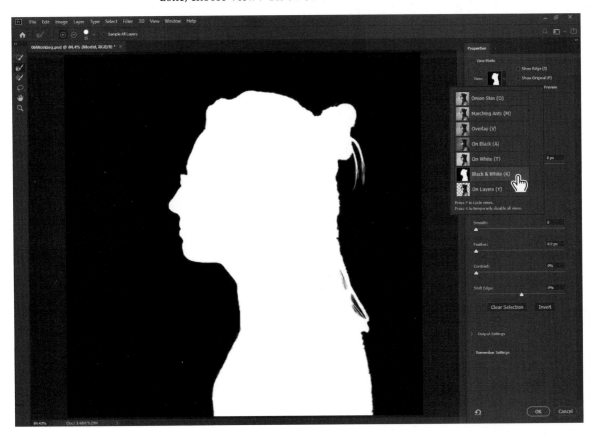

If you see hairs or other details that are masked but should be revealed, drag the Refine Edge brush over them. The finer the details you want to mask, the smaller you should set the Refine Edge brush size. It's OK if the brush size is slightly larger than the details you want to mask, and you don't have to drag the Refine Edge Brush tool precisely.

If you see Refine Edge Brush tool mistakes that need to be erased, such as inner areas incorrectly added to the mask, drag the Refine Edge Brush tool over the mistakes while holding down the Alt (Windows) or Option (Mac) key.

Adjusting Global Refinements

At this point the mask is in good shape, but needs to be tightened up a little. You can tune the overall appearance of the mask edge by adjusting the Global Refinements settings.

1 Click the View menu in the View Mode section, and choose On Layers. This lets you preview adjustments over the Magazine Background layer, which is behind the Model layer.

2 In the Global Refinements section, move the sliders to create a smooth, unfeathered edge along the face. The optimal settings depend on the selection you created, but they'll probably be similar to ours. We moved the Smooth slider to 5 to create a smoother outline, Contrast to 20% to make the transitions along the selection border more abrupt, and Shift Edge to −15% to move the selection border inward and help remove unwanted background colors from selection edges. (Adjusting Shift Edge to a positive number would move the border outward.)

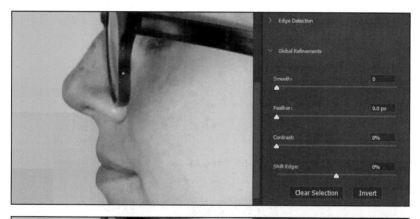

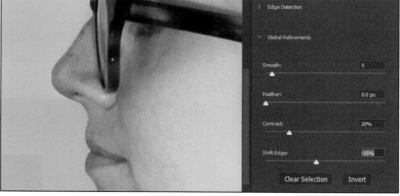

3 Take one more look at this preview of the current mask over the Magazine Background layer, and make any remaining corrections as needed.

Completing the mask

When you're satisfied with the mask preview, you can create its final output as a selection, a layer with transparency, a layer mask, or a new document. For this project, we want to use this as a layer mask on the Model layer, which was selected when you entered Select and Mask.

1 If the Output Settings are hidden, click the disclosure icon (⟩) to reveal them.

2 Zoom in to 200% or more so that you can more easily see the light fringing around the face edge that's due to the Model layer's original background color seeping in behind the mask.

3 Select Decontaminate Colors to suppress those color fringes. If Decontaminate Colors creates unwanted artifacts, reduce the Amount until the effect looks the way you want. We set Amount to 25%.

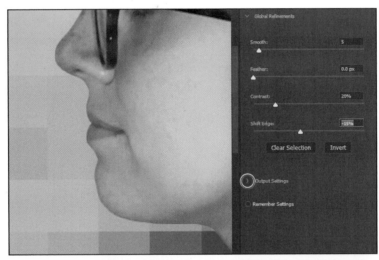

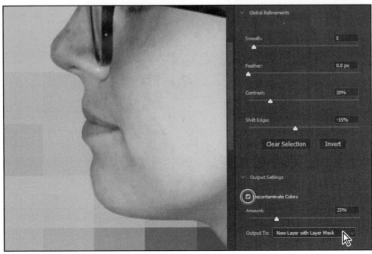

4 Choose New Layer With Layer Mask from the Output To menu. Then click OK.

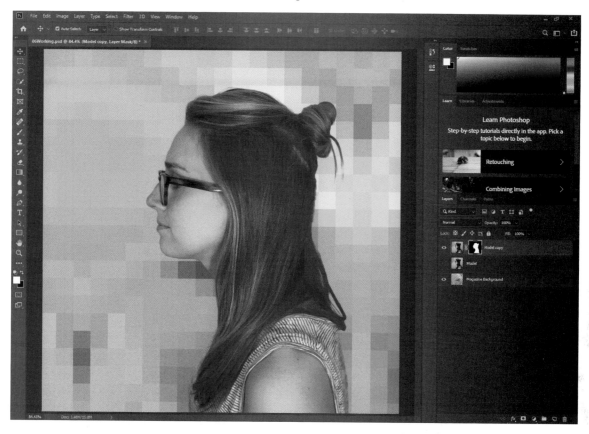

Clicking OK exits Select and Mask. In the Layers panel, the Model Copy layer now has a layer mask (pixel mask) that was generated by Select and Mask.

The layer was copied because using the Decontaminate Colors option requires that new pixels be generated. The original Model layer is preserved, and automatically hidden; if you wanted to start over you could delete the Model Copy layer and begin again using the original Model layer.

> ● **Note:** If you had not selected Decontaminate Colors, it would have been possible to choose a Layer Mask output option that would have added a layer mask to the Model layer without copying it.

If the mask isn't perfect, you can continue to edit it at any time. When a layer mask thumbnail is selected in the Layers panel, you can click the Select and Mask button in the Properties panel, in the options bar (if a selection tool is active), or choose Select > Select and Mask.

5 Save your work.

Creating a quick mask

You'll create a quick mask to change the color of the glasses frames. First, you'll clean up the Layers panel.

1   Hide the Magazine Background layer so you can concentrate on the model. Make sure the Model copy layer is selected.

2   Click the Edit In Quick Mask Mode button in the Tools panel. (By default, you have been working in Standard mode.)

In Quick Mask mode, a red overlay appears as you make a selection, masking the area outside the selection the way a rubylith, or red acetate, was used to mask images in traditional print shops. (This idea is similar to the Overlay view mode you saw in Select and Mask.) You can apply changes only to the unprotected area that is visible and selected. Notice that the highlight color for the selected layer in the Layers panel is red, indicating you're in Quick Mask mode.

3   In the Tools panel, select the Brush tool (✐).

4   In the options bar, make sure that the mode is Normal. Open the Brush pop-up panel, and select a small brush with a diameter of **13** px and a Hardness of **100**%. Click outside the panel to close it.

5   Paint the earpiece of the glasses frames. The area you paint will appear red, creating a mask.

6 Continue painting with the Brush tool to mask the earpiece of the frames and the frame around the lenses. Reduce the brush size to paint around the lenses. You can stop where the earpiece goes under the hair.

In Quick Mask mode, Photoshop operates in grayscale mask mode, where shades of gray correspond to degrees of mask transparency. When using a painting or editing tool in Quick Mask mode, keep these principles in mind:

- Painting with black adds to the mask (the red overlay), subtracting from the selected area.

- Painting with white erases the mask, adding to the selected area.

- Painting with gray adds semitransparent areas to the mask, where darker shades are more transparent (more masked).

7 Click the Edit In Standard Mode button to exit Quick Mask Mode.

The unmasked area is selected. Exiting Quick Mask mode converts the Quick Mask into a selection.

8 Choose Select > Inverse to select the area you originally masked.

9 Choose Image > Adjustments > Hue/Saturation. The selection is converted to a layer mask that restricts the Hue/Saturation adjustment to the unmasked area.

10 In the Hue/Saturation dialog box, change the Hue to **+70**. The new green color fills the glasses frame. Click OK.

▶ **Tip:** If you want to keep the selection for future use, save it as an alpha channel (Select > Save Selection); otherwise it will be lost as soon as the area is deselected.

 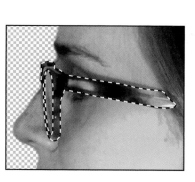

11 Choose Select > Deselect.

Manipulating an image with Puppet Warp

The Puppet Warp feature gives you flexibility in manipulating an image. You can reposition areas, such as hair or an arm, just as you might pull the strings on a puppet. Place pins wherever you want to control movement. You'll use Puppet Warp to tilt the model's head back, so she appears to be looking up.

1   Zoom out so you can see the entire model.

2   With the Model Copy layer selected in the Layers panel, choose Edit > Puppet Warp.

A mesh appears over the visible areas in the layer—in this case, the mesh appears over the model. You'll use the mesh to place pins where you want to control movement (or to ensure there is no movement).

3   Click to add pins around the body and along the base of the head. Each time you click, Puppet Warp adds a pin. Around ten to twelve pins should work.

The pins you've added around the shirt will keep it in place as you tilt the head.

4   Select the pin at the nape of the neck. A blue dot appears in the center of the pin to indicate that it's selected.

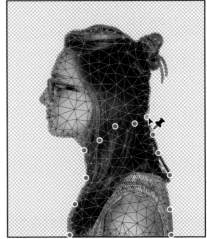

5   Press Alt (Windows) or Option (Mac). A larger circle appears around the pin and a curved double arrow appears next to it. Continue pressing Alt or Option as you drag the pointer to rotate the head backwards. You can see the angle of rotation in the options bar; you can enter **170** there to rotate the head back.

6   When you're satisfied with the rotation, click the Commit Puppet Warp button (✓) in the options bar, or press Enter or Return.

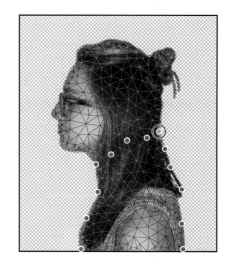

● **Note:** Be careful not to Alt-click or Option-click the dot itself, or you'll delete the pin.

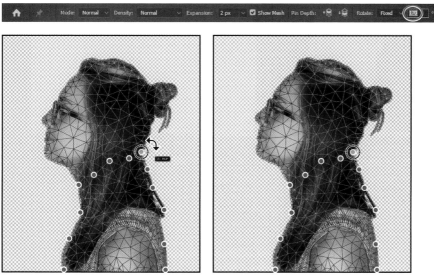

7   Save your work so far.

Using an alpha channel to create a shadow

Just as different information in an image is stored on different layers, channels also let you access specific kinds of information. Alpha channels store selections as grayscale images. Color information channels store information about each color in an image; for example, an RGB image automatically has red, green, blue, and composite channels.

To avoid confusing channels and layers, think of channels as containing an image's color and selection information, and think of layers as containing painting, shapes, text, and other content.

You'll use an alpha channel to set up a selection, which you'll then fill with black on a layer to create the actual shadow.

You've already created a mask of the model. To create a shadow, you want to duplicate that mask and then shift it. You'll use an alpha channel to make that possible.

1   In the Layers panel, Ctrl-click (Windows) or Command-click (Mac) the layer thumbnail icon in the Model Copy layer. The masked area is selected.

2   Choose Select > Save Selection. In the Save Selection dialog box, make sure New is chosen in the Channel menu. Then name the channel **Model Outline**, and click OK.

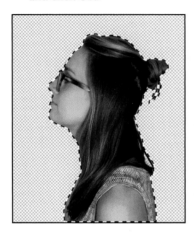 

Nothing changes in the Layers panel or in the image window. However, a new channel named Model Outline has been added to the Channels panel.

About alpha channels

As you work in Photoshop, you will eventually encounter alpha channels. It's a good idea to know a few things about them.

- An image can contain up to 56 channels, including all color and alpha channels.

- All channels are 8-bit grayscale images, capable of displaying 256 levels of gray.

- You can specify a name, color, mask option, and opacity for each channel. (The opacity affects the preview of the channel, not the image.)

- All new channels have the same dimensions and number of pixels as the original image.

- You can edit the mask in an alpha channel using the painting tools, editing tools, and filters.

- You can convert alpha channels to spot-color channels.

3 Click the Create A New Layer icon (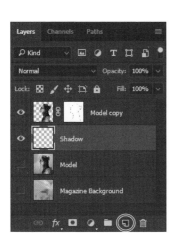) at the bottom of the Layers panel. Drag the new layer below the Model Copy layer, so that the shadow will be below the image of the model. Double-click the new layer's name, and rename it **Shadow**.

4 With the Shadow layer selected, choose Select > Select and Mask.

5 Click the View menu in the View Mode section, and choose On Black.

6 In Select and Mask, move the Shift Edge slider to **+36**%.

7 In the Output Settings section, make sure Selection is selected in the Output To menu, and then click OK.

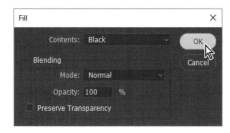

8 Choose Edit > Fill. In the Fill dialog box, choose Black from the Contents menu, and then click OK.

The Shadow layer displays a filled-in black outline of the model. Shadows aren't usually as dark as the person that casts them. You'll reduce the layer opacity.

9 In the Layers panel, change the layer opacity to **30%**.

The shadow is in exactly the same position as the model, where it can't be seen. You'll shift it.

10 Choose Select > Deselect to remove the selection.

11 Choose Edit > Transform > Rotate. Rotate the shadow by hand, or enter **−15°** in the Rotate field in the options bar. Then drag the shadow to the left, or enter **545** in the X field in the options bar. Click the Commit Transform button (✓) in the options bar, or press Enter or Return, to accept the transformation.

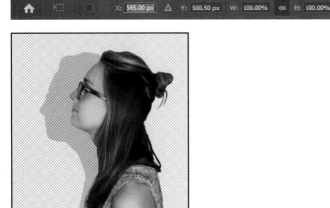

12 Click the eye icon for the Magazine Background layer to make it visible, and delete the Model layer (the one without the mask).

13 Choose File > Save to save your work so far.

Your magazine cover is ready to go!

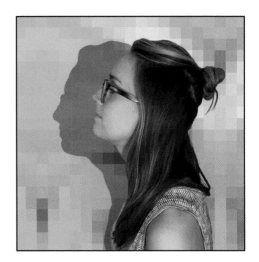

Review questions

1 What is the benefit of using a quick mask?

2 When you have a selection created by a quick mask, what happens when you deselect?

3 When you save a selection as an alpha channel, where is the alpha channel stored?

4 How can you edit a mask in a channel once you've saved it?

5 How do channels differ from layers?

Review answers

1 Quick masks are helpful for creating one-time selections. In addition, using a quick mask is an easy way to edit a selection using the painting tools.

2 As with any other selection, a quick mask selection disappears when you deselect it.

3 Alpha channels are stored in the Channels panel, along with the visible color channels.

4 You can paint in an alpha channel using black, white, and shades of gray.

5 Alpha channels are storage areas for saved selections. All layers set to be visible will be present in printed or exported output. But only the color channels are visible in printed or exported output; alpha channels are not. Layers contain information about image content, while alpha channels contain information about selections and masks.

7 TYPOGRAPHIC DESIGN

Lesson overview

In this lesson, you'll learn how to do the following:

- Use guides to position text in a composition.
- Make a clipping mask from type.
- Merge type with other layers.
- Preview fonts.
- Format text.
- Distribute text along a path.
- Control type and positioning using advanced features.

This lesson will take less than an hour to complete. Please log in to your account on peachpit.com to download the lesson files for this chapter, or go to the Getting Started section at the beginning of this book and follow the instructions under "Accessing the Lesson Files and Web Edition."

As you work on this lesson, you'll preserve the start files. If you need to restore the start files, download them from your Account page.

PROJECT: MAGAZINE COVER LAYOUT

Photoshop provides powerful, flexible text tools so you can add type to your images with great control and creativity.

About type

Type in Photoshop consists of vector-based shapes that describe the letters, numbers, and symbols of a typeface. Many typefaces are available in more than one format, the most common formats being TrueType and OpenType (see "OpenType in Photoshop" later in this lesson). Type 1 or PostScript fonts are older font formats that are still in use.

When you add type to a document in Photoshop, the characters are composed of pixels and have the same resolution as the image file—zooming in on characters shows jagged edges. However, Photoshop preserves the vector-based type outlines and uses them when you scale or resize type, save a PDF or EPS file, or print the image to a PostScript printer. As a result, you can produce type with crisp, resolution-independent edges, apply effects and styles to type, and transform its shape and size.

Getting started

In this lesson, you'll work on the layout for the cover of a technology magazine. You'll start with the artwork you created in Lesson 6: The cover has a model, her shadow, and the orange background. You'll add and stylize type for the cover, including warping the text.

You'll start the lesson by viewing an image of the final composition.

1 Start Photoshop, and then immediately hold down Ctrl+Alt+Shift (Windows) or Command+Option+Shift (Mac) to restore the default preferences. (See "Restoring Default Preferences" on page 5.)

2 When prompted, click Yes to delete the Adobe Photoshop Settings file.

● **Note:** If Bridge is not installed, you'll be prompted to download and install it. See page 3 for more information.

3 Choose File > Browse In Bridge to open Adobe Bridge.

4 In the Favorites panel on the left side of Bridge, click the Lessons folder, and then double-click the Lesson07 folder in the Content panel.

5 Select the 07End.psd file. Increase the thumbnail size to see the image clearly by dragging the thumbnail slider to the right.

● **Note:** Though this lesson starts where Lesson 6 left off, use the 07Start.psd file. We've included a path and a sticky note in the start file that won't be in the 06Working.psd file you saved.

You'll apply the type treatment in Photoshop to finish the magazine cover. All of the type controls you need are available in Photoshop, so you don't have to switch to another application to complete the project.

6 Double-click the 07Start.psd file to open it in Photoshop.

7 Choose File > Save As, rename the file **07Working.psd**, and click Save.

8 Click OK in the Photoshop Format Options dialog box.

9 Choose Graphic and Web from the Workspace Switcher in the options bar.

The Graphic and Web workspace displays the Character and Paragraph panels that you'll use in this lesson, along with the Glyphs and Layers panels.

Creating a clipping mask from type

A *clipping mask* is an object or a group of objects whose shape masks other artwork so that only areas that lie within the clipping mask are visible. In effect, you are clipping the artwork to conform to the shape of the object (or mask). In Photoshop, you can create a clipping mask from shapes or letters. In this exercise, you'll use letters as a clipping mask to allow an image in another layer to show through the letters.

Adding guides to position type

The 07Working.psd file includes a background layer, which will be the foundation for your typography. You'll start by zooming in on the work area and using ruler guides to help position the type.

1 Choose View > Fit On Screen to see the whole cover clearly.

2 Choose View > Rulers to display rulers along the left and top borders of the image window.

▶ **Tip:** If you find it difficult to position the vertical ruler guide exactly at 4.25", holding down Shift will snap the guide to the 4.25" ruler tick mark.

3 Drag a vertical guide from the left ruler to the center of the cover (4.25").

Adding point type

Now you're ready to add type to the composition. You can create horizontal or vertical type anywhere in an image. You can enter *point type* (a single letter, word, or line) or *paragraph type*. You will do both in this lesson. First, you'll create point type.

1 In the Layers panel, select the Background layer.

2 Select the Horizontal Type tool (**T**), and, in the options bar, do the following:

 • Choose a serif typeface, such as Minion Pro Regular, from the Font Family pop-up menu.

 • Type **144 pt** for the Size, and press Enter or Return.

 • Click the Center Text button.

3 In the Character panel, change the Tracking value to **100**.

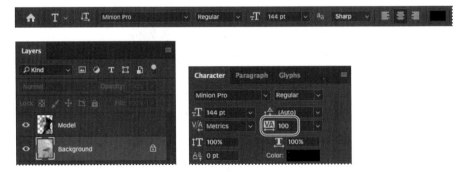

The Tracking value specifies the overall space between letters, which affects the density in a line of text.

4   Click on the center guide you added to set an insertion point, and type
    DIGITAL in all capital letters. Then click the Commit Any Current Edits
    button (✔) in the options bar.

Note: In some versions of Photoshop CC 2019, a new text layer may be created with left alignment even if you specified another alignment before clicking the Horizontal Type tool. You can fix this by applying center alignment after the text layer is created.

Note: After you type, you must commit your editing in the layer by clicking the Commit Any Current Edits button, switching to another tool or layer, or clicking away from the text layer. You cannot commit to current edits by pressing Enter or Return; doing so merely creates a new line of type.

The word "DIGITAL" is added to the cover, and it appears in the Layers panel as
a new type layer named DIGITAL. You can edit and manage the type layer as you
would any other layer. You can add or change the text, change the orientation of
the type, apply anti-aliasing, apply layer styles and transformations, and create
masks. You can move, restack, and copy a type layer, or edit its layer options, just as
you would for any other layer.

The text is big enough, but not modern enough, for this magazine's style. You'll
apply a different font.

5   Double-click the "DIGITAL" text.

6   Open the Font Family pop-up menu in the options bar. Move the cursor over
    the fonts, either with the mouse or using arrow keys.

When the cursor is over a font name, Photoshop temporarily applies that font to
the selected text so you can preview the font in context.

7   Select Myriad Pro Semibold, and then click the Commit Any Current Edits button (✓) in the options bar.

That's much more appropriate.

8   Select the Move tool, and drag the "DIGITAL" text to move it to the top of the cover, if it's not there already.

9   Choose File > Save to save your work so far.

Making a clipping mask and applying a shadow

You added the letters in black, the default text color. However, you want the letters to appear to be filled with an image of a circuit board, so you'll use the letters to make a clipping mask that will allow another image layer to show through.

1   Choose File > Open, and open the circuit_board.tif file, which is in the Lesson07 folder.

2   Choose Window > Arrange > 2-Up Vertical. The circuit_board.tif and 07Working.psd files appear onscreen together. Click the circuit_board.tif file to ensure that it's the active window.

3   With the Move tool selected, hold down the Shift key as you drag the Background layer from the Layers panel in the circuit_board.tif file onto the center of the 07Working.psd file.

Pressing Shift as you drag centers the circuit_board.tif image in the composition.

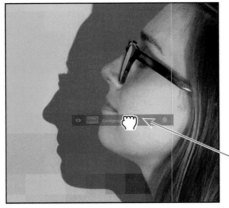

A new layer—Layer 1—appears in the Layers panel for the 07Working.psd file. This new layer contains the image of the circuit board, which will show through the type. But before you make the clipping mask, you'll resize the circuit board image, as it's currently too large for the composition.

4   Close the circuit_board.tif file without saving any changes to it.

5   In the 07Working.psd file, select Layer 1, and then choose Edit > Transform > Scale.

6   Hold down Alt (Windows) or Option (Mac) as you drag a corner handle on the bounding box for the circuit board, and resize it to approximately the same width as the area of text.

Pressing Alt or Option keeps it centered.

7   Reposition the circuit board so that the image covers the text, and commit the transformation by clicking away from the circuit board layer.

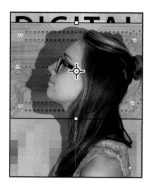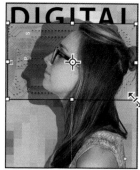

8   Double-click the Layer 1 name, and change it to **Circuit Board**. Then press Enter or Return, or click away from the name in the Layers panel, to apply the change.

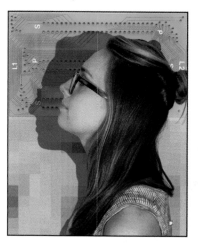

Tip: You can also make a clipping mask by holding down the Alt (Windows) or Option (Mac) key and clicking between the Circuit Board and DIGITAL type layers.

9   Select the Circuit Board layer, if it isn't already selected, and choose Create Clipping Mask from the Layers panel menu (≡).

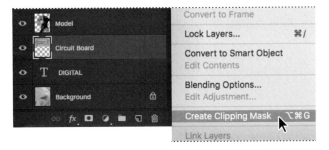

The circuit board now shows through the DIGITAL letters. A small arrow in the Circuit Board layer and the underlined type layer name indicate the clipping mask is applied. Next, you'll add an inner shadow to give the letters depth.

10 Select the DIGITAL layer to make it active. Then, click the Add A Layer Style button (*fx*) at the bottom of the Layers panel, and choose Inner Shadow from the pop-up menu.

11 In the Layer Style dialog box, change the Blend Mode to Multiply, Opacity to **48**%, Distance to **18**, Choke to **0**, and Size to **16**. Then click OK.

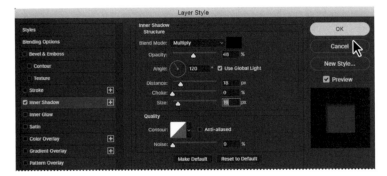

12 Choose File > Save to save your work so far.

Paragraph and Character Styles

If you frequently work with type in Photoshop, or if you need to consistently format a significant amount of type in an image, then paragraph and character styles can help you work more efficiently. A paragraph style is a collection of type attributes that you can apply to an entire paragraph with a single click. A character style is a collection of attributes that you can apply to individual characters. You can work with these styles by opening their panels: Choose Window > Paragraph Styles and Window > Character Styles.

The concept of type styles in Photoshop is similar to that in page layout applications such as Adobe InDesign and word-processing applications such as Microsoft Word. However, styles behave a little differently in Photoshop. For the best results working with type styles in Photoshop, keep the following in mind:

- By default, all text you create in Photoshop has the Basic Paragraph style applied. The Basic Paragraph style is defined by your text defaults, but you can change its attributes.

- Deselect all layers before you create a new style.

- If the selected text has been changed from the current paragraph style (usually the Basic Paragraph style), those changes (considered overrides) persist even when you apply a new style. To ensure that all the attributes of a paragraph style are applied to text, apply the style, and then click the Clear Override button in the Paragraph Styles panel.

- You can use the same paragraph and character styles across multiple files. To save the current styles as defaults for all new documents, choose Type > Save Default Type Styles. To use your default styles in an existing document, choose Type > Load Default Type Styles.

Creating type on a path

In Photoshop, you can create type that follows along a path that you create with a pen or shape tool. The direction the type flows depends on the order in which anchor points were added to the path. When you use the Horizontal Type tool to add text to a path, the letters are perpendicular to the baseline of the path. If you change the location or shape of the path, the type moves with it.

You'll create type on a path to make it look as if questions are coming from the model's mouth. We've already created the path for you.

1   In the Layers panel, select the Model layer.

2   Choose Window > Paths to show the Paths panel.

3   In the Paths panel, select the path named Speech Path.

The path appears to be coming out of the model's mouth.

4   Select the Horizontal Type tool.

5   In the options bar, click the Right Align Text button.

Julieanne Kost is an official Adobe Photoshop evangelist.

Tool tips from the Photoshop evangelist

Type tool tricks

- Shift-click in the image window with the Horizontal Type tool to create a new type layer—in case you're close to another block of type and Photoshop tries to autoselect the existing type layer.

- Double-click the thumbnail icon of any type layer in the Layers panel to select all of the type on that layer.

- With any text selected, right-click (Windows) or Control-click (Mac) on the text to access the context menu. Choose Check Spelling to run a spell check.

6 In the Character panel, select the following settings:

- Font Family: Myriad Pro Regular

- Font Style: Regular

- Font Size (T): **14** pt

- Tracking (VA): **−10**

- Color: White

- All Caps (TT)

7 Move the Type tool over the path. When a small slanted line appears across the I-bar, click the end of the path closest to the model's mouth, and type **What's new with games?**

● **Note:** In some versions of Photoshop CC 2019, a new text layer may be created with left alignment even if you specified another alignment before clicking the Horizontal Type tool. You can fix this by applying center alignment after the text layer is created.

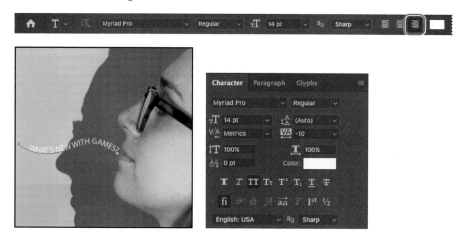

8 Select the word "GAMES?" and change its font style to Bold. Click the Commit Any Current Edits button (✓) in the options bar.

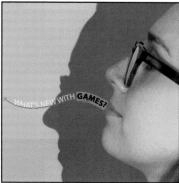

9   Click the Layers tab to bring it forward. In the Layers panel, select the What's new with games? layer, and then choose Duplicate Layer from the Layers panel menu. Name the new layer **What's new with music?**, and click OK.

You can't see the duplicate text layer yet, because it's exactly on top of the original text layer.

10   With the Type tool, select "GAMES," and replace it with **music**. Click the Commit Any Current Edits button in the options bar.

11   Choose Edit > Free Transform Path. Rotate the left side of the path approximately 15 degrees, and then shift the path up above the first path and a little to the right, as in the image below. Click the Commit Transform button in the options bar.

12   Repeat steps 9–11, replacing the word "GAMES" with **phones**. Rotate the left side of the path approximately –15 degrees, and move it below the original path.

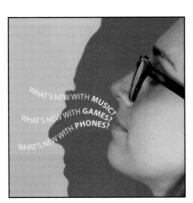 

13   Choose File > Save to save your work so far.

Warping point type

The text on a curvy path is more interesting than straight lines would be, but you'll warp the text to make it more playful. *Warping* lets you distort type to conform to a variety of shapes, such as an arc or a wave. The warp style you select is an attribute of the type layer—you can change a layer's warp style at any time to change the overall shape of the warp. Warping options give you precise control over the orientation and perspective of the warp effect.

1   If necessary, zoom or scroll to move the visible area of the image window so that the sentences to the left of the model are in the center of the screen.

2   Right-click (Windows) or Control-click (Mac) the What's new with games? layer in the Layers panel, and choose Warp Text from the context menu.

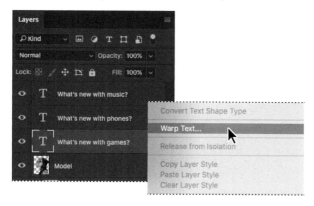

3   In the Warp Text dialog box, choose Wave from the Style menu, and select the Horizontal option. Specify the following values: Bend, **+33**%; Horizontal Distortion, **−23**%; and Vertical Distortion, **+5**%. Then click OK.

The Bend slider specifies how much warp is applied. Horizontal Distortion and Vertical Distortion determine the perspective of the warp.

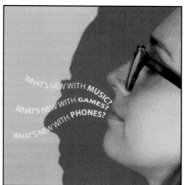

The words "What's new with games?" appear to float like a wave on the cover.

4 Repeat steps 2 and 3 to warp the other two text layers you typed on a path.

5 Save your work.

Designing paragraphs of type

All of the text you've written on this cover so far has been a few discrete words or lines—point type. However, many designs call for full paragraphs of text. You can design complete paragraphs of type in Photoshop; you can even apply paragraph styles. You don't have to switch to a dedicated page layout program for sophisticated paragraph type controls.

Using guides for positioning

You will add paragraphs to the cover in Photoshop. First, you'll add some guides to the work area to help you position the paragraphs.

1 If necessary, zoom or scroll so that you can see the entire top half of the document.

2 Drag a guide from the left vertical ruler, placing it approximately ¼" from the right side of the cover.

3 Drag a guide down from the top horizontal ruler, placing it approximately 2" from the top of the cover.

Adding paragraph type from a sticky note

You're ready to add the text. In a real-world design environment, the text might be provided to you in a word-processing document or the body of an email message, which you could copy and paste into Photoshop. Or you might have to type it in. Another easy way to add a bit of text is for the copywriter to attach it to the image file in a sticky note, as we've done for you here.

1   Select the Move tool, and then double-click the yellow sticky note in the lower right corner of the image window to open it in the Notes panel. Expand the Notes panel, if necessary, to see all the text.

2   In the Notes panel, select all the text. Press Ctrl+C (Windows) or Command+C (Mac) to copy the text to the clipboard. Close the Notes panel.

3   Select the Model layer. Then, select the Horizontal Type tool (**T**).

4   Press Shift as you click where the guidelines intersect at about ¼" from the right edge and 2" from the top of the cover. Continue to hold the Shift key as you start to drag a text box down and to the left. Then release the Shift key, and continue dragging until the box is about 4 inches wide by 8 inches high, the top and right edges aligned with the guides you just added.

5   Press Ctrl+V (Windows) or Command+V (Mac) to paste the text. The new text layer is at the top of the Layers panel, so the text appears in front of the model.

6   Select the first three lines ("The Trend Issue"), and then apply the following settings in the Character panel:

   • Font Family: Myriad Pro (or another sans serif font)

   • Font Style: Regular

   • Font Size ($_T$T): **70** pt

   • Leading ($_A^A$): **55** pt

   • Tracking (𝖵𝖠): **50**

   • Alignment: Right

   • Color: White

▶ **Tip:** Press Shift as you start to drag a text box to ensure that Photoshop creates a new text layer instead of selecting an existing text layer.

● **Note:** If the text isn't visible, make sure the new type layer is above the Model layer in the Layers panel.

▶ **Tip:** If you paste text and it includes unwanted formatting, you can instead choose the Edit > Paste Without Formatting command in Photoshop to remove all formatting from the pasted text.

● **Note:** *Leading* determines the vertical space between lines.

7 Select just the word "Trend," and change the Font Style to Bold.

You've formatted the title. Now you'll format the rest of the text.

8 Select the rest of the text you pasted. In the Character panel, select the following:

- Font Family: Myriad Pro
- Font Style: Regular
- Font Size: **22** pt
- Leading: **28** pt
- Tracking: **0**
- Deselect All Caps (**TT**)

The text looks good, but it's all the same. You'll make the headlines stand out more.

9 Select the "What's Hot!" text, and then change the following in the Character panel:

- Font Style: Bold
- Font Size: **28** pt

10 Repeat step 9 for the "What's Not!" subhead.

11 Select the word "TREND." Then, in the Character panel, change the text color to green.

12 Finally, click the Commit Any Current Edits button in the options bar.

13 Save your changes.

OpenType in Photoshop

OpenType is a cross-platform font file format developed jointly by Adobe and Microsoft. The format uses a single font file for both Mac and Windows, so you can move files from one platform to another without font substitution or reflowed text. OpenType offers widely expanded character sets and layout features, such as swashes and discretionary ligatures, that aren't available in traditional PostScript and TrueType fonts. This, in turn, provides richer linguistic support and advanced typography control. Here are some highlights of OpenType.

The OpenType menu The Character panel menu includes an OpenType submenu that displays all available features for a selected OpenType font, including ligatures, alternates, and fractions. Dimmed features are unavailable for that typeface; check marks appear next to features that have been applied.

Discretionary ligatures To add a discretionary ligature to two OpenType letters, such as "th" in the Bickham Script Standard typeface, select them in the file, and choose OpenType > Discretionary Ligatures from the Character panel menu.

Swashes Adding swashes or alternate characters works the same way as discretionary ligatures: Select the letter, such as a capital "T" in Bickham Script, and choose OpenType > Swash to change the ordinary capital into a dramatically ornate (swash) "T."

True fractions To create true fractions, type the fraction's characters—for example, 1/2. Then, select the characters, and from the Character panel menu, choose OpenType > Fractions. Photoshop applies the true fraction (½).

Color fonts While you can apply a color to a font in Photoshop, a format called OpenType-SVG allows multiple colors and gradients to be part of the font design itself. For example, a color font may provide the letter A in solid blue as well as solid red and in a blue-to-green gradient.

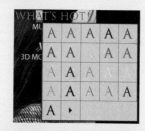

Emoji fonts Another example of OpenType-SVG fonts are emoji fonts, since OpenType-SVG allows vector graphics to be used as font characters. The Photoshop font family menu indicates color and emoji fonts with an OpenType SVG icon (⬛).

Variable fonts When you want a certain font weight but Regular is too thin and Bold is too thick, you can use a Variable Font that lets you customize attributes such as weight, width, and slant in the Properties panel. The Photoshop font family menu indicates variable fonts with an OpenType VAR icon (⬛).

Note that some OpenType fonts have more options than others.

> **Tip:** Want to know if a character has OpenType alternates? Just select it. If a thick underline appears under a selected character, moving the pointer over that character reveals the alternate glyphs available for that character in the font applied to it. You can select from those glyphs just as you can in the Glyphs panel, or you can click a triangle to open the Glyphs panel.

Adding a rounded rectangle

You're almost done with the text for the magazine cover. All that remains is to add the volume number in the upper right corner. First, you'll create a rectangle with rounded corners to serve as a background for the volume number.

1 Select the Rounded Rectangle tool (◯) in the Tools panel.

2 Draw a rectangle in the space above the letter "L" in the upper right corner of the cover, placing its right edge along the guide.

3 In the Properties panel, type **67** px for the width.

4 Click the fill color swatch in the Properties panel, and select the Pastel Yellow Orange swatch in the third row. Make sure the stroke is set to No Color.

By default, all the corners in the rectangle have the same radius, but you can adjust the radius for each corner separately. You can even return to edit the corners later if you want to. You'll change the rectangle so that only the lower left corner is rounded, changing the others to right angles.

5 In the Properties panel, click to deselect the Link Together Corner Radius Values icon (∞). Then change the bottom left corner to **16** px, and set all the others to **0** px.

6 With the Move tool, drag the rectangle to the top of the image so it hangs down like a ribbon and its right edge is next to the ruler guide.

7 Select Show Transform Controls in the options bar. Drag the bottom of the rectangle down so that it's close to the letter "L." (If you're not sure how long to make it, refer to the 07End.psd file.) Then click the Commit Transform button (✔).

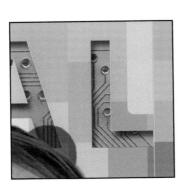

Adding vertical text

You're ready to add the volume number on top of the ribbon.

1   Choose Select > Deselect Layers. Then select the Vertical Type tool (↓T), which is hidden under the Horizontal Type tool.

2   Press the Shift key, and click near the bottom of the rectangle you just created.

Pressing the Shift key as you click ensures that you create a new text box instead of selecting the title.

3   Type **VOL 9**.

The letters are too large to view. You'll need to change their size to see them.

4   Choose Select > All, and then, in the Character panel, select the following:

   • Font Family: a sans-serif typeface, such as Myriad Pro

   • Font Style: a light or narrow style, such as Condensed

   • Font size: **15** pt

   • Tracking: **10**

   • Color: Black

5   Click the Commit Any Current Edits button (✔) in the options bar. Your vertical text now appears as the layer named VOL 9. Use the Move tool (✛) to center it in the ribbon, if necessary.

Saving as Photoshop PDF

The type you've added consists of vector-based outlines, which remain crisp and clear as you zoom in or resize them. However, if you save the file as a JPEG or TIFF image, Photoshop rasterizes the type, so you lose that flexibility. When you save a Photoshop PDF file, vector type is included.

You can preserve other Photoshop editing capabilities in a Photoshop PDF file too. For example, you can retain layers, color information, and even notes.

To ensure you can edit the file later, select Preserve Photoshop Editing Capabilities in the Save Adobe PDF dialog box.

To preserve any notes in the file and convert them to Acrobat comments when you save to PDF, select Notes in the Save area of the Save As dialog box.

You can open a Photoshop PDF file in Acrobat or Photoshop, place it in another application, or print it. For more information about saving as Photoshop PDF, see Photoshop Help.

▶ **Tip:** Want a design to have a familiar look, but not with the exact font that look is known for? Try **Font Similarity**. Choose a font in the Font Family menu in either the Type tool options bar or the Character panel. You'll see options at the top of the font list; click the Show Similar Fonts button.

The font list will now show the 20 most similar fonts available either on your system or from Typekit.

Now, you'll clean up a bit.

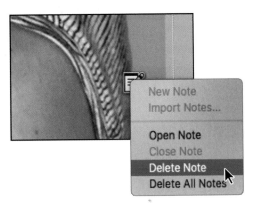

6   Click the note to select it. Then right-click (Windows) or Control-click (Mac), and choose Delete Note from the context menu; click Yes to confirm that you want to delete the note.

7   Hide the guides: Choose the Hand tool (✋), and then press Ctrl+; (Windows) or Command+; (Mac). Then zoom out to get a nice look at your work.

8   Choose File > Save to save your work.

Congratulations! You've added and stylized all of the type on the Digital magazine cover. Now that the magazine cover is ready to go, you'll flatten it and prepare it for printing.

9   Choose File > Save As, rename the file **07Working_flattened**, and click Save. Click OK if you see the Photoshop Format Options dialog box.

The Glyphs panel

The Glyphs panel lists all characters available for a font, including specialized characters and alternate versions such as swashes. Above the font name and style menus is a row of recently used glyphs. It's blank if you haven't used any glyphs yet. A menu under the font name lets you display a writing system such as Arabic, or a category of characters such as punctuation or currency symbols. A black dot in the bottom right corner of a character's box indicates that alternates are available for that character; click and hold the mouse on the character to view its alternate glyphs or to choose one to enter into a text layer.

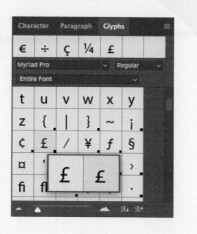

▶ **Tip:** Use the Glyphs panel (Window > Glyphs) to access the full range of alternate characters in OpenType fonts. When editing text, double-click a character in the Glyphs panel to add it to the text.

Keeping a layered version lets you return to the 07Working.psd file in the future to edit it.

10 Choose Layer > Flatten Image.

11 Choose File > Save, and then close the document window.

▶ **Tip:** When preparing a Photoshop file for high-resolution output, if it contains vector shapes and text layers, consult with your output service provider about the best format to use and whether the file should be flattened.

Extra credit

Using Match Fonts to keep your projects consistent

We want to identify a font that was used in an earlier issue, for text that says "Premiere Issue" (see the file MatchFont.psd in the Lesson07 folder). We'd like to use that font for other text inside the magazine. But the only available file is flattened, so the original type layer is lost. Because no type layer is available, it's impossible to select the text to find out which font was used. Fortunately, you don't have to guess which font is in the image because, in Photoshop CC, you can let the Match Font feature figure it out for you. Thanks to the magic of intelligent imaging analysis, using just a picture of a Latin font, Photoshop CC can use machine learning to detect which font it is. Match Font then shows you a list of similar fonts. Match Font is also useful for identifying fonts in photos, such as in the text on a sign in a street scene.

1   Open MatchFont.psd in the Lesson07 folder.

2   Select the area containing the mystery font. Keep the selection close to the text.

3   Choose Type > Match Font. Photoshop displays a list of fonts similar to the font in the image, including fonts currently active on your system and fonts from Typekit.

4   To list only the fonts on your computer, deselect Show Fonts Available To Sync From Typekit.

5   Select a script font that most closely resembles the font in the image from the list of fonts that Match Font determined to be similar. Your Match Font results may look different than ours.

6   Click OK. Photoshop selects the font you clicked, so you can now create new text with it.

Review questions

1 How does Photoshop treat type?

2 How is a text layer the same as or different from other layers in Photoshop?

3 What is a clipping mask, and how do you make one from type?

Review answers

1 Type in Photoshop consists of vector-based shapes that describe the letters, numbers, and symbols of a typeface. When you add type to an image in Photoshop, the characters appear on a text layer at the same resolution as the image file. As long as the type layer exists, Photoshop preserves the type outlines so that the text remains sharp when you scale or resize type, save a PDF or EPS file, or print the image to a high-resolution printer.

2 Type that is added to an image appears in the Layers panel as a text layer that can be edited and managed in the same way as any other kind of layer. You can add and edit the text, change the orientation of the type, and apply anti-aliasing as well as move, restack, copy, and change the options for layers.

3 A clipping mask is an object or group whose shape masks other artwork so that only areas that lie within the shape are visible. To use a text layer as a clipping mask, make sure the layer you want to reveal is directly above the text layer, select the layer you want to show through the letters, and choose Create Clipping Mask from the Layers panel menu.

8 VECTOR DRAWING TECHNIQUES

Lesson overview

In this lesson, you'll learn how to do the following:

- Differentiate between bitmap and vector graphics.
- Draw straight and curved paths using the Pen tool.
- Save paths.
- Draw and edit shape layers.
- Draw custom shapes.
- Import and edit a Smart Object from Adobe Illustrator.
- Use Smart Guides.

This lesson will take about 90 minutes to complete. Please log in to your account on peachpit.com to download the lesson files for this chapter, or go to the Getting Started section at the beginning of this book and follow the instructions under "Accessing the Lesson Files and Web Edition."

As you work on this lesson, you'll preserve the start files. If you need to restore the start files, download them from your Account page.

PROJECT: COFFEE SHOP SIGN

Unlike bitmap images, vector graphics retain their crisp edges when you enlarge them to any size. You can draw vector shapes and paths in your Photoshop images and add vector masks to control what is shown in an image.

About bitmap images and vector graphics

Before working with vector shapes and vector paths, it's important to understand the basic differences between the two main categories of computer graphics: *bitmap images* and *vector graphics*. You can use Photoshop to work with either type of graphic; in fact, you can combine both bitmap and vector data in an individual Photoshop image file.

Bitmap images, technically called *raster images*, are based on a grid of dots known as *pixels*. Each pixel is assigned a specific location and color value. In working with bitmap images, you edit groups of pixels rather than objects or shapes. Because bitmap graphics can represent subtle gradations of shade and color, they are appropriate for continuous-tone images such as photographs or artwork created in painting programs. A disadvantage of bitmap graphics is that they contain a fixed number of pixels. As a result, they can lose detail and appear jagged when scaled up on screen or printed at a lower resolution than they were created for.

Vector graphics are made up of lines and curves defined by mathematical objects called *vectors*. These graphics retain their crispness whether they are moved, resized, or have their color changed. Vector graphics are appropriate for illustrations, type, and graphics such as logos that may be scaled to different sizes.

Logo drawn as vector art

Logo rasterized as bitmap art

About paths and the Pen tool

In Photoshop, the outline of a vector shape is called a *path*. A path is a curved or straight line segment you draw using the Pen tool, Freeform Pen tool, Curvature Pen tool, or a shape tool. The Pen tool draws paths with the greatest precision; shape tools draw rectangles, ellipses, and other shape paths; the Freeform Pen tool draws paths as if you were drawing with a pencil on paper.

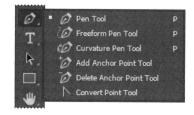

Paths can be open or closed. An open path (such as a wavy line) has two distinct endpoints. A closed path (such as a circle) is continuous. The type of path you draw affects how it can be selected and adjusted.

Paths that have no fill or stroke do not print when you print your artwork. This is because paths are vector objects that contain no pixels, unlike the bitmap shapes drawn by the Pencil tool and other painting tools. If you want a path to have a fill or stroke, create it as a *shape*. A shape is a layer based on vector objects instead of pixels. Unlike a path, you can apply colors and effects to a shape layer.

Getting started

In this lesson, you'll draw a path around a coffee cup in an image, and create another path inside the handle. You'll subtract one selection from the other so that a lightning bolt shape (provided in the Shapes panel) knocks out of the cup shape. Finally, you'll import an Illustrator title treatment as a Smart Object and apply a color and emboss effect.

Before you begin, you'll view the image you'll be creating—a sign for a fictitious coffee shop.

1   Start Photoshop, and then immediately hold down Ctrl+Alt+Shift (Windows) or Command+Option+Shift (Mac) to restore the default preferences. (See "Restoring Default Preferences" on page 5.)

2   When prompted, click Yes to delete the Adobe Photoshop Settings file.

3   Choose File > Browse In Bridge.

4   In the Favorites panel, click the Lessons folder, and then double-click the Lesson08 folder in the Content panel.

5   Select the 08End.psd file, and press the spacebar to see it in full-screen view.

To create this sign, you'll trace the coffee cup in an image, and use that tracing to make a vector logo. You'll resize that logo and combine it with an Illustrator typographic logo imported as a Smart Object. First, you'll practice making paths and selections using the Pen tool.

6   When you've finished looking at the 08End.psd file, press the spacebar again. Then double-click the 08Practice_Start.psd file to open it in Photoshop.

7   Choose File > Save As, rename the file **08Practice_Working.psd**, and click Save. If the Photoshop Format Options dialog box appears, click OK.

Drawing with the Pen tool

▶ **Tip:** The Curvature Pen tool offers a potentially simpler way to draw precise vector paths; consider learning it if you find the Pen tool to be challenging to use. The Pen tool is taught here because it's a traditional way to precisely draw the vector paths and shapes that are used in many applications.

You'll use the Pen tool to select the coffee cup. The cup has long, smooth, curved edges that would be difficult to select using other methods.

The Pen tool works a little differently from most Photoshop tools. We've created a practice file which you can use to get familiar with the Pen tool before making your Kailua Koffee sign.

Paths include anchor points (smooth and corner) and segments (straight and curved). You'll get a feel for the Pen tool by drawing a straight path, a simple curve, and then an S-curve before you practice tracing the coffee cup.

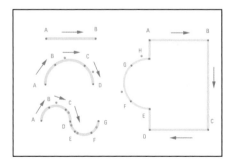

Creating paths with the Pen tool

You can use the Pen tool to create paths that are straight or curved, open or closed. If you're unfamiliar with the Pen tool, it can be confusing to use at first. Understanding the elements of a path and how to create those elements with the Pen tool makes paths much easier to draw.

To create a straight path, click the mouse button. The first time you click, you set the starting point. Each time that you click thereafter, a straight line is drawn between the previous point and the current point. To draw complex straight-segment paths with the Pen tool, simply click each time you want to add a new segment.

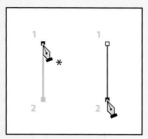

Creating a straight line

To create a curved path, click to place an anchor point, drag to create a direction line for that point, and then click to place the next anchor point. Each direction line ends in two direction points; the positions of direction lines and points determine the size and shape of the curved segment. Moving the direction lines and points reshapes the curves in a path.

Smooth curves are connected by anchor points called *smooth points*. Sharply curved paths are connected by *corner points*. When you move a direction line on a smooth point, the curved segments on both sides of the point adjust simultaneously, but when you move a direction line on a corner point, only the curve on the same side of the point as the direction line is adjusted.

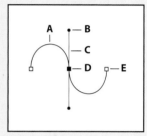

A. *Curved line segment*
B. *Direction point*
C. *Direction line*
D. *Selected anchor point*
E. *Unselected anchor point*

Path segments and anchor points can be moved after they're drawn, either individually or as a group. When a path contains more than one segment, you can drag individual anchor points to adjust individual segments of the path, or select all of the anchor points in a path to edit the entire path. Use the Direct Selection tool to select and adjust an anchor point, a path segment, or an entire path.

Creating a closed path differs from creating an open path in the way that you end it. To end an open path, press Enter or Return. To create a closed path, position the Pen tool pointer over the starting point, and click. Closing a path automatically ends the path. After the path closes, the Pen tool pointer appears with a small ∗, indicating that your next click will start a new path.

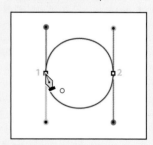

Creating a closed path

As you draw paths, a temporary storage area named Work Path appears in the Paths panel. It's a good idea to save work paths, and it's essential if you use multiple discrete paths in the same image file. If you deselect an existing Work Path in the Paths panel and then start drawing again, a new work path will replace the original one, which will be lost. To save a work path, double-click it in the Paths panel, type a name in the Save Path dialog box, and click OK to rename and save the path. The path remains selected in the Paths panel.

First, you'll configure the Pen tool options and the work area.

1   In the Tools panel, select the Pen tool (⬥).

2   In the options bar, select or verify the following settings:

    •   Choose Shape from the Tool Mode pop-up menu.

    •   In the Path Options menu, make sure that Rubber Band is not selected.

    •   Make sure that Auto Add/Delete is selected.

    •   Choose No Color from the Fill pop-up menu.

    •   Choose a green color from the Stroke pop-up menu.

    •   Enter **4 pt** for the stroke width.

    •   In the Stroke Options window, choose Center (the second option) from the Align menu.

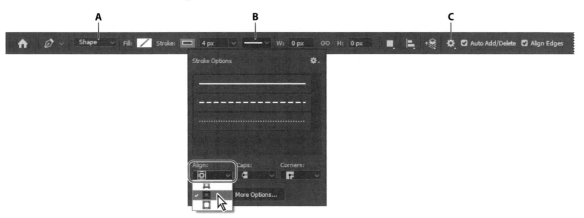

A. Tool Mode menu   **B.** Stroke Options menu   **C.** Path Options menu

Drawing a straight line

You'll start by drawing a straight line. Anchor points mark the ends of path segments; the straight line you'll draw is a single path segment with two anchor points.

1   Click the Paths tab to bring that panel to the front of the Layers panel group.

The Paths panel displays thumbnail previews of the paths you draw. Currently, the panel is empty, because you haven't started drawing.

2   If necessary, zoom in so that you can easily see the lettered points and blue dots on the shape template. Make sure you can see the whole template in the image window, and be sure to reselect the Pen tool after you zoom.

3 Click point A on the first shape, and release the mouse button. You've created an anchor point.

4 Click point B. You've created a straight line with two anchor points.

5 Press Enter or Return to stop drawing.

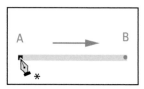
Note: If a tutorial pop-up for the Curvature Pen tool appears, you do not need to read it at this time. It will probably close on its own, or you can close it.

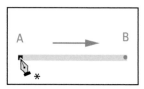
Create an anchor point.

Click to create a straight line.

Complete the path.

The path you drew appears in the Paths panel and as a new layer in the Layers panel.

> **Tip:** It can be useful to see both the Paths and Layers panels at the same time, so if they're currently overlapping each other, consider pulling them apart so you can see them simultaneously.

Drawing curves

On curved segments, selecting an anchor point displays two direction lines (smooth points) or one direction line (corner point). Direction lines end in direction points, and the positions of the direction lines and direction points determine the size and shape of the curved segment. You'll create curved lines, using smooth points.

1 Click A on the semicircle, and release the mouse to create the first anchor point.

2 Click point B, but don't release the mouse button. Instead, drag the cursor to the blue dot to the right of point B to create a curved path segment and a smooth anchor point. Then release the mouse button.

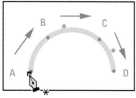
Create an anchor point.

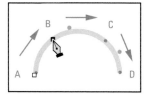
Click and hold.

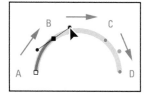
Drag to curve the path segment.

Smooth anchor points have two linked direction lines. When you move one, the curved segments on both sides of the path adjust simultaneously.

3   Click point C, and drag down to the blue dot below. Then release the mouse button. You've created a second curved path segment and another smooth point.

4   Click point D, and release the mouse to create the final anchor point. Press Enter or Return to complete the path.

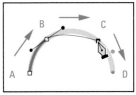 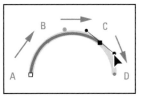 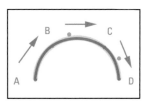

Click C to create a point.   Drag to curve the segment.   Click D to finish the semicircle.

When drawing a freehand path using the Pen tool, use as few points as possible to create the shape you want. The fewer points you use, the smoother the curves are—and the more efficient your file is.

Using the same techniques, you'll draw an S-shaped curve.

5   Click point A, and then click point B; then drag the cursor to the first blue dot.

6   Continue with points C, D, E, and F, in each case clicking the point and then dragging to the corresponding blue dot.

7   Click point G to create the final anchor point, and then press Enter or Return to complete the path.

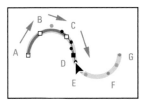 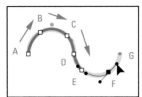 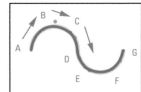

This shape is on its own layer in the Layers panel. Only one path is in the Paths panel because the work path for the second shape overwrote the work path for the first one.

Notice that the curves you drew with the Pen tool are much smoother and easier to precisely control than if you had drawn them freehand.

Drawing a more complex shape

Now that you've got the idea, you'll have a chance to draw a more complex object: the outline of a coffee cup.

1   Click point A on the shape on the right side to set the first anchor point.

2   Press the Shift key as you click point B. Pressing the Shift key constrains the line so that it is perfectly straight.

3   Press the Shift key as you click points C, D, and E to create straight path segments.

4　Click point F, and drag to the blue dot to create a curve. Then release the mouse button.

5　Click point G, and drag to the blue dot to create another curve. Then release the mouse button.

6　Click point H. Then press Alt (Windows) or Option (Mac) as you click point H again to create a corner point.

When you move a direction line on a corner point, only the curve on the same side of the point as the direction line is adjusted, so you can create a sharp transition between two segments.

7　Click point A to draw the final path segment and close the path. Closing a path automatically ends the drawing; you don't need to press Enter or Return.

▶ **Tip:** Why is it useful to create paths using points and handles, instead of drawing directly as with a real pen or pencil? Because it's difficult for most people to draw curves and straight lines without bumps or other errors. Points and handles let you draw absolutely perfect curves and straight lines. If you prefer to draw normally, use the Freeform Pen tool.

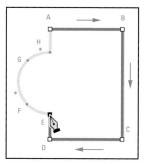
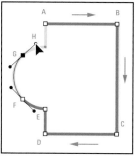
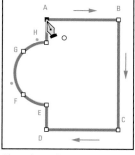

Start with straight segments.　*Drag to create a curve.*　*Close the path.*

8　Close the file without saving changes.

Tracing a shape from a photo

Now you're ready to draw a path around the coffee cup in the image. You'll use the techniques you've practiced to draw a path around the outside of the cup and another one inside the handle.

1　Open the 08Start.psd file in Photoshop.

The image includes three layers: the background layer and two template layers to guide you as you draw shapes.

2 Choose File > Save As, rename the file **08Working.psd**, and click Save. Click OK in the Photoshop Format Options dialog box.

3 With the Pen tool selected, click point A. Photoshop creates a new layer for the shape.

4 Click point B, and drag the cursor to the red dot on the right to create the initial curve.

▶ **Tip:** When tracing, adjust the magnification of the document window so you can clearly see the outline that you're tracing.

▶ **Tip:** If you'd like to try tracing the cup without using the dots to guide you, hide the Outside Cup layer in the Layers panel.

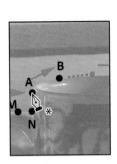 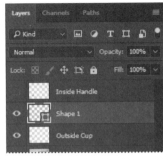 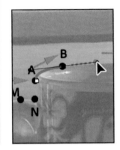

5 Click point C, and drag to the red dot to its right.

6 Continue tracing the cup, clicking each point, and dragging the cursor to the corresponding red dots when you need to create a curve.

7 Close the shape by clicking point A again.

▶ **Tip:** If the path is difficult to see as you draw it, click the Path Options menu (the gear) in the options bar, and customize Thickness and Color. These options affect only the visibility of the path while drawing; they do not affect the Fill and Stroke settings that determine how the shape appears when printed or exported.

8 Evaluate your path. If you want to adjust any segments, use the Direct Selection tool to select a point, and then move its direction lines to edit the segment.

9 Press Enter or Return to deselect the path, and save your work so far.

Adding a second shape to a path

You've drawn a path that outlines the exterior of the cup, but you want the inside of the handle to be transparent. You'll draw a shape to isolate the inside of the cup handle.

1 Hide the Outside Cup layer, and make the Inside Handle layer visible.

2 Make sure Shape 1 is selected in the Layers panel, and then, in the Paths panel, select Shape 1 Shape Path.

3 Make sure the Pen tool is selected, and choose Subtract Front Shape from the Path Operations pop-up menu in the options bar.

Options in the Path Operations menu determine how multiple shapes interact with each other in a path. After you draw the cup outline, you'll subtract the inside of the handle from it.

4 Click point A to begin drawing. Then click point B, drag to the next red dot, and release the mouse button.

5 Continue drawing, clicking and dragging as indicated at points C and D.

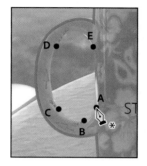 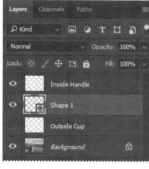

Note: If your green cup outline and Layers panel don't appear exactly as they do in the figure at the left, choose Edit > Step Backward until Shape 2 disappears from the Layers panel, press Enter or Return to deselect the path, and start again at step 2.

6 Click point E, drag slightly down to the red dot, and release. Then, press Alt (Windows) or Option (Mac) as you click point E again, to convert the point to a corner point.

Converting point E to a corner point enables you to draw a straight path segment between it and point A. If point E remained a smooth point, the path between points E and A would be slightly curved.

7 Click point A to close the shape and stop drawing.

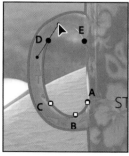 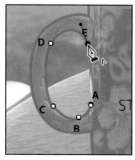 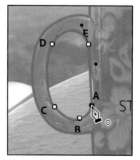

Create curved path.   Convert E to corner point.   Create final straight segment.

Now you'll save the path to use later.

ADOBE PHOTOSHOP CC CLASSROOM IN A BOOK (2019 RELEASE) **199**

8 In the Paths panel, double-click Shape 1 Shape Path, type **Cup Outline** in the Save Path dialog box, and click OK to save it; then, still in the Paths panel, click in an empty area to deselect all paths.

You won't need the Shape 1, Outside Cup, and Inside Handle layers any more, so you'll delete them.

> **Tip:** When you want to delete a range of contiguous layers, Shift-click the first and last layers in the range to select them, and then click the Delete Layer icon in the Layers panel.

9 In the Layers panel, select the Shape 1 layer, and then click the Delete Layer icon (🗑) at the bottom of the Layers panel. Click Yes if you're asked to confirm the deletion. This will also remove the Shape 1 Shape Path from the Paths panel. In the same way, delete the Inside Handle and Outside Cup layers.

10 Choose File > Save to save your work.

Working with defined custom shapes

Photoshop includes several predefined custom shapes in the Custom Shape Picker, but you can also create your own.

Converting a path to a shape

You'll define the cup outline path as a custom shape that you can use for the logo. The shape will be available in the Custom Shape Picker.

1 Select the Cup Outline path in the Paths panel.

2 Choose Edit > Define Custom Shape.

3 Name the shape **Coffee Cup**, and click OK.

4   Select the Custom Shape tool (🖾), hidden under the Rectangle tool (⬜) in the Tools panel.

5   In the options bar, click the Shape icon to open the Custom Shape Picker, and scroll to the bottom of the picker. The shape you added should be the last one displayed. Click to select the Coffee Cup shape.

6   Position the Custom Shape tool near the top left corner of the document. Hold down the Shift key to maintain original proportions, and start dragging down and to the right. When the logo is about 2 inches tall, release the mouse button, and then release the Shift key.

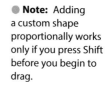 **Note:** Adding a custom shape proportionally works only if you press Shift before you begin to drag.

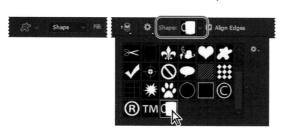 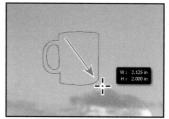

7   Double-click the name of the Shape 1 layer in the Layers panel, and name it **Coffee Cup**.

Changing the fill color of a shape layer

You've created a custom shape from your path, and you've used the Custom Shape tool to draw the shape on the image. But it's just an outline. You'll add a fill.

1   Make sure the Coffee Cup layer is selected in the Layers panel.

2   Select the Pen tool (✒) in the Tools panel.

3   In the options bar, select Black for the Fill color and No Color for the stroke.

The coffee cup shape is now solid black.

4   Press Enter or Return to deselect the coffee cup path.

Subtracting shapes from a shape layer

After you create a shape layer, you can subtract new shapes from it. You'll add some interest to the coffee cup shape by subtracting a lightning bolt shape from it, allowing the background to show through.

1   In the Tools panel, select the Custom Shape tool.

2   In the Paths panel, select Coffee Cup Shape Path.

3   In the options bar, choose Subtract Front Shape from the Path Operations menu. The pointer now appears as cross-hairs with a small minus sign ($-|_-$).

4   Select the lightning bolt from the Custom Shape Picker (it's in the second row). Position the pointer at the upper left corner of the black coffee cup.

5   Start at the upper left corner of the black coffee cup, and drag down to the bottom right.

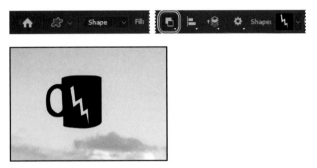

Importing a Smart Object

Smart Objects are layers that you can edit in Photoshop nondestructively; that is, changes you make to the image remain editable and don't affect the actual image pixels, which are preserved. Regardless of how often you scale, rotate, skew, or otherwise transform a Smart Object, it retains its sharp, precise edges.

You can import vector objects from Adobe Illustrator as Smart Objects. If you later edit the original object in Illustrator, the changes will be reflected in the placed Smart Object in your Photoshop image file.

When you place a file as a Smart Object, you can link it or embed it. If you link it, Photoshop remembers the folder path to the placed file so that you can easily update it by editing the original file, and it includes a preview image of the Smart Object in the Photoshop file. If you embed a Smart Object, Photoshop includes the entire object in the Photoshop file without storing the path to the original file. However, you can convert an embedded Smart Object to a linked Smart Object; this exports the embedded object as a linked file stored in a folder you choose.

You'll work with a Smart Object now by placing a Kailua Koffee logotype that was created in Illustrator.

1   Select the Move tool (✛) in the Tools panel.

2   Select the Coffee Cup layer, and choose File > Place Linked. Select the Logotype.eps file in the Lesson08 folder, and click Place.

The Kailua Koffee logotype is added to the middle of the composition, inside a bounding box with adjustable handles. A new layer, Logotype, appears in the Layers panel.

3   Drag the logotype object to the upper left corner of the sign, just to the right of the coffee cup logo, and then drag a corner to make the text object larger—large enough that it fills the top portion of the image, as in the following illustration. When you've finished, confirm the transformation using any of the methods you have learned, such as clicking away from the layer.

▶ **Tip:** You can place a file as a linked Smart Object by holding down Alt (Windows) or Option (Mac) as you drag and drop the file into a Photoshop document window.

When you apply the transformation, the layer thumbnail icon changes to show a link icon, indicating that the Logotype layer is a linked Smart Object.

As with any shape layer or Smart Object, you can continue to edit its size and shape if you'd like. Simply select the layer, choose Edit > Free Transform to access the control handles, and drag to adjust them. Or, select the Move tool (✛), and select Show Transform Controls in the options bar. Then adjust the handles.

● **Note:** A placed file always imports with a transformation bounding box active, so that you can scale and position it. You must apply it even if you make no changes.

▶ **Tip:** When a linked Smart Object is selected in the Layers panel, you can see and adjust its options in the Properties panel, including the path to the linked file.

Adding color and depth to a shape using layer styles

You created the shape with a black fill. Now you'll make it snazzier by changing the fill color and adding a Bevel & Emboss effect.

1   With the Logotype layer selected, choose Color Overlay from the Add A Layer Style menu (fx) at the bottom of the Layers panel.

2   In the Layer Style dialog box, choose a dark red or burgundy color.

● **Note:** Be sure to click the words "Bevel & Emboss." If you click only the check box, Photoshop applies the layer style with its default settings, but you won't see the options.

3   Click Bevel & Emboss on the left side of the Layer Style dialog box to add another layer style. Accept the defaults for the Bevel & Emboss layer style, and click OK.

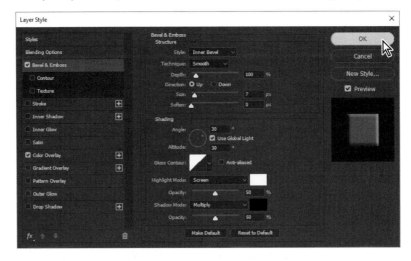

The Color Overlay and Bevel & Emboss layer styles affect the Logotype layer. You'll copy them to the Coffee Cup layer.

4   Press Alt (Windows) or Option (Mac) as you drag the layer effects indicator (*fx*) from the Logotype layer onto the Coffee Cup layer.

5   Clean up the Paths panel by deleting the Cup Outline path.

6   Choose File > Save to save your work. The coffee shop sign is complete.

7   Close the file.

Extra Credit

Using Creative Cloud Libraries with linked Smart Objects

When you organize and share your design assets using Creative Cloud Libraries, you and your team can use those library items in many Creative Cloud desktop and mobile apps. Let's take a look:

1   Open 08End.psd. If the Libraries panel isn't open, choose Window > Libraries.

2   In the Libraries panel menu, choose Create New Library, and name it **Kailua Koffee**.

3   In the Layers panel, select the Background layer. In the Layers panel menu, choose Convert to Smart Object. This layer is now named "Layer 0."

4   Select the Move tool. Drag the layer from the document window (not the Layers panel) into the Kailua Koffee library.

5   Repeat steps 3 and 4 for the Logotype layer and the Coffee Cup layer.

Now all three elements will appear in Creative Cloud applications and mobile apps. Because each item is a linked Smart Object, you can edit the logo in the Kailua Koffee library and it will update in all documents that use it. To edit a library item, just double-click it in the Libraries panel. (Note that the Logotype graphic is an EPS file that Photoshop cannot edit.)

Adding colors

1   With the Eyedropper tool, click the red mug in the document window. Then choose Select > Deselect Layers.

2   At the bottom of the Libraries panel, click the Add Content button (+), make sure the Foreground Color swatch is selected, and click Add. That adds the color you sampled to the current library. Use the same method to sample a light blue from the sky in the background, and add that color to your library too.

Collaborating

When you share a Creative Cloud Library, your team always has the current version of those assets. In the Libraries panel menu, choose Collaborate, and fill in the Invite Collaborators screen that appears in your web browser. Collaborators will see the library you shared in their Creative Cloud applications (to utilize this feature, you must have a Creative Cloud account and be logged in).

Adding assets to libraries using Adobe mobile apps

Use Adobe mobile apps—such as Adobe Capture CC—to record color themes, shapes, and brushes from real life and add them to your Creative Cloud libraries. Library assets you add with mobile apps are automatically synced to your Creative Cloud account, so you'll see the new assets in your Libraries panel when you return to your computer.

Extra credit

Smart Guides

Let's take this design to the next level. You can use the coffee cup logo to make a repeated motif at the bottom of the sign. Smart Guides can help you position the images evenly.

1   In 08Working.psd, choose View > Show, and make sure Smart Guides are enabled. If there's a check mark next to Smart Guides, they're on. Otherwise, select Smart Guides to enable them.

2   Select the Coffee Cup layer. Then select the Move tool, and hold down the Alt (Windows) or Option (Mac) key as you drag the cup logo to the lower left corner of the sign. The Alt or Option key copies the selected object; the magenta lines that appear are Smart Guides that align the copy to the center or edges of the original, as long as you keep the object snapped to the guides. Without Smart Guides, you'd have to also press Shift to keep the copy aligned.

3   Choose Edit > Free Transform. Then press Shift to maintain the proportions as you scale the cup to about half its original size. Press Enter or Return to confirm the transformation.

4   Make sure the Move tool and the Coffee Cup copy layer are still selected, and then press Alt or Option as you drag the coffee cup copy to the right until the measurements displayed in pink show you that the images are 4.5 inches apart. Again, keep the copy snapped to the Smart Guides as you drag, and use the transformation value display to see how far you've dragged and the space between objects.

5   Select the second image on the bottom, and repeat step 4. This time, when you drag the image 4.5 inches, Photoshop displays the distance between each of the sets of images.

6   Repeat step 5 so you have a total of four equally spaced logos.

206   LESSON 8   Vector Drawing Techniques

Review questions

1 What is the difference between a bitmap image and a vector graphic?

2 How can you create a custom shape?

3 What tool can you use to move and resize paths and shapes?

4 What are vector Smart Objects, and what is the benefit of using them?

Review answers

1 Bitmap, or raster, images are based on a grid of pixels and are appropriate for continuous-tone images such as photographs or artwork created in painting programs. Vector graphics are made up of shapes based on mathematical expressions and are appropriate for illustrations, type, and drawings that require clear, smooth lines.

2 To create a custom shape, select a path, and then choose Edit > Define Custom Shape. Name the shape; it will appear in the Custom Shape Picker.

3 You use the Direct Selection tool to move, resize, and edit shapes. You can also modify and scale a selected shape or path by choosing Edit > Free Transform.

4 Vector Smart Objects are vector objects that you can place and edit in Photoshop without a loss of quality. Regardless of how often you scale, rotate, skew, or otherwise transform a vector Smart Object, it retains sharp, precise edges. A great benefit of using vector Smart Objects is that you can edit the original object in its original application, such as Illustrator, and the changes will be reflected in the placed Smart Object in your Photoshop image file.

9 ADVANCED COMPOSITING

Lesson overview

In this lesson, you'll learn how to do the following:

- Apply and edit Smart Filters.

- Use the Liquify filter to distort an image.

- Apply color effects to selected areas of an image.

- Apply filters to create various effects.

- Use the History panel to return to a previous state.

- Upscale a low-resolution image for high-resolution printing.

This lesson will take about an hour to complete. Please log in to your account on peachpit.com to download the lesson files for this chapter, or go to the Getting Started section at the beginning of this book and follow the instructions under "Accessing the Lesson Files and Web Edition."

As you work on this lesson, you'll preserve the start files. If you need to restore the start files, download them from your Account page.

PROJECT: MONSTER MOVIE POSTER DESIGN

Monster makeup imagery courtesy of Russell Brown, with illustration by John Connell

Filters can transform ordinary images into extraordinary digital artwork. Smart Filters let you edit those transformations at any time. The wide variety of features in Photoshop lets you be as creative as you want to be.

Getting started

In this lesson, you'll assemble a montage of images for a movie poster as you explore filters in Photoshop. First, look at the final project to see what you'll be creating.

1 Start Photoshop, and then immediately hold down Ctrl+Alt+Shift (Windows) or Command+Option+Shift (Mac) to restore the default preferences. (See "Restoring Default Preferences" on page 5.)

2 When prompted, click Yes to delete the Adobe Photoshop Settings file.

3 Choose File > Browse In Bridge.

● **Note:** If Bridge isn't installed, you'll be prompted to install it when you choose Browse In Bridge. For more information, see page 3.

4 In Bridge, choose Favorites from the menu on the left, and then click the Lessons folder. Double-click the Lesson09 folder.

5 View the 09_End.psd thumbnail. Move the slider at the bottom of the Bridge window if you need to zoom in to see the thumbnail more clearly.

This file is a movie poster that comprises a background, a monster image, and several smaller images. Each image has had one or more filters or effects applied to it.

The monster is composed of an image of a perfectly normal (though slightly threatening) guy with several ghoulish images applied. These monstrous additions are courtesy of Russell Brown, with illustration by John Connell.

6 In Bridge, navigate to the Lesson09/Monster_Makeup folder, and open it.

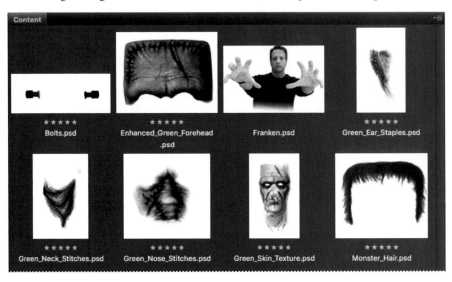

7 Shift-click the first and last items to select all the files in the Monster_Makeup folder, and then choose Tools > Photoshop > Load Files Into Photoshop Layers.

Photoshop imports all the selected files as individual layers in a new Photoshop file. The designer used a red layer color to indicate components of the monster's look.

8 In Photoshop, choose File > Save As. Choose Photoshop for the Format, and name the new file **09Working.psd**. Save it in the Lesson09 folder. Click OK in the Photoshop Format Options dialog box.

Arranging layers

Your image file contains eight layers, imported in alphabetical order. In their current positions, they don't make a very convincing monster. You'll rearrange the layer order and resize their contents as you start to build your monster.

1 Zoom out or scroll so that you can see all the layers on the artboard.

2 In the Layers panel, drag the Monster_Hair layer to the top of the layer stack.

3 Drag the Franken layer to the bottom of the layer stack.

4 Select the Move tool (✛), and then move the Franken layer (the image of the person) to the bottom of the page.

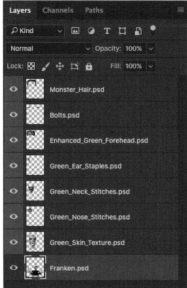

5 In the Layers panel, Shift-select every layer except the Franken layer, and choose Edit > Free Transform.

6   Drag down from a corner of the selection to resize all the selected layers to about 50% of their original size. (Watch the width and height percentages in the options bar.)

7   With the Free Transform bounding box still active, position the layers over the head of the Franken layer. Then press Enter or Return to commit the transformation.

8   Zoom in to see the head area clearly.

9   Hide all layers except the Green_Skin_Texture and Franken layers.

10 Select only the Green_Skin_Texture layer, and use the Move tool to center it over the face.

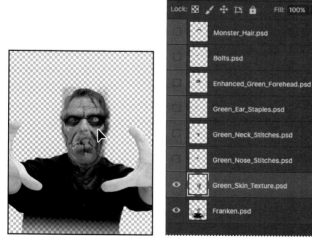

▶ **Tip:** If magenta Smart Guides appear, making it difficult to position the Green_Skin_Texture layer, hold down the Control key to temporarily disable snapping to Smart Guides as you drag. Or permanently disable them by deselecting the View > Show > Smart Guides command.

▶ **Tip:** For more
detailed control over
how the texture fits
the face, choose Edit >
Transform > Warp, drag
the transform grid
or handles, and then
press Return or Enter to
commit the changes.

11 Choose Edit > Free Transform again to adjust the fit of the texture to the face. Using the eyes and mouth as a guide, press arrow keys to nudge the entire layer into position. Drag the side handles on the bounding box to adjust the width and height. When you've positioned the skin texture, press Enter or Return to commit the transformation.

12 Save your file.

Using Smart Filters

Unlike regular filters, which permanently change an image, Smart Filters are nondestructive: They can be adjusted, turned off and on, and deleted. However, you can apply Smart Filters only to a Smart Object.

Applying the Liquify filter

You'll use the Liquify filter to tighten the eye openings and change the shape of the monster's face. Because you want to be able to adjust the filter settings later, you'll use the Liquify filter as a Smart Filter. So you'll first need to convert the Green_Skin_Texture layer to a Smart Object.

1 Make sure the Green_Skin_Texture layer is selected in the Layers panel, and then choose Filter > Convert for Smart Filters. This creates a Smart Object. Click OK if you're asked to confirm the conversion to a Smart Object.

2 Choose Filter > Liquify.

Photoshop displays the layer in the Liquify dialog box.

3 In the Liquify dialog box, click the disclosure triangle next to Face-Aware Liquify to close that group of options.

You already explored Face-Aware Liquify in Lesson 5. While Face-Aware Liquify is a quick and powerful way to modify facial features, the amount of face editing you can do with those options is limited. In this lesson, you'll try some of the more manual Liquify techniques, which you may prefer when you want to create a more expressive face. Hiding the Face-Aware Liquify options makes it easier to concentrate on the other options in the Liquify dialog box.

4   Select Show Backdrop, and then choose Behind from the Mode menu. Set the Opacity to **75**.

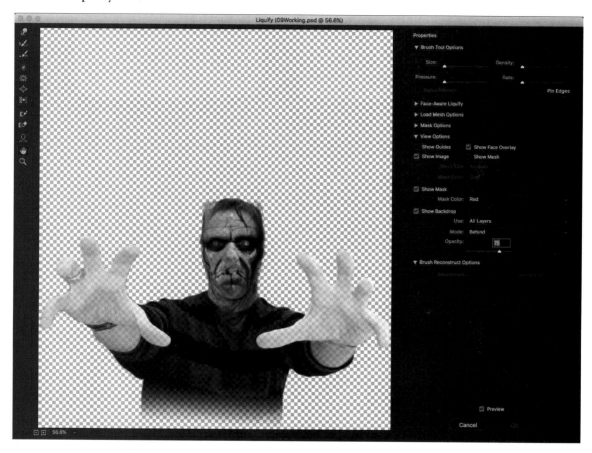

5   Select the Zoom tool (Q) from the Tools panel on the left side of the dialog box, and zoom in to the eye area.

6   Select the Forward Warp tool (⌖) (the first tool).

The Forward Warp tool pushes pixels forward as you drag.

7   In the Brush Tool Options area, set the Size to **150** and Pressure to **75**.

8 With the Forward Warp tool, pull the right eyebrow down to close the eye opening. Then pull up from under the eye.

9 Repeat step 8 on the left eyebrow and under-eye area. You might prefer to use the Forward Warp tool differently for each eye, to create an even scarier face.

10 When you've closed the gap around the eyes, click OK.

Because you've applied the Liquify filter as a Smart Filter, you can freely remove or change your Liquify edits later without losing image quality, by double-clicking the Smart Object in the Layers panel.

Positioning other layers

Now that you've got the skin texture in place, you'll move the other layers into position, working up from the lowest layers in the Layers panel.

1 Make the Green_Nose_Stitches layer visible, and select it in the Layers panel.

2   Choose Edit > Free Transform, and then position the layer over the nose, resizing it as necessary. Press Enter or Return to commit the transformation.

► **Tip:** If you only need to move a layer, you can simply drag it with the Move tool. In these steps, choosing Edit > Free Transform lets you both move and resize a layer.

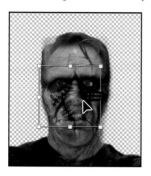
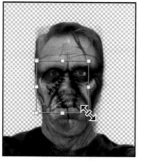
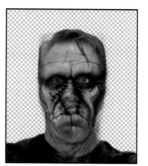

You'll repeat the process to position the rest of the layers.

3   Make the Green_Neck_Stitches layer visible, and select it. Then move it over the neck. If you need to adjust it, choose Edit > Free Transform, resize it, and press Enter or Return.

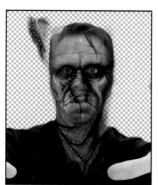
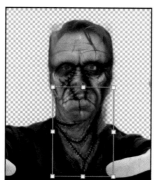

4   Make the Green_Ear_Staples layer visible, and select it. Move the staples over his right ear. Choose Edit > Free Transform, resize and reposition the staples, and then press Enter or Return.

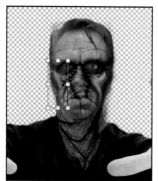

Tip: Remember that you can position and size a selected layer using any combination of the Move tool, the Edit > Free Transform command, and nudging by pressing arrow keys. Use whatever tools get the job done!

5   Make the Enhanced_Green_Forehead layer visible, and select it. Move it over the forehead; it's probably a bit large. Choose Edit > Free Transform, resize the forehead to fit the space, and press Enter or Return.

6   Make the Bolts layer visible, and select it. Drag the bolts so they're positioned on either side of the neck. Choose Edit > Free Transform, and resize them so that they fit snugly against the neck. When you have them in position, press Enter or Return to commit the transformation.

 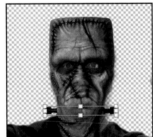

7   Lastly, make the Monster_Hair layer visible, and select it. Move it over the forehead. Choose Edit > Free Transform, and then resize the hair so it fits properly against the forehead. Press Enter or Return to commit the change.

8   Save your work so far.

Editing a Smart Filter

With all the layers in position, you can further refine the eye openings and experiment with the bulges in the eyebrows. You'll return to the Liquify filter to make those adjustments.

1 In the Layers panel, double-click Liquify, listed under Smart Filters in the Green_Skin_Texture layer.

Photoshop opens the Liquify dialog box again. This time, all the layers are visible in Photoshop, so when Show Backdrop is selected, you see them all. Sometimes it's easier to make changes without a backdrop to distract you. Other times, it's useful to see your edits in context.

2 Zoom in to see the eyes more closely.

3 Select the Pucker tool (🟅) in the Tools panel, and click on the outer corner of each eye.

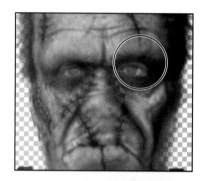

The Pucker tool moves pixels towards the center of the brush as you click or hold the mouse button, or drag.

4 Select the Bloat tool (◈), and click the outer edge of an eyebrow to expand it; do the same for the other eyebrow.

The Bloat tool moves pixels away from the center of the brush as you click or drag.

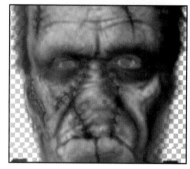

5 Experiment with the Pucker, Bloat, and other tools in the Liquify filter to customize the monster's face. Remember that you can change the brush size and other settings. You can choose Edit > Undo for individual steps, but if you want to start over, it's easiest to click Cancel, and then return to the Liquify dialog box.

6 When you're happy with the monster's face, click OK and save your work.

▶ **Tip:** The Pucker, Bloat, and other tools on the left side of the Liquify panel provide more control over Liquify distortions than the Face-Aware Liquify options, and they work on any part of an image. But Face-Aware Liquify is easier for quick and subtle adjustments to facial features.

Painting a layer

There are many ways to paint objects and layers in Photoshop. One of the simplest is to use the Color blending mode and the Brush tool. You'll use this method to paint the exposed skin green on your monster.

1   Select the Franken layer in the Layers panel.

2   Click the Create A New Layer button () at the bottom of the Layers panel.

Photoshop creates a new layer, named Layer 1.

▶ **Tip:** To learn more about blending modes, including a description of each one, see "Blending modes" in Photoshop Help.

3   With Layer 1 selected, choose Color from the Blending Mode menu at the top of the Layers panel.

The Color blending mode combines the luminance of the base color (the color already on the layer) with the hue and saturation of the color you're applying. It's a good blending mode to use when you're coloring monochrome images or tinting color images.

4   In the Tools panel, select the Brush tool (✐). In the options bar, select a **60**-pixel brush with a Hardness of **0**.

5   Press Alt or Option to temporarily switch to the Eyedropper tool. Sample a green color from the forehead. Then release the Alt or Option key to return to the Brush tool.

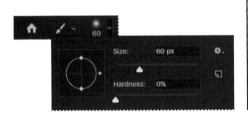

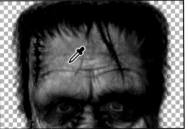

6   Ctrl-click or Command-click the thumbnail in the Franken layer to select
    its contents.

 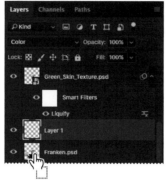

Usually, you select an entire layer in the Layers panel. When you do that, the layer is active, but there isn't actually an active selection. When you Ctrl-click or Command-click the thumbnail of the layer, Photoshop selects the contents of the layer, so you have an active selection. It's a quick way to select all of the contents of a layer—but only the contents of that specific layer.

7   Make sure Layer 1 is still selected in the Layers panel, and then use the Brush
    tool to paint over the hands and arms. You can paint quickly where the hands
    are against transparent areas, because painting outside the selection has no effect.
    However, remember that the shirt is part of the selection, so you need to be
    more careful as you paint the skin where it abuts the shirt colors.

▶ **Tip:** To change the brush size as you paint, press the bracket keys on your keyboard. The Left Bracket key ([) decreases the brush size; the Right Bracket (]) increases it.

8   Paint any areas of the face or neck where
    the original flesh color shows through
    the Green_Skin_Texture layer.

9   When you're happy with the green skin,
    choose Select > Deselect. Save your work.

Adding a background

You've got a good-looking monster. Now it's time to put him in his spooky environment. To easily move the monster onto a background, you'll first merge the layers.

1   Make sure all the layers are visible. Then choose Merge Visible from the Layers panel menu.

Photoshop merges all the layers into one, named Layer 1.

2   Rename Layer 1 **Monster**.

3   Choose File > Open. Navigate to and open the Backdrop.psd file in the Lesson09 folder.

4   Choose Window > Arrange > 2-Up Vertical to display both the monster and backdrop files.

5 Click the 09Working.psd file to make it active.

6 Select the Move tool (✛), drag the Monster layer, and then drop it onto the Backdrop.psd file. Position the monster so his hands are just above the movie title.

7 Close the 09Working.psd file, saving the changes when prompted.

From now on, you'll work on the movie poster file itself.

8 Choose File > Save As, and save the file with the name **Movie-Poster.psd**. Click OK in the Photoshop Format Options dialog box.

Using the History panel to undo edits

You've used the Edit > Undo command to back out of the last change you applied. You can also choose Edit > Redo to reapply a change you just undid. Choosing either command repeatedly steps you back or forward through multiple edits.

You can choose Edit > Toggle Last State to undo and redo only the most recent change. For a quick before/after comparison of your last edit, press the Toggle Last State keyboard shortcut: Ctrl+Alt+Z (Windows) or Command+Option+Z (Mac).

A more visual way to step backward and forward through your changes is to use the History panel; choose Window > History to see it. The History panel shows you a list of your changes. To go back to a certain edit (for example, four steps ago), just select it in the History panel, and continue working from that point.

Applying filters and effects

You'll add a tombstone to the poster, and you'll experiment with filters and effects to see what works, using the History panel to reverse course if necessary.

1   In Photoshop, choose File > Open.

2   Navigate to the Lesson09 folder, and double-click the T1.psd file to open it.

The tombstone image is plain, but you'll add texture and color to it.

▶ **Tip:** A quick way to do step 3 is to press the D key, the keyboard shortcut for setting the foreground color to the default of black and the background color to the default of white.

3   In the Tools panel, click the Default Foreground And Background Colors icon (⬚) to return the foreground color to black.

You'll start by adding a little atmosphere to the tombstone.

4   Choose Filter > Render > Difference Clouds.

The original is dull.   Clouds add drama.

You'll leave the top of the tombstone in focus, but blur the rest using an iris blur. The default blur settings will work fine.

5   Choose Filter > Blur Gallery > Iris Blur.

6   In the image window, drag the Iris Blur ellipse up so that the top of the tombstone is in focus and the rest is not. Then click OK.

By default, the ellipse is centered.   Shift the focus higher.

You'll use adjustment layers to make the image darker and change its color.

7   Click the Brightness/Contrast icon (☀) in the Adjustments panel. Then, in the Properties panel, move the Brightness slider to **70**.

8   Click the Channel Mixer icon (◉) in the Adjustments panel.

9   In the Properties panel, choose Green from the Output Channel menu, and then change the Green value to **+37** and the Blue value to **+108**.

The tombstone takes on a green cast. You can use the Channel Mixer adjustment to make these types of creative color adjustments to an image. The Channel Mixer is also popular as an alternative to the Black & White adjustment for converting color images to black and white, and for tinting effects. It's also useful for some advanced color correction techniques.

Tip: The Exposure adjustment is primarily intended for correcting HDR images, but in this lesson it's used as a creative effect.

10 Click the Exposure icon in the Adjustments panel. In the Properties panel, move the Exposure slider to **+.90** to brighten the lighter areas of the image.

Undoing multiple steps

The tombstone certainly looks different than it did when you started, but it doesn't quite match the tombstones that are already in the poster. You'll use the History panel to revisit the steps you've taken.

1 Choose Window > History to open the History panel. Drag the bottom of the panel down so that you can see everything in it.

The History panel records the recent actions you've performed on the image. The current state is selected.

2 Click the Blur Gallery state in the History panel.

The states below the selected state are dimmed, and the image has changed. The color is gone, as are the Brightness/Contrast settings. At this point, the Difference Clouds filter has been run and the iris blur has been applied. Everything else has been removed. There are no adjustment layers listed in the Layers panel.

3 Click the Modify Channel Mixer Layer state in the History panel.

Many of the states are restored. The color has returned, along with the brightness and contrast settings. There are two adjustment layers in the Layers panel. However, the states below the one you selected remain dimmed, and the Exposure adjustment layer is not listed in the Layers panel.

You'll return almost to the beginning to apply different effects to the tombstone.

4 Click Difference Clouds in the History panel.

Everything following that state is dimmed.

5 Choose Filter > Noise > Add Noise.

Adding noise will give the tombstone a grainier look.

6 In the Add Noise dialog box, set the Amount to **3**%, select Gaussian, and select Monochromatic. Then click OK.

The states that were dimmed are no longer in the History panel. Instead, the History panel has added a state for the task you just performed (Add Noise), following the state you had selected (Difference Clouds). You can click any state to return to that point in the process, but as soon as you perform a new task, Photoshop deletes all dimmed states.

● **Note:** The Lighting Effects filter is unavailable if Use Graphics Processor is not selected in the Performance Preferences dialog box. If the graphics hardware in your computer does not support the Use Graphics Processor option, skip steps 7–12.

7   Choose Filter > Render > Lighting Effects.

8   In the options bar, choose Flashlight from the Presets menu.

9   In the Properties panel, click the Color swatch, select a light blue color, and then click OK.

10 In the image window, drag the light source to the upper third of the tombstone, centered over the letters "RIP."

11 In the Properties panel, change the Ambience to **46**.

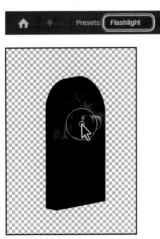

12 Click OK in the options bar to accept the Lighting Effects settings.

The tombstone is ready to join the others in your movie poster.

13 Save the file, then choose Window > Arrange > Tile All Vertically.

14 With the Move tool, drag the tombstone you just created to the Movie-Poster.psd file. Click OK if you see a color management warning.

15 Drag the tombstone to the bottom left corner, with the top third of it showing.

16 Choose File > Save to save the Movie-Poster.psd file. Then close the T1.psd file without saving it.

You've had a chance to try out some new filters and effects, and to use the History panel to backtrack. By default, the History panel retains only the last 50 states. You can change the number of levels in the History panel by choosing Edit > Preferences > Performance (Windows) or Photoshop CC > Preferences > Performance (Mac), and entering a different value for History States.

Upscaling a low-resolution image

Low-resolution images are fine—even desirable—for web pages and social media. If you need to enlarge them, though, they may not contain enough information for high-quality printing. To scale an image up in size, Photoshop needs to resample it. That is, it needs to create new pixels where none existed, approximating their values. The Preserve Details (Enlargement) algorithm in Photoshop gives the best results when you upscale low-resolution images.

In your movie poster, you want to use a low-resolution image that was posted on a social media site. You'll need to resize it without compromising quality for your printed poster.

1   Choose File > Open, navigate to the Lesson09 folder, and open the Faces.jpg file.

2   Zoom in to 300%, so you can see the pixels.

3   Choose Image > Image Size.

4   Make sure the Resample option is selected.

5   Change the width and height measurements to Percent, and then change their values to **400**%.

The width and height are linked by default, so that images resize proportionally. If you need to change the width and height separately for a project, click the link icon to unlink the values.

6   Drag in the preview window to pan so that you can see the glasses.

7   In the Resample menu, choose Bicubic Smoother (Enlargement). The image looks less rough than it did before.

The Resample menu includes options that control how to adjust the image for enlargement or reduction. Automatic is the default and it picks a method based on whether you're enlarging or reducing, but you may find that another option might look better depending on the image.

8   With the Resample option still selected, choose Preserve Details (Enlargement) from the Resample menu.

The Preserve Details option results in a sharper enlargement than Bicubic Smoother, but it has emphasized the existing noise in the image.

● **Note:** Your version of Photoshop CC 2019 may display a "Preserve Details 2.0" option in the Resample menu. This is an upgraded version of Preserve Details provided as a Technology Preview for comparison with the older Preserve Details option. Use the option that produces better results for the image you're scaling up.

9 Move the Reduce Noise slider to **50**% to smooth the image.

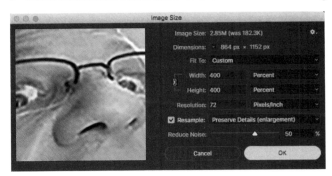

10 Click and hold in the preview window to see the original image, so you can compare it to the current settings. You can also compare the current settings to the Bicubic Smoother option by switching between them in the Resample menu. When upscaling or downscaling, choose the Resample method that produces the best balance between preserving details and smoothing pixel jagginess, and then use Reduce Noise to remove noise that remains. If the Reduce Noise value removes too much detail, lower it.

11 Click OK.

Now you'll paste the image into a feathered selection on the poster.

12 Choose Select > All, and then choose Edit > Copy.

13 Select the Movie-Poster.psd tab to bring it to the front, and then select the Elliptical Marquee tool (◯), hidden under the Rectangular Marquee tool (⬚).

14 In the options bar, enter **50** px for Feather to soften the edge of the pasted image.

15 Draw an oval in the upper right corner of the poster, above the monster's head. The oval should overlap the window and fire escape.

16 Make sure Layer 1 is selected, and then choose Edit > Paste Special > Paste Into. Click OK if you see the Paste Profile Mismatch dialog box.

17 Select the Move tool (✛), and center the pasted image in the feathered area.

18 In the Layers panel, choose Luminosity from the Blending Mode menu, and move the Opacity slider to **50**%.

19 Choose File > Save. Then close the Faces.jpg file without saving it.

Review questions

1 What are the differences between using a Smart Filter and a regular filter to apply effects to an image?

2 What do the Bloat and Pucker tools in the Liquify filter do?

3 What does the History panel do?

Review answers

1 Smart Filters are nondestructive: They can be adjusted, turned off and on, and deleted at any time without altering the pixels of a layer. In contrast, regular filters permanently change a layer or image; once applied, they cannot be removed. A Smart Filter can be applied only to a Smart Object layer.

2 The Bloat tool moves pixels away from the center of the brush; the Pucker tool moves pixels toward the center of the brush.

3 The History panel records recent steps you've performed in Photoshop. You can return to an earlier step by selecting it in the History panel.

10 PAINTING WITH THE MIXER BRUSH

Lesson overview

In this lesson, you'll learn how to do the following:

- Customize brush settings.

- Clean the brush.

- Mix colors.

- Create a custom brush preset.

- Use wet and dry brushes to blend color.

 This lesson will take about an hour to complete. Please log in to your account on peachpit.com to download the lesson files for this chapter, or go to the Getting Started section at the beginning of this book and follow the instructions under "Accessing the Lesson Files and Web Edition."

As you work on this lesson, you'll preserve the start files. If you need to restore the start files, download them from your Account page.

PROJECT: DIGITAL PAINTING

The Mixer Brush tool gives you flexibility, color-mixing
abilities, and brush strokes as if you were painting on
a physical canvas.

About the Mixer Brush

In previous lessons, you've used brushes in Photoshop to perform various tasks. The Mixer Brush is unlike other brushes in that it lets you mix colors with each other. You can change the wetness of the brush and how it mixes the brush color with the color already on the canvas.

Some Photoshop brush types can have realistic bristles, so you can add textures that resemble those in paintings you might create in the physical world. While this is a great feature in general, it's particularly useful when you're using the Mixer Brush. Combining different bristle settings and brush tips with different wetness, paint-load, and paint-mixing settings gives you opportunities to create exactly the look you want.

Getting started

In this lesson, you'll get acquainted with the Mixer Brush as well as the brush tip and bristle options available in Photoshop. Start by taking a look at the final projects you'll create.

1 Start Photoshop, and then immediately hold down Ctrl+Alt+Shift (Windows) or Command+Option+Shift (Mac) to restore the default preferences. (See "Restoring Default Preferences" on page 5.)

2 When prompted, click Yes to delete the Adobe Photoshop Settings file.

3 Choose File > Browse In Bridge to open Adobe Bridge.

● **Note:** If Bridge isn't installed, you'll be prompted to install it when you choose Browse In Bridge. For more information, see page 3.

4 In Bridge, click Lessons in the Favorites panel. Double-click the Lesson10 folder in the Content panel.

5 Preview the Lesson10 end files.

You'll use the palette image to explore brush options and learn to mix colors. You'll then apply what you've learned to transform the landscape image into a painting.

● **Note:** If you use Photoshop for digital painting, consider using a graphics tablet with a pressure-sensitive stylus, such as a Wacom Intuos. If your stylus transmits information such as pressure, angle, and rotation, Photoshop can apply that data to your brush as you paint.

6 Double-click 10Palette_Start.psd to open the file in Photoshop.

7 Choose File > Save As, and name the file **10Palette_Working.psd**. Click OK if the Photoshop Format Options dialog box appears.

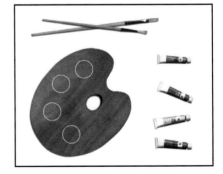

8 Click the Choose a Workspace icon at the top right corner of the application frame, and choose the Painting workspace.

Selecting brush settings

The practice image includes a palette and four tubes of color, which you'll use to sample the colors you're working with. You'll change settings as you paint different colors, exploring brush tip settings and wetness options.

1 Select the Zoom tool (🔍), and zoom in to see the tubes of paint.

2 Select the Eyedropper tool (💉), and click the red tube to sample its color.

The foreground color changes to red.

3 Select the Mixer Brush tool (💧) in the Tools panel. (When another workspace is selected, you may find the Mixer Brush hidden under the Brush tool [🖌].)

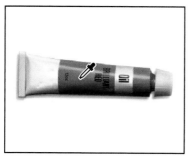

Note: When you hold down the Eyedropper tool on the image, Photoshop displays a sampling ring that previews the color you're selecting. The sampling ring is available if Photoshop can use the graphics processor on your computer (see the Performance panel in Photoshop preferences).

4 Choose Window > Brush Settings to open the Brush Settings panel. Select the first brush.

The Brush Settings panel contains brush presets and several options for customizing brushes.

Tip: Looking for a specific brush name in the Brush Settings panel? Hover the pointer over a brush thumbnail, and its name will pop up in a tool tip.

Experimenting with wetness options and brushes

The effect of the brush is determined by the Wet, Load, and Mix fields in the options bar. *Wet* controls how much paint the brush picks up from the canvas. *Load* controls how much paint the brush holds when you begin painting (as with a physical brush, it runs out of paint as you paint with it). *Mix* controls the ratio of paint from the canvas and paint from the brush.

You can change these settings separately. However, it's faster to select a standard combination from the pop-up menu.

1 In the options bar, choose Dry from the pop-up menu of blending brush combinations.

When you select Dry, Wet is set to 0%, Load to 50%, and Mix is not applicable. With the Dry preset, you paint opaque color; you cannot mix colors on a dry canvas.

2 Paint in the area above the red tube. Solid red appears. As you continue painting without releasing the mouse, the paint eventually fades and runs out.

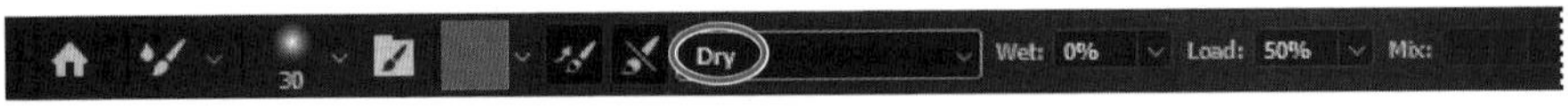

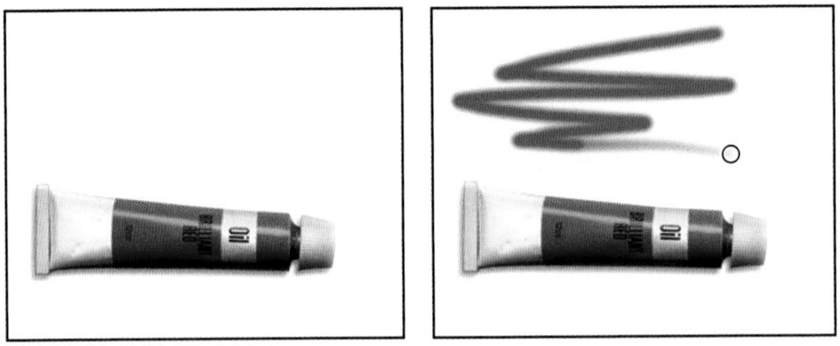

● **Note:** You can also sample paint by Alt-clicking or Option-clicking the Mixer Brush tool. This samples the area within the brush size as an image, unless you selected Load Solid Colors Only in the Current Brush Load menu in the options bar.

3 With the Eyedropper tool, sample the blue color from the blue tube of paint.

4 Select the Mixer Brush. For the blue paint, in the Brush Settings panel we chose the Round Sketch Ballpoint Pen brush (the first brush in the second row). Choose Wet from the pop-up menu in the options bar.

If the brush you select doesn't match the one shown here, resize the Brush Settings panel so that the brush thumbnails display six columns across.

5 Paint above the blue tube. The paint mixes with the white background.

● **Note:** If you aren't getting the same results from the brushes, make sure the Background layer is selected in the Layers panel.

6 Choose Dry from the menu in the options bar, and then paint again above the blue tube. A much darker, more opaque blue appears, and doesn't mix with the white background.

7 Sample the yellow color from the yellow paint tube, and then select the Mixer brush. For the yellow paint, in the Brush Settings panel we chose the Pencil KTW 1 brush (the fourth brush in the second row). Choose Dry from the menu in the options bar, and then paint in the area over the yellow paint tube.

● **Note:** If the brushes in your Brush Settings panel don't match the ones shown in this chapter, open the Brushes panel, Shift-select all brushes and brush folders in the list, click the Delete Brush button (🗑), click OK to confirm, and then choose Restore Default Brushes from the Brushes panel menu.

8 Choose Very Wet from the menu in the options bar, and then paint some more. Now the yellow mixes with the white background.

9 Sample the green color from the green paint tube, and then select the Mixer brush. For the green paint, in the Brush Settings panel we chose the Hard Round 30 brush (the sixth brush in the fifth row). Choose Dry from the menu in the options bar.

10 Draw a zigzag line above the green paint tube.

Mixing colors

● **Note:** Depending on the complexity of your project and the performance of your computer, you may need to be patient. Mixing colors can be an intensive process.

You've used wet and dry brushes, changed brush settings, and mixed the paint with the background color. Now, you'll focus more on mixing colors with each other as you add paint to the painter's palette.

1   Zoom out just enough to see the full palette and the paint tubes.

2   Select the Paint mix layer in the Layers panel, so the color you paint won't blend with the brown palette on the Background layer.

The Mixer Brush tool mixes colors only on the active layer unless you select Sample All Layers in the options bar.

3   Use the Eyedropper tool to sample the red color from the red paint tube, and then select the Mixer brush. In the Brush Settings panel, select the Soft Round 30 brush (the first brush in the first row). Then choose Wet from the pop-up menu in the options bar, and paint in the top circle on the palette.

4   Click the Clean The Brush After Each Stroke icon (✖) in the options bar to deselect it.

▶ **Tip:** If the paint tubes are covered by the Brush Settings panel, feel free to rearrange your workspace to make room. For example, collapse or close panels you aren't using. But make sure you can still see the Layers panel.

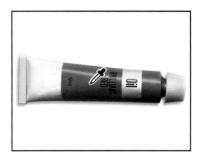

5   Use the Eyedropper tool to sample the blue color from the blue paint tube, and then use the Mixer Brush tool to paint in the same circle, mixing the red with the blue until the color becomes purple.

You can use the Eyedropper tool to sample a color when the layer that contains the color (in this case, the Background layer) isn't selected.

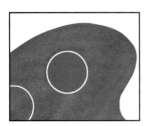

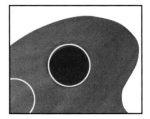

6 Use the Eyedropper tool to sample the purple color from the circle you just painted, and then paint in the next circle.

7 In the options bar, choose Clean Brush from the Current Brush Load pop-up menu. The preview changes to indicate transparency, meaning the brush has no paint loaded.

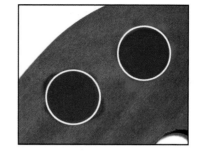

Tip: Use the Eyedropper tool to sample the color, since it's on a different layer.

To remove the paint load from a brush, you can choose Clean Brush in the options bar. To replace the paint load in a brush, sample a different color.

If you want Photoshop to clean the brush after each stroke, select the Clean The Brush After Each Stroke icon (✘) in the options bar. To load the brush with the foreground color after each stroke, select the Load The Brush After Each Stroke icon (✔) in the options bar. By default, both of these options are selected.

8 Use the Eyedropper tool to sample the blue color from the blue paint tube, and then paint blue in half of the next circle.

9 Sample the yellow color from the yellow paint tube, and slowly paint over the blue with a wet brush to mix the two colors.

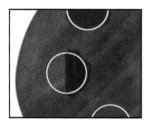
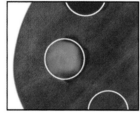

10 Fill the last circle with yellow and red paint, mixing the two with a wet brush to create an orange color.

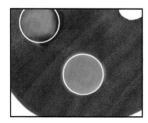

11 Hide the Circles layer in the Layers panel to remove the outlines on the palette. You've mixed paint colors on a digital palette!

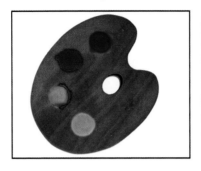
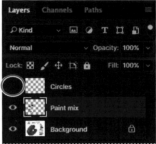

12 Choose File > Save, and close the document.

Julieanne Kost is an official Adobe Photoshop evangelist.

Tool tips from the Photoshop evangelist

Mixer Brush shortcuts

There are no default keyboard shortcuts for the Mixer Brush tool, but you can create your own.

To create custom keyboard shortcuts:

1   Choose Edit > Keyboard Shortcuts.

2   Choose Tools from the Shortcuts For menu.

3   Scroll down to the bottom of the list.

4   Select a command, and then enter a custom shortcut. You can create shortcuts for the following commands:

• Load Mixer Brush

• Clean Mixer Brush

• Toggle Mixer Brush Auto-Load

• Toggle Mixer Brush Auto-Clean

• Toggle Mixer Brush Sample All Layers

• Sharpen Erodible Tips

Mixing colors with a photograph

When you come up with a great brush, you probably want to save all of its settings so that you can use that brush again in a later project. While Photoshop already has a Tool Preset feature that lets you save tool settings, brushes have more options than most tools. For this reason, Photoshop has convenient Brush Presets that can remember everything about a brush.

Tip: If you've used earlier versions of Photoshop, you'll find that the Brush Presets in Photoshop CC 2018 or later are simpler and more powerful than in previous versions.

Earlier, you mixed colors with a white background and with each other. Now, you'll use a photograph as your canvas. You'll add colors and mix them with each other and with the background colors to transform a photograph of a landscape into a painting.

1 Choose File > Open. Double-click the 10Landscape_Start.jpg file in the Lesson10 folder to open it.

2 Choose File > Save As. Rename the file **10Landscape_Working.jpg**, and click Save. Click OK in the JPEG Options dialog box.

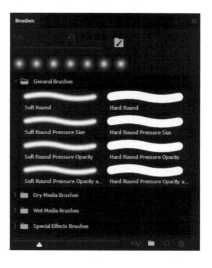

Photoshop includes numerous brush presets, which are very handy. But if you need a different brush for your project, you might find it easier to create your own brush preset or download brush presets that another artist has created and shared online. In the following exercises, you'll load, edit, and save custom brush presets.

Loading custom brush presets

The Brushes panel displays visual samples of the strokes created by different brushes. If you already know the name of the brush you want to use, it can be easier to display the brushes by name. You'll list them by name now, so you can find your preset for the next exercise.

Tip: If you have enough space on your screen, you can see more brushes at once by making the Brushes panel wider or taller.

1 Open the Brushes panel, and then expand one of the brush preset groups to see how the brushes are organized.

Now you'll load brush presets that you'll use for this exercise. Loading brush presets is how you use brush presets that you've downloaded or purchased from another artist.

▶ Tip: If you want to share your custom brushes with others or back them up, select the brushes or brush groups, and choose Export Selected Brushes from the Brushes panel menu.

2   Click the Brushes panel menu, and choose Import Brushes.

3   Navigate to the Lesson10 folder, select CIB Landscape Brushes.abr, and click Open or Load. The CIB Landscape Brushes group appears at the end of the Brushes panel list.

4   Click to expand the CIB Landscape Brushes group, revealing the brushes it contains.

Some of the presets contain not only a stroke preview and a name, but also a color swatch. That's because a color can be part of a brush preset.

Creating a custom brush preset

For the next exercise, you'll create and save a variation on a brush preset that exists in the CIB Landscape Brushes you just imported.

1   Select the Mixer Brush, and then, in the CIB Landscape Brushes group in the Brushes panel, select the Round Fan Brush. You'll use this brush preset as the starting point for the brush preset you'll create.

2   Change the following settings in the Brush Settings panel:

- Size: **36** px

- Shape: Round Fan

- Bristles: **35**%

- Length: **32**%

- Thickness: **2**%

- Stiffness: **75**%

- Angle: **0**°

- Spacing: **2**%

3 Click the Foreground color swatch in the Tools panel. Select a medium-light blue color (we chose R=86, G=201, B=252).

4 In the options bar, choose Dry.

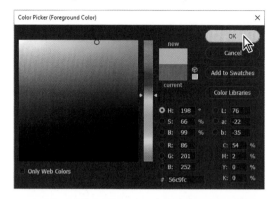

Now it's time to save the settings as a brush preset.

5 Choose New Brush Preset from the Brush Settings panel menu.

6 Name the brush **Sky Brush**, select all of the options in the New Brush dialog box, and then click OK.

▶ **Tip:** The options in the New Brush dialog box make it possible to save the brush size, the tool settings, and the brush color in the preset.

Your new brush is saved in the CIB Landscape Brushes group because it was based on a brush preset from that group. Feel free to reorganize your brush presets any way you like by dragging and dropping presets into brush preset groups within the Brushes panel. You can create a brush preset group by clicking the Create a New Group button (▢) at the bottom of the Brushes panel. You can change the order of the Brushes panel list and organize brush preset groups into subgroups.

Painting and mixing colors
with brush presets

You'll paint the sky first, using the brush preset you just created.

1 Select the Sky Brush from the Brushes panel.

Presets are saved on your system, so they're available when you work with any image.

2 Paint over the sky, moving in close to the trees. Because you're using a dry brush, the blue paint isn't mixing with the colors beneath it.

3 Select the Clouds Brush.

4 Use this brush to scrub diagonally in the upper right corner of the sky, blending the two colors with the background color.

When you're satisfied with the sky, move on to the grass and trees.

Live Tip Brush Preview

When you use a brush with a bristle tip, the Live Tip Brush Preview helps you visualize interactive brush attributes, such as the direction of the bristles as you paint, especially when using a stylus that supports features such as tilt angle.

● **Note:** The Live Tip Brush Preview is available if Photoshop supports the graphics processor on your computer (see the Performance panel in Photoshop preferences).

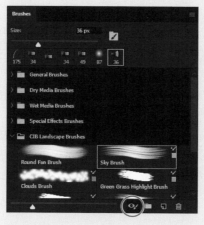

To show or hide the Live Tip Brush Preview, click the Toggle The Live Tip Brush Preview button at the bottom of the Brushes or Brush Settings panel. The default Photoshop brushes don't display the Live Tip Brush Preview because they don't use bristle tips, but the CIB Landscape Brushes do use bristle tips.

5   Select the Green Grass Highlight Brush. Then paint short vertical strokes over the darker grass areas so that they become bright green grass.

Tip: If you want to create less jittery strokes with the Mixer Brush, like near the edges of the trees, try increasing the Set Smoothing for Stroke percentage in the options bar.

6 Select the Foreground Tree Brush, and then paint the darker areas of the tree. Then select the Background Trees Brush, and paint the two smaller trees on the right side of the painting. Select the Tree Highlights Brush, and paint the lighter areas of the trees. These are Wet brushes so that you can blend colors.

Tip: For different effects, paint in different directions or customize the brush size or other settings. With the Mixer Brush tool, you can go wherever your artistic instincts lead you.

So far, so good. The brown grasses are all that remain to be painted.

7 Select the Brown Grass Brush. Paint along the brown grass with up-and-down strokes for the look of a field. Use the same brush to paint the trunk of the tree.

8 Select the Foreground Grass Brush. Then paint using diagonal strokes to blend the colors in the grass.

9 Choose File > Save, and close the document.

Voilà! You've created a masterpiece with your paints and brushes, and there's no mess to clean up.

Brushes from Kyle T. Webster

In 2017, award-winning brush designer Kyle T. Webster joined Adobe. At the same time, Adobe acquired the popular brush collections at KyleBrush.com. Kyle has drawn for *The New Yorker*, *TIME*, *The New York Times*, *The Wall Street Journal*, *The Atlantic*, *Entertainment Weekly*, Scholastic, Nike, IDEO, and many other distinguished editorial, advertising, publishing, and institutional clients. His illustration work has been recognized by the Society of Illustrators, Communications Arts, and American Illustration. Kyle now works closely with Adobe product teams on the development of future brushes for Adobe Creative Cloud.

To add the Kyle T. Webster brushes to Photoshop, open the Brushes panel (Window > Brushes), and choose Get More Brushes from the Brushes panel menu. After you download a brush pack and with Photoshop running, double-click the downloaded ABR file to add its brushes as a new group in the Brushes panel.

Painting with Symmetry

If you're painting a design that uses symmetry, try the Paint Symmetry brush option. When a brush type that supports Paint Symmetry is selected, you'll see the Paint Symmetry icon (🦋) in the options bar. Click that icon, and select the type of symmetry axis you want; it appears as a guide object in the document. Move, scale, or rotate the guide if you want, and then press Enter or Return. As you paint with Paint Symmetry, each of your brushstrokes is repeated across the axes you set up.

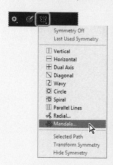

You might use a single axis for simple mirror symmetry, but you can also use multiple axes arranged in different ways. For example, you can use horizontal and vertical axes to design tiles, or radial axes to design mandalas.

The axes are actually paths, so you can see and edit them in the Paths panel. You can even create your own custom axis. Draw with a tool such as the Pen, Curvature Pen, or Custom Shape tool in Path mode (not Shape mode). With the path selected in the Paths panel, choose Make Symmetry Path from the Paths panel menu.

Painting gallery

The painting tools and brush tips in Photoshop let you create all kinds of painting effects.

The following pages show examples of art created with the brush tips and tools in Photoshop.

Image © Megan Lee, www.megan-lee.com

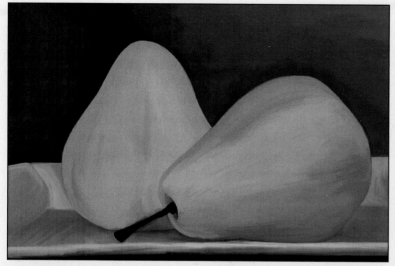

Image © Victoria Pavlov, pavlovphotography.com

Image © sholby, www.sholby.net

Image © sholby, www.sholby.net

Image © sholby, www.sholby.net

Continues on next page

Painting gallery (continued)

Review questions

1 What does the Mixer Brush do that other brushes don't?

2 How do you load a mixer brush with color?

3 How do you clean a brush?

4 What is the name of the panel that you use to manage brush presets?

5 What is the Live Tip Brush Preview, and how can you hide it?

Review answers

1 The Mixer Brush mixes the current brush color with colors on the canvas.

2 You can load color on a mixer brush by sampling a color, either by using the Eyedropper tool or keyboard shortcuts (Alt-click or Option-click). Or, you can choose Load Brush from the pop-up menu in the options bar to load the brush with the foreground color.

3 To clean a brush, choose Clean Brush from the pop-up menu in the options bar.

4 You manage brush presets in the Brushes panel.

5 The Live Tip Brush Preview shows you the direction the brush strokes are moving. To hide or show the Live Tip Brush Preview, click the Toggle The Live Tip Brush Preview icon at the bottom of the Brushes panel or the Brush Settings panel.

11 EDITING VIDEO

Lesson overview

In this lesson, you'll learn how to do the following:

- Create a video timeline in Photoshop.

- Add media to a video group in the Timeline panel.

- Add motion to still images.

- Animate type and effects using keyframes.

- Add transitions between video clips.

- Include audio in a video file.

- Render a video.

 This lesson will take about 90 minutes to complete. Please log in to your account on peachpit.com to download the lesson files for this chapter, or go to the Getting Started section at the beginning of this book and follow the instructions under "Accessing the Lesson Files and Web Edition."

As you work on this lesson, you'll preserve the start files. If you need to restore the start files, download them from your Account page.

PROJECT: FAMILY VIDEO FROM MOBILE PHONE

You can edit video files in Photoshop using many
of the same effects you use to edit image files. You
can create a movie from video files, still images, Smart
Objects, audio files, and type layers; apply transitions;
and animate effects using keyframes.

Getting started

In this lesson, you'll edit a video that was shot using a smartphone. You'll create a video timeline, import clips, add transitions and other video effects, and render the final video. First, look at the final project to see what you'll be creating.

1   Start Photoshop, and then immediately hold down Ctrl+Alt+Shift (Windows) or Command+Option+Shift (Mac) to restore the default preferences. (See "Restoring Default Preferences" on page 5.)

2   When prompted, click Yes to delete the Adobe Photoshop Settings file.

● **Note:** If Bridge isn't installed, you'll be prompted to install it when you choose Browse In Bridge. For more information, see page 3.

3   Choose File > Browse In Bridge.

4   In Bridge, select the Lessons folder in the Favorites panel. Then, double-click the Lesson11 folder in the Content panel.

5   Double-click the 11End.mp4 file to open it in the default video player for your system, such as QuickTime Player (Mac) or Movies & TV (Windows).

6   Click the Play button to view the final video.

The short video is a compilation of clips from a day at the beach. It includes transitions, layer effects, animated text, and a musical track.

7   Close the video player, and return to Bridge.

8   Double-click the 11End.psd file to open it in Photoshop.

About the Timeline panel

If you've used a video-editing application such as Adobe Premiere® Pro or Adobe After Effects®, the Timeline panel is probably familiar. You use the Timeline panel to assemble and arrange video clips, images, and audio files for a movie file. You can edit the duration of each clip, apply filters and effects, animate attributes such as position and opacity, mute sound, add transitions, and perform other standard video-editing tasks without ever leaving Photoshop.

1 Choose Window > Timeline to open the Timeline panel.

Each video clip or image included in the project is represented in a box in the Timeline panel and as a layer in the Layers panel. Video clips have a blue background in the Timeline panel; image files have a purple background. At the bottom of the Timeline panel is the audio track.

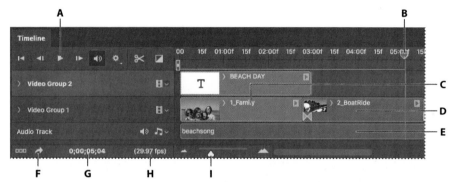

A. Play button **B.** Playhead **C.** Image file **D.** Video clip **E.** Audio track **F.** Render Video button
G. Current time **H.** Frame rate **I.** Control Timeline Magnification slider

The timeline contents should appear visible as in the figure above. If they're collapsed against the left side so that content titles and previews aren't visible, drag the magnification slider (below the timeline) to the right to see time in more detail.

2 Click Play in the Timeline panel to view the movie.

The playhead moves across the time ruler, displaying each frame of the movie.

3 Press the spacebar to pause playback.

4 Drag the playhead to another point in the time ruler.

The playhead's time location determines what appears in the document window.

When you work with video, Photoshop displays guidelines across the document window. To minimize the chance that your content will be cut off along the edges of some televisions, keep important content within the center area marked by the guides.

5 When you've finished exploring the end file, close it, but leave Photoshop open. Don't save any changes you might have made.

Creating a new video project

Working with video is a little different from working with still images in Photoshop. You may find it easiest to create the project first, and then import the assets you'll be using. You'll choose the video preset for this project, and then add nine video and image files to include in your movie.

Creating a new file

Photoshop includes several film and video presets for you to choose from. You'll create a new file and select an appropriate preset.

1 In the Start workspace, click the Create New button, or choose File > New.

2 Name the file **11Working.psd**.

● **Note:** The video in this lesson was shot using an Apple iPhone, so one of the HDV presets is appropriate. The 720p preset provides good quality without providing too much data for easy online streaming.

3 Click Film & Video in the document type bar at the top of the dialog box.

4 In the Blank Document Presets section, choose HDV/HDTV 720p.

5 Accept the default settings for the other options, and click Create.

6 Choose File > Save As, and save the file in the Lesson11 folder.

Importing assets

Photoshop provides tools specifically for working with video, such as the Timeline panel, which may already be open because you previewed the end file. To ensure you have access to the resources you need, you'll select the Motion workspace and organize your panels. Then you'll import the video clips, images, and audio file you need to create the movie.

1 Choose Window > Workspace > Motion.

2 Pull up the top edge of the Timeline panel so that the panel occupies the bottom half of the workspace.

3 Select the Zoom tool (🔍), and then click Fit Screen in the options bar so that you can see the entire canvas within the top half of the screen.

4 In the Timeline panel, click Create Video Timeline. Photoshop creates a new video timeline, including two default tracks: Layer 0 and Audio Track.

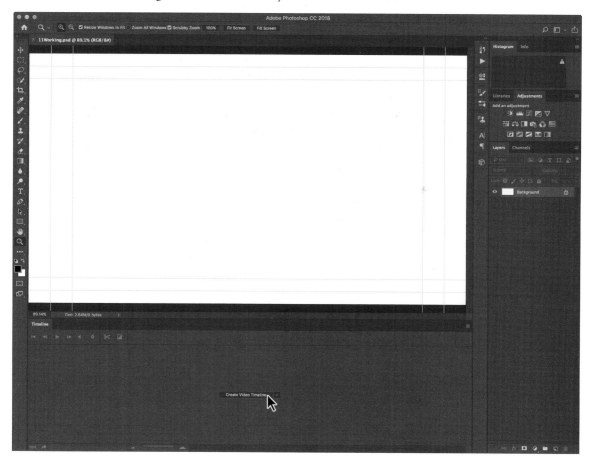

5 Click the Video menu in the Layer 0 track, and choose Add Media.

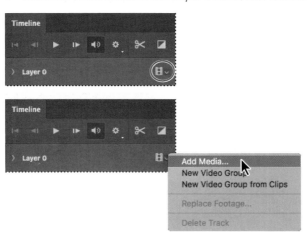

6 Navigate to the Lesson11 folder.

Note: If the media appear in reverse order, choose Edit > Undo, and when you choose Add Media again, make sure you select 1_Family.jpg first and then Shift-select 6_Sunset.jpg. Also, it will be easiest to Shift-select the media if the files are sorted by name.

7 Shift-select the video and photo assets numbered 1–6, and click Open.

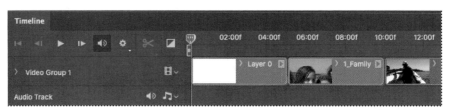

Photoshop imports all six of the assets you selected onto the same track, now named Video Group 1, in the Timeline panel. It displays still images with a purple background and video clips with a blue background. In the Layers panel, the assets appear as individual layers within the layer group named Video Group 1. You don't need the Layer 0 layer, so you'll delete it.

8 Select Layer 0 in the Layers panel, and click the Delete Layer button at the bottom of the panel. Click Yes to confirm the deletion.

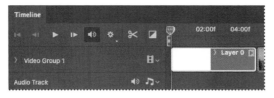

Changing the duration and size of clips in the timeline

The clips are of very different lengths, meaning they'd play for different amounts of time. For this video, you want all the clips to be the same length, so you'll shorten them all to 3 seconds. The length of a clip (its *duration*) is measured in seconds and frames: 03:00 is 3 seconds; 02:25 is 2 seconds and 25 frames.

1 Drag the Control Timeline Magnification slider to the right at the bottom of the Timeline panel to zoom in on the timeline. You want to be able to see a thumbnail of each clip and enough detail in the time ruler that you can accurately change the duration of each clip.

● **Note:** You're shortening each clip to the same length here, but you can have clips of varying lengths, depending on what's appropriate for the project.

2 Drag the right edge of the first clip (1_Family) to 03:00 on the time ruler. Photoshop displays the end point and the duration as you drag so that you can find the right stopping point.

3 Drag the right edge of the second clip (2_BoatRide) to a duration of 03:00.

Shortening a video clip this way doesn't change its speed; it removes part of the clip from the video. In this case, you want to use the first three seconds of each clip. If you wanted to use a different portion of a video clip, you would shorten the clip from each end. As you drag the end point of a video clip, Photoshop displays a preview so you can see which part of the clip is included.

4 Repeat step 3 for each of the remaining clips so that each has a duration of 3 seconds.

▶ **Tip:** To quickly change the duration of a video clip, click the arrow in the upper right corner, and then type a new Duration value. This option isn't available for still images.

The clips are now the right duration, but some of the images are the wrong size for the canvas. You'll resize the first image before continuing.

5 Select the 1_Family layer in the Layers panel. The clip is also selected in the Timeline panel.

6 Click the triangle in the upper right corner of the 1_Family clip in the Timeline panel to open the Motion panel.

▶ **Tip:** The arrow on the left side of a clip (next to the clip's thumbnail) reveals the attributes you can animate using keyframes. The arrow on the right side of a clip opens the Motion panel.

7 Choose Pan & Zoom from the menu, and make sure Resize To Fill Canvas is selected. Then click an empty area of the Timeline panel to close the Motion panel.

The image resizes to fit the canvas. However, you applied the effect only to quickly resize the image and not to pan and zoom, so you'll remove the effect.

8 Open the Motion panel from the 1_Family clip again, and choose No Motion from the menu. Click an empty area of the Timeline panel to close the Motion panel.

9 Choose File > Save. Click OK in the Photoshop Format Options dialog box.

Animating text with keyframes

Keyframes let you control animation, effects, and other changes that occur over time. A keyframe marks the point in time where you specify a value, such as a position, size, or style. To create a change over time, you must have at least two keyframes: one for the state at the beginning of the change and one for the state at the end. Photoshop interpolates the values for the positions in between so that the change takes effect smoothly over the specified time. You'll use keyframes to animate a movie title (Beach Day) from left to right over the opening image.

1 Click the Video pop-up menu in the Video Group 1 track, and choose New Video Group. Photoshop adds Video Group 2 to the Timeline panel.

2   Select the Horizontal Type tool (**T**), and then click on the left edge of the image, about halfway down from the top.

Photoshop creates a new type layer, named Layer 1, in the Video Group 2 track. The type layer initially includes "Lorem Ipsum" placeholder text.

3   In the options bar, select a sans serif font such as Myriad Pro, set the type size to **600** pt, and select white for the type color.

4   Type **BEACH DAY**, replacing the selected placeholder text. Click the check mark (✓) in the options bar to commit the text to the layer.

The text is large enough that it doesn't all fit on the image. That's okay; you'll animate it to move across the image.

5   In the Layers panel, change the opacity for the BEACH DAY layer to **25%**.

6   In the Timeline panel, drag the end point of the type layer to 03:00 so that it has the same duration as the 1_Family layer.

7   Click the arrow to the left of the BEACH DAY clip title to display the clip's attributes.

8   Make sure the playhead is at the beginning of the time ruler.

9   Click the stopwatch icon (⏱) next to the Transform property to set an initial keyframe for the layer.

The keyframe appears as a yellow diamond in the timeline.

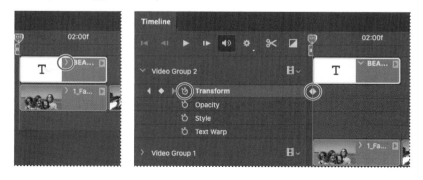

10 Select the Move tool (✛), and use it to drag the type layer over the canvas so that the tops of each letter are slightly clipped at the edge of the canvas. Drag it to the right so that only the left edge of the letter "B" in the word "BEACH" is visible on the canvas. The keyframe you set in step 9 ensures that the text will be in this position at the beginning of the movie.

▶ **Tip:** Photoshop displays the playhead's location in the lower left corner of the Timeline panel.

11 Move the playhead to the last frame of the first clip (02:29).

12 Press the Shift key as you drag the type layer to the left over the canvas so that only the right edge of the "Y" in the word "DAY" is visible. Pressing the Shift key ensures that the type moves straight across as you drag.

Because you've changed the position, Photoshop creates a new keyframe.

13 Move the playhead across the first three seconds of the time ruler to preview the animation. The title moves across the image.

14 Click the arrow to the left of the title of the BEACH DAY text clip to close the clip's attributes, and then choose File > Save to save your work so far.

Creating effects

One of the benefits of working with video files in Photoshop is that you can create effects using adjustment layers, styles, and simple transformations.

Adding adjustment layers to video clips

You've used adjustment layers with still images throughout this book. They work just as well on video clips. When you apply an adjustment layer in a video group, Photoshop applies it only to the layer immediately below it in the Layers panel.

1   Select the 3_DogAtBeach layer in the Layers panel.

2   In the Timeline panel, move the playhead to the beginning of the 3_DogAtBeach layer so you can see the effect as you apply it.

3   In the Adjustments panel, click the Black & White button.

4   In the Properties panel, leave the default preset, and select Tint. The default tint color creates a sepia effect that works well for this clip. You can experiment with the sliders and the tint color to modify the black-and-white effect to your taste.

● **Note:** If you had imported the video file using the Place command, so that it was not in a video group, to limit the adjustment layer to a single video layer you would have to set up the adjustment layer as a clipping mask, as you did on page 98.

5   Move the playhead across the 3_DogAtBeach clip in the Timeline panel to preview the effect.

Animating a zoom effect

Even simple transformations become interesting effects when you animate them. You'll use animation to zoom in on the 4_Dogs clip.

1   Move the playhead to the beginning of the 4_Dogs clip in the Timeline panel (09:00).

2   Click the arrow at the top right corner of the 4_Dogs clip to display the Motion panel.

3   Choose Zoom from the pop-up menu, and choose Zoom In from the Zoom menu. On the Zoom From grid, select the upper left corner to zoom in from that point. Make sure Resize To Fill Canvas is selected, and then click an empty area of the Timeline panel to close the Motion panel.

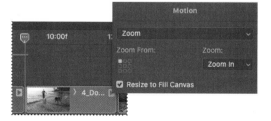

4   Drag the playhead across the clip to preview the effect.

You'll enlarge the image in the last keyframe to make the zoom more dramatic.

5   Click the arrow to the left of the title of the 4_Dogs clip to reveal the attributes for the clip.

There are two keyframes, which appear as yellow diamonds under the clip on the timeline: one for the beginning of the Zoom In effect, and one for the end.

 **Tip:** You can move to the next keyframe by clicking the right arrow next to the attribute in the Timeline panel. Click the left arrow to move to the previous keyframe.

6   Click the right triangle next to the Transform attribute (under Video Group 1 on the left side of the Timeline panel) to move the playhead to the last keyframe if it's not already there, and choose Edit > Free Transform. Then enter **120%** for Width and Height in the options bar. Click the Commit Transform button (✓) to confirm the transformation.

7   Drag the playhead across the 4_Dogs clip in the time ruler to preview the animation again.

8   Choose File > Save.

Animating an image to create a motion effect

You'll animate another transformation to create the appearance of motion. You want the image to begin with the diver's legs and end with his hands.

1   Move the playhead to the end of the 5_Jumping clip (14:29), and select the clip. Press Shift while you move the image down in the document window so that the hands are near the top of the canvas, putting the diver in the final position.

2　Click the arrow to the left of the clip title to display the clip's attributes, and click the stopwatch icon for the Position attribute to add a keyframe (a yellow diamond icon) under the clip.

3　Move the playhead to the beginning of the clip (12:00). Press Shift while you move the image up so that the feet are near the bottom of the canvas.

Photoshop adds a second keyframe under the clip to complete the animation.

4　Move the playhead across the time ruler to preview the animation.

5　Close the clip's attributes. Then choose File > Save to save your work so far.

Adding the Pan & Zoom effect

You can easily add features similar to the pan and zoom effects used in documentaries. You'll add them to the sunset to bring the video to a dramatic close.

1　Move the playhead to the beginning of the 6_Sunset clip.

2　Click the arrow at the top right corner of the clip to display its Motion panel. Choose Pan & Zoom from the pop-up menu, choose Zoom Out from the Zoom menu, and make sure Resize To Fill Canvas is selected. Then click an empty area of the Timeline panel to close the Motion panel.

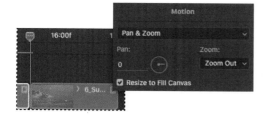

3　Move the playhead across the last clip to preview the effects.

Adding transitions

Simply drag and drop to add transitions, such as fading one clip into another.

1 Click the Go To First Frame button (◄) in the upper left corner of the Timeline panel to return the playhead to the beginning of the time ruler.

2 Click the Transition button (▧) near the upper left corner of the Timeline panel. Select Cross Fade, and change the Duration value to **.25** s (a quarter of a second).

3 Drag the Cross Fade transition and drop it where the 1_Family and 2_BoatRide clips meet.

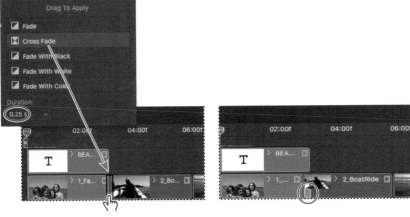

Photoshop adjusts the ends of the clips to apply the transition and adds a white transition icon in the lower left corner of the second clip.

4 Drag Cross Fade transitions between each of the other clips.

5 Drag a Fade With Black transition onto the end of the final clip.

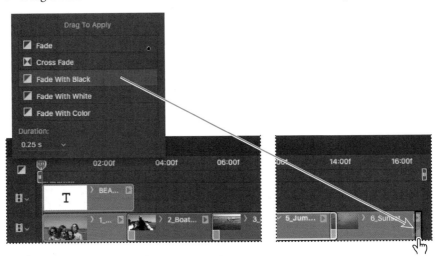

6 To make the transition smoother, extend the Fade With Black transition by stretching its left side to about one-third the total length of the clip.

7 Choose File > Save.

Adding audio

You can add a separate audio track to a video file in Photoshop. In fact, the Timeline panel includes an audio track by default. You'll add an MP3 file to play as the soundtrack for this short video.

1 Click the musical-note icon in the Audio Track at the bottom of the Timeline panel, and choose Add Audio from the pop-up menu.

▶ **Tip:** You can also add an audio track by clicking the + sign at the far right end of the track in the Timeline panel.

2 Select the beachsong.mp3 file from the Lesson11 folder, and click Open.

The audio file is added to the timeline, but it's much longer than the video. You'll use the Split At Playhead tool to shorten it.

3 Move the playhead to the end of the 6_Sunset clip. With the audio file still selected, click the Split At Playhead tool (✂) in the Timeline panel.

The audio file is clipped at that point, becoming two audio clips.

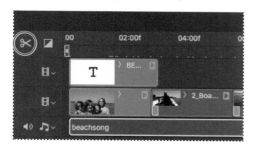
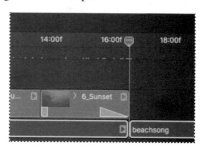

4 Select the second audio file segment, the one that begins after the end of the 6_Sunset clip. Press the Delete key on your keyboard to delete the selected clip.

Now the audio file is the same length as the video. You'll add a fade so that it ends smoothly.

5 Click the small arrow at the right edge of the audio clip to open the Audio panel. Then enter **3** seconds for Fade In and **5** seconds for Fade Out.

6 Click an empty area of the Timeline panel to close the Audio panel, and save your work so far.

Muting unwanted audio

So far, you've previewed portions of the video by moving the playhead across the time ruler. Now you'll preview the entire video using the Play button in the Timeline panel, and then mute any extraneous audio from the video clips.

1 Click the Play button (▶) in the upper left corner of the Timeline panel to preview the video so far.

It's looking good, but there is some unwanted background noise from the video clips. You'll mute that extra sound.

2 Click the small triangle at the right end of the 2_BoatRide clip.

3 Click the Audio tab to see audio options, and then select Mute Audio. Click an empty area of the Timeline panel to close the Audio/Video panel.

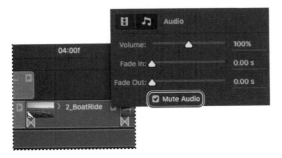

4 Click the small triangle at the right end of the 3_DogAtBeach clip.

5 Click the Audio tab to see audio options, and then select Mute Audio. Click an empty area of the Timeline panel to close the panel.

6 Play the timeline to check your audio changes, and then save your work.

Rendering video

You're ready to render your project to video. Photoshop provides several rendering options. You'll select options appropriate for streaming video to share on the YouTube website. For information about other rendering options, see Photoshop Help.

1 Choose File > Export > Render Video, or click the Render Video button (→) in the lower left corner of the Timeline panel.

2 Name the file **11Working.mp4**.

3 Click Select Folder, and then navigate to the Lesson11 folder, and click OK or Choose.

4 From the Preset menu, choose YouTube HD 720p 29.97.

5 Click Render.

● **Note:** The choices in the Preset menu depend on the selection in the Format menu. For the YouTube options to be available in the Preset menu, the Format menu must be set to H.264.

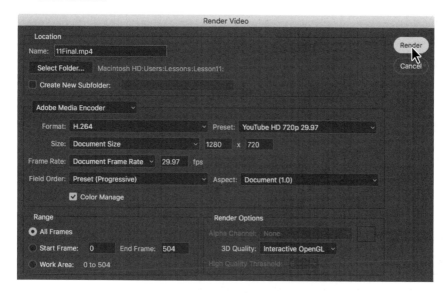

Photoshop displays a progress bar as it exports the video. Depending on your system, the rendering process may take several minutes.

6 Save your work.

 Depending on your system, this may take a while.

▶ Tip: When a video is selected in Bridge, you can play it inside Bridge by pressing the spacebar on your keyboard. This plays the video in the Preview panel in Bridge. Double-clicking a video opens it in your system's default video player.

7   Locate the 11Working.mp4 file in the Lesson11 folder in Bridge. Double-click it to view the video you made using Photoshop!

Review questions

1 What are keyframes, and how do you use them to create an animation?

2 How do you add a transition between clips?

3 How do you render a video?

Review answers

1 A keyframe marks the point in time where you specify a value, such as a position, size, or style. To create a change over time, you must have at least two keyframes: one for the state at the beginning of the change and one for the state at the end. To create an initial keyframe, click the stopwatch icon next to the attribute you want to animate for the layer. Photoshop creates additional keyframes each time you change the values of that attribute.

2 To add a transition, click the Transition button near the upper left corner of the Timeline panel, and then drag a transition onto a clip.

3 To render a video, choose File > Export > Render Video, or click the Render Video button in the lower left corner of the Timeline panel. Then select the video settings that are appropriate for your intended output.

12

WORKING WITH CAMERA RAW

Lesson overview

In this lesson, you'll learn how to do the following:

- Open a proprietary camera raw image in Adobe Camera Raw.

- Adjust tone and color in a raw image.

- Sharpen an image in Camera Raw.

- Synchronize settings for multiple images.

- Open a Camera Raw image as a Smart Object in Photoshop.

- Apply Camera Raw as a filter in Photoshop.

 This lesson will take about an hour to complete. Please log in to your account on peachpit.com to download the lesson files for this chapter, or go to the Getting Started section at the beginning of this book and follow the instructions under "Accessing the Lesson Files and Web Edition."

As you work on this lesson, you'll preserve the start files. If you need to restore the start files, download them from your Account page.

PROJECT: ADVANCED PHOTO RETOUCHING

Raw images give you greater flexibility, especially
in setting color and tone. Camera Raw lets you tap into
that potential. It can be a useful tool even when you're
starting with a JPEG or TIFF image, or when you apply
it as a filter in Photoshop.

Getting started

● **Note:** We used Adobe Camera Raw 11, which was the current version at the time of publication. Adobe updates Camera Raw frequently; if you're using a later version, some of the steps in this lesson may not match what you see.

● **Note:** If you haven't installed Bridge, you'll be prompted to do so when you choose Browse In Bridge. For more information, see page 3.

In this lesson, you'll edit several digital images using Photoshop and Adobe Camera Raw, which comes with Photoshop. You'll use a variety of techniques to touch up and improve the appearance of digital photographs. You'll start by viewing the before and after images in Adobe Bridge.

1 Start Photoshop, and then immediately hold down Ctrl+Alt+Shift (Windows) or Command+Option+Shift (Mac) to restore the default preferences. (See "Restoring Default Preferences" on page 5.)

2 When prompted, click Yes to delete the Adobe Photoshop Settings file.

3 Choose File > Browse In Bridge to open Adobe Bridge.

4 In the Favorites panel in Bridge, click the Lessons folder. Then, in the Content panel, double-click the Lesson12 folder to open it.

5 Adjust the thumbnail slider, if necessary, so that you can see the thumbnail previews clearly. Then look at the 12A_Start.crw and 12A_End.psd files.

12A_Start.crw   12A_End.psd

The original photograph of a Spanish-style church is a camera raw file, so it doesn't have the usual .psd or .jpg file extension you've worked with so far in this book.

It was shot with a Canon Digital Rebel camera and has the Canon proprietary .crw file extension. You'll process this camera raw image to make it brighter, sharper, and clearer, and then save it as a JPEG file for the web and as a PSD file so that you could work on it further in Photoshop.

6   Compare the 12B_Start.nef and 12B_End.psd thumbnail previews.

12B_Start.nef   *12B_End.psd*

This time, the start file was taken with a Nikon camera, and the raw image has an .nef extension. You'll perform color corrections and image enhancements in Camera Raw and Photoshop to achieve the end result.

About camera raw files

A *camera raw* file contains unprocessed picture data from a digital camera's image sensor. Raw sensor data has not yet been converted to a standard RGB color image file. Many digital cameras can save images in camera raw format. The advantage of camera raw files is that they let the photographer—rather than the camera—interpret the image data and make adjustments and conversions. (In contrast, shooting JPEG images with your camera permanently applies in-camera processing to the image.) Because the camera doesn't apply image processing to a camera raw photo, you can use Adobe Camera Raw to set the white balance, tonal range, contrast, color saturation, and sharpening with more freedom than

Note: Camera raw files are typically unique to each camera model's sensor. If you have CRW files from three different Canon camera models and NEF files from three Nikon models, chances are those represent six different formats. If you buy a new camera, you might need an Adobe Camera Raw update that adds support for its raw format.

after the raw image is converted to a standard RGB image. Camera raw files are like undeveloped film: You can go back and reprocess the file at any time to achieve the results you want. To create camera raw files, set your digital camera to save files in its own, possibly proprietary, raw file format. When you download the file from your camera, it has a filename extension such as .nef (from Nikon) or .crw (from Canon). In Bridge or Photoshop, you can process camera raw files from a myriad of supported digital cameras from Canon, Fuji, Leica, Nikon, and other makers—and even process multiple images simultaneously. You can then export the proprietary camera raw files to DNG, JPEG, TIFF, or PSD file format.

You can process camera raw files obtained from supported cameras, but you can also open TIFF and JPEG images in Camera Raw, which includes some editing features that aren't in Photoshop. However, you won't have the same flexibility with white balance and other settings if you're using a TIFF or JPEG image. Although Camera Raw can open and edit a camera raw image file, it cannot save a camera raw format image back to a proprietary camera raw format. However, Adobe Camera Raw can save to the open Adobe DNG camera raw format.

Processing files in Camera Raw

When you make adjustments to an image in Camera Raw, such as straightening or cropping the image, Photoshop and Bridge preserve the original file data. This way, you can edit the image as you desire, export the edited image, and keep the original intact for different or improved adjustments in the future.

Opening images in Camera Raw

You can open Camera Raw from either Bridge or Photoshop, and you can apply the same edits to multiple files simultaneously. This is especially useful if you're working with images that were all shot in the same environment, and which therefore need the same lighting and other adjustments.

Camera Raw provides extensive controls for adjusting white balance, exposure, contrast, sharpness, tone curves, and much more. In this exercise, you'll edit one image, and then apply the settings to similar images.

1 In Bridge, open the Lessons/Lesson12/Mission folder, which contains three shots of the Spanish church you previewed earlier.

2 Shift-click to select all of the images—Mission01.crw, Mission02.crw, and Mission03.crw—and then choose File > Open In Camera Raw.

A. *Filmstrip*

B. *Filmstrip divider (drag to adjust)*

C. *Toolbar*

D. *RGB values*

E. *Image adjustment tabs*

F. *Histogram*

G. *Camera Raw Settings menu*

H. *Save selected images*

I. *Zoom levels*

J. *Click to display workflow options*

K. *Multi-image navigation controls*

L. *Adjustment options*

The Camera Raw dialog box displays a large preview of the first image, and a filmstrip down the left side displays all open images. The histogram in the upper right corner shows the tonal range of the selected image; the workflow options link below the preview window displays the selected image's color space, bit depth, size, and resolution. Tools along the top of the dialog box let you zoom, pan, straighten, and make other adjustments to the image. Tabbed panels on the right side of the dialog box give you more nuanced options for adjusting the image: You can correct the white balance, adjust the tone, sharpen the image, remove noise, adjust color, and make other changes. You can also save settings as a preset, and then apply them later.

The Camera Raw options on the right side are generally organized for good results by simply using the tabbed panels from left to right, and then making adjustments within each panel from top to bottom. But it's OK for you to adjust the options in any order, and you don't have to adjust every option.

You will explore these controls now as you edit the first image file.

3 Click each thumbnail in the filmstrip to preview all the images before you begin. Or, you can click the Forward button under the main preview window to cycle through them. When you've seen all three, select the Mission01.crw image again.

Choosing an Adobe Raw profile

An *Adobe Raw profile* controls the overall color rendering of an image. Adjustments you make are applied on top of the rendering of the selected profile, and you can change the profile at any time.

Tip: You can use Creative profiles to apply a visual style to an image. Click the Browse Profiles icon to the right of the Profile menu, scroll down to see the list of profile categories (such as Artistic, B&W, Modern, and Vintage), select one, and click Done.

1   If the Basic panel isn't already displayed on the right side of the dialog box, click the Basic button (⬤) to open it.

2   Choose Adobe Landscape from the Profile menu.

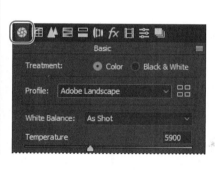

Note: Profiles in Adobe Camera Raw are different than the ICC color profiles used by your display or printer.

The default profile, Adobe Color, is a general-purpose profile. Adobe Landscape emphasizes colors in nature like trees and skies, and works well for this image. The goal of Adobe Portrait is natural representation of skin tones, and Adobe Vivid adds punchy color contrast. Adobe Monochrome provides a high-quality conversion to black and white.

Adjusting white balance

An image's white balance reflects the color conditions under which it was captured. A digital camera records the white balance at the time of exposure; this is the value that initially appears in the Camera Raw dialog box image preview.

White balance comprises two components. The first is *temperature*, which is measured in kelvins and determines the level of "coolness" or "warmth" of the image—that is, its cool blue-green tones or warm yellow-red tones. The second component is *tint*, which compensates for magenta or green color casts in the image.

Tip: As long as an image is in raw format, you can adjust settings such as white balance with a lot of freedom. After a raw image is converted to a standard format (such as JPEG), its adjustment range is more limited before image quality starts to break down.

Depending on the settings you're using on your camera and the environment in which you're shooting (for example, with artificial light or mixed light sources), you may want to adjust the white balance for the image. If you plan to modify the white balance, make that the first thing you do, as it will affect all other changes in the image.

By default, As Shot is selected in the White Balance menu. Camera Raw applies the white balance settings that were in your camera at the time of exposure. Camera Raw includes several White Balance presets, which you can use as a starting point to see different lighting effects.

1   Choose Cloudy from the White Balance menu.

Tip: Adjusting white balance is easiest when there is only one light source. When a scene is lit by multiple light sources with different color characteristics, you may have to manually choose a white balance setting and also make local color corrections.

Camera Raw adjusts the temperature and tint for a cloudy day. Sometimes a preset is an instant fix. In this case, though, there's still a blue cast to the image. You'll adjust the white balance manually.

2 Select the White Balance tool (🖊) at the top of the Camera Raw dialog box.

To set an accurate white balance, select an object that should be white or gray. The spot where you click becomes a reference for neutral white balance; Camera Raw shifts the image colors accordingly.

3 Click the white clouds in the image. The lighting of the image changes.

4 Click a different area of the clouds. The lighting shifts.

You can use the White Balance tool to find the best lighting for the scene quickly and easily. Click areas that should be neutral. Clicking different areas changes the lighting without making any permanent changes to the file, so you can experiment freely.

5 Click the white area of the small sign in front of the church. This removes most of the color casts.

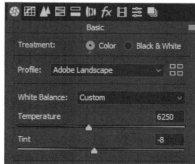

Tip: To expand Camera Raw to fill the screen, click the Toggle Full Screen Mode button ( ) on the far right side of the toolbar, or press F.

6 To see the changes you've made, click the preview mode button ( ) at the bottom of the window, and choose Before/After Left/Right from the pop-up menu.

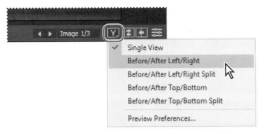

Camera Raw displays the Before image on the left and the After image on the right so you can compare them.

7 To see only the After image again, choose Single View from the preview mode pop-up menu. If you prefer, you can leave both views visible so you can see how the image changes as you continue to alter it.

Making tonal adjustments in Camera Raw

The group of sliders in the middle of the Basic panel affects the tonal distribution of the image. Except for Contrast, moving a slider to the right lightens the affected areas of the image, and moving it to the left darkens those areas. Exposure sets the overall brightness of the image. The Highlights and Shadows sliders increase detail in the highlights and the shadows, respectively. The Whites slider defines the *white point*, or the lightest tone of the image. Conversely, the Blacks slider sets the *black point*, or the darkest tone in the image.

Dragging the Contrast slider to the right moves darker and lighter midtones away from the midtone; dragging left moves those tones toward the midtone. For more nuanced contrast adjustments, you can use the Clarity slider, which adds depth to an image by increasing local contrast, especially around the midtones.

▶ **Tip:** For the best effect, increase the Clarity slider until you see halos near the edge details, and then reduce the setting slightly.

The Saturation slider adjusts the intensity of all colors in the image equally. The Vibrance slider has a greater effect on undersaturated colors. You can use it to bring life to a background without oversaturating any skin tones in the image, for example.

You can use the Auto option to let Camera Raw attempt to correct the image tone, or you can select your own settings.

1 Click Auto in the Basic panel.

 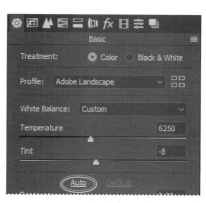

Camera Raw changes several settings in the Basic panel, and the image is greatly improved. The Auto feature often produces a useful image because its corrections are based on advanced Adobe Sensei machine learning technology. This makes Auto a quick way to both reach a good starting point for edits, and, if you like the results, to study and learn from the adjustments made by Auto. However, in this exercise, you'll return to the default settings and adjust them yourself.

2 Click Default in the Basic panel.

3 Change the sliders as follows:

- Exposure: **+0.50**
- Contrast: **+0**
- Highlights: **-20**
- Shadows: **+70**
- Whites: **+20**
- Blacks: **−10**
- Clarity: **+20**
- Dehaze: **+0**
- Vibrance: **+20**
- Saturation: **+0**

These settings brighten the image, especially the dark shadow areas, and boost color without oversaturating it.

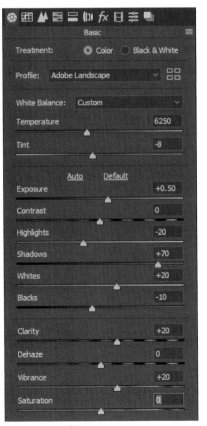

About the Camera Raw histogram

The histogram in the upper right corner of the Camera Raw dialog box simultaneously shows the red, green, and blue channels of the selected image, and updates interactively as you adjust settings. As you move any tool over the preview image, the RGB values for the area under the pointer appear below the histogram. Selecting the top left or right square indicates where on the image current settings are clipping (losing details) in the shadows or highlights, respectively.

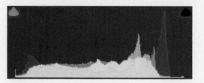

▶ **Tip:** Indications of clipped shadows or highlights don't always mean you've overcorrected an image. For example, a clipped specular highlight (such as a reflection of the sun or a studio light on metal) is acceptable because a specular highlight has no detail to lose.

Applying sharpening

Photoshop offers several sharpening filters, but when an image is in raw format it's often a good idea to use the Sharpening controls in Camera Raw. The Sharpening controls are in the Detail panel. To see the effect of sharpening in the preview panel, you must view the image at 100% or greater.

1 Double-click the Zoom tool (🔍) on the left side of the toolbar to zoom in to 100%. Then select the Hand tool (✋), and pan the image to see the cross at the top of the mission tower.

2 Click the Detail button (▲) to open the Detail panel.

The Amount slider determines how much sharpening Camera Raw applies. Typically, you'll want to exaggerate the amount of sharpening at first, and then adjust it after you've set the other sliders.

3 Move the Amount slider to **100**.

The Radius slider determines the pixel area Camera Raw analyzes as it sharpens the image. For most images, you'll get the best results if you keep the radius low, even below one pixel. A larger radius can begin to cause an unnatural look, almost like a watercolor.

4 Move the Radius slider to **0.9**.

The Detail slider determines how much detail you'll see. Even when this slider is set to 0, Camera Raw performs some sharpening. Typically, you'll want to keep the Detail setting relatively low.

5 Move the Detail slider to **25**, if it isn't already there.

The Masking slider determines which parts of the image Camera Raw sharpens. When the Masking value is high, Camera Raw sharpens only those parts of the image that have strong edges.

▶ **Tip:** Press Alt (Windows) or Option (Mac) as you drag the Masking slider; the white areas indicate the areas Camera Raw will sharpen.

6 Move the Masking slider to **61**.

After you've adjusted the Radius, Detail, and Masking sliders, you can lower the Amount slider to finalize the sharpening.

7 Decrease the Amount slider to **70**.

▶ **Tip:** If you have difficulty seeing the effects of sharpening, change the zoom level to at least 100%.

Sharpening the image gives stronger definition to the details and edges. The Masking slider lets you target the sharpening effect to edges and lines in the image, so that artifacts don't appear in unfocused or solid areas.

When you make adjustments in Camera Raw, the original file data is preserved. Your adjustment settings for the image are stored either in the Camera Raw database file or in a separate "sidecar" XMP file that accompanies the original image file in the same folder. These XMP files retain the adjustments you made in Camera Raw when you move the image file to a different storage medium or computer.

Synchronizing settings across images

All three of the mission images were shot at the same time under the same lighting conditions. Now that you've made the first one look great, you can automatically apply the same settings to the other two images using the Synchronize command.

1   In the upper left corner of the Camera Raw dialog box, click the Filmstrip menu button, and choose Select All to select all of the images in the filmstrip.

2   Click the Filmstrip menu button again, and choose Sync Settings.

The Synchronize dialog box appears, listing all the settings you can apply to the images. By default, all options except Crop, Spot Removal, and Local Adjustments are selected. You can accept the default for this project, even though you didn't change all the settings.

3   Click OK in the Synchronize dialog box.

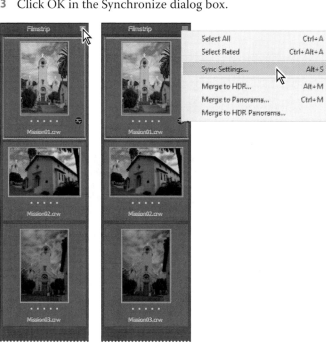
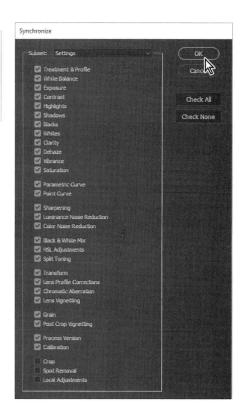

When you synchronize the settings across all of the selected images, the thumbnails update to reflect the changes you made. To preview the images, click each thumbnail in the filmstrip.

Saving Camera Raw changes

You can save your changes in different ways for different purposes. First, you'll save the images with adjustments as low-resolution JPEG files that you can share on the web. Then, you'll save one image, Mission01, as a Photoshop file that you can open as a Smart Object in Photoshop. When you open an image as a Smart Object in Photoshop, you can return to Camera Raw at any time to make further adjustments.

1   In the Camera Raw dialog box, click the Filmstrip menu button, and choose Select All to select all three images.

2   Click Save Images in the lower left corner.

3   In the Save Options dialog box, do the following:

   • Choose Save In Same Location from the Destination menu.

   • In the File Naming area, leave "Document Name" in the first box.

   • Choose JPEG from the Format menu, and set the Quality level to High (8–9).

   • In the Color Space area, choose sRGB IEC61966-2.1 from the Space menu.

   • In the Image Sizing area, select Resize To Fit, and then choose Long Side from the Resize To Fit menu.

   • Enter **800** pixels. This will set the long side of an image to 800 pixels whether it's a portrait (tall) or landscape (wide) image. When you choose Long Side, the dimension of the short side will automatically be adjusted proportionally.

   • Type **72** pixels/inch for the Resolution value.

These settings will save your corrected images as smaller, downsampled JPEG files, which you can share with colleagues on the web. They'll be resized so that most viewers won't need to scroll to see the entire image when it opens. Your files will be named Mission01.jpg, Mission02.jpg, and Mission03.jpg.

4 Click Save.

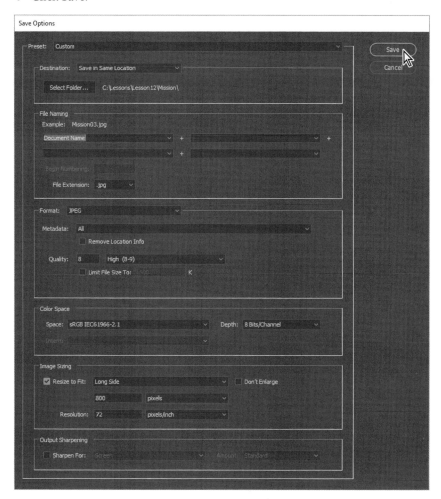

In the Camera Raw dialog box, a readout in the bottom left corner indicates how many images have been processed until all the images have been saved. The CRW thumbnails still appear in the Camera Raw dialog box. In Bridge, however, you now also have JPEG versions as well as the original CRW image files, which you can continue to edit or leave for another time.

Now you'll open a copy of the Mission01 image in Photoshop.

Note: If you see a message that says "Skip loading optional and third-party plug-ins?" click No. The message appears if the Shift key is held down when Photoshop starts up.

5   Select the Mission01.crw image thumbnail in the filmstrip in the Camera Raw dialog box. Then press the Shift key, and click Open Object at the bottom of the dialog box.

▶ **Tip:** To make the Open Object button the default, click the underlined workflow options link at the bottom of the Camera Raw dialog box, select Open In Photoshop As Smart Objects, and click OK.

The Open Object button opens the image as a Smart Object layer in Photoshop; you can double-click the Smart Object thumbnail in the Layers panel to open Camera Raw and continue making raw-based adjustments at any time.

If, instead, you had clicked Open Image, the image would open as a standard Photoshop layer, and no more raw format edits would be possible. The Open Image button changes into the Open Object button when you Shift-click it.

6   In Photoshop, choose File > Save As. In the Save As dialog box, choose Photoshop for the format, rename the file **Mission_Final.psd**, navigate to the Lesson12 folder, and click Save. Click OK if the Photoshop Format Options dialog box appears. Then close the file.

About saving files in Camera Raw

Every camera model saves raw images in a unique format, but Adobe Camera Raw can process many raw file formats. Camera Raw processes the raw files with default image settings based on built-in camera profiles for supported cameras and on the EXIF (Exchangeable Image File format) data recorded by digital cameras. EXIF data can include exposure and lens information.

You can save the proprietary files in DNG format (the format saved by Adobe Camera Raw), JPEG, TIFF, and PSD. All of these formats can be used to save RGB and CMYK continuous-tone, bitmapped images, and all of them except DNG are also available in the Photoshop Save and Save As dialog boxes.

- The **DNG (Adobe Digital Negative)** format contains raw image data from a digital camera and metadata that defines what the image data means. DNG is meant to be an industry-wide standard format for raw image data, helping photographers manage the variety of proprietary raw formats and providing a compatible archival format. (You can save this format only from the Camera Raw dialog box.)

- The **JPEG (Joint Photographic Experts Group)** file format is commonly used to display photographs and other continuous-tone RGB images on the web. Higher-resolution JPEG compresses file size by selectively discarding data, starting with the visual information that our eyes are least likely to notice. The greater the compression, the lower the image quality.

- **TIFF (Tagged Image File Format)** is a flexible format supported by virtually all paint, image-editing, and page layout applications. It can save Photoshop layers. TIFF images can also be produced by most applications that control image capture hardware such as scanners.

- **PSD format** is the Photoshop native file format. Because of the tight integration between Adobe products, other Adobe applications such as Adobe Illustrator and Adobe InDesign can directly import PSD files and preserve many Photoshop features.

After you open a file in Photoshop, you can save or export it in many more formats, including Large Document Format (PSB), Photoshop PDF, GIF, or PNG. There's also a Photoshop Raw format (RAW) that you should not confuse with camera raw files; Photoshop Raw is a specialized technical file format that is not commonly used by photographers and designers.

For more information about file formats in Camera Raw and Photoshop, see Photoshop Help.

Applying advanced color correction

You'll use Levels, the Healing Brush tool, and other Photoshop features to enhance the image of this model.

Adjust the white balance in Camera Raw

The original image of the bride has a slight color cast. You'll start your color corrections in Camera Raw, setting the white balance and adjusting the overall tone of the image.

1   In Bridge, navigate to the Lesson12 folder. Select the 12B_Start.nef file, and choose File > Open In Camera Raw.

2   In Camera Raw, select the White Balance tool (✒), and then click a white area in the model's dress to adjust the temperature and remove a green color cast.

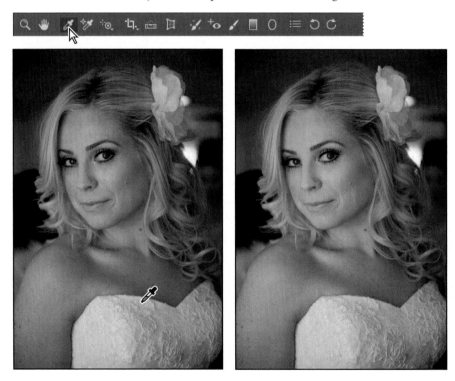

3 Adjust other sliders in the Basic panel to brighten and intensify the image:

- Increase Exposure to **+0.30**.
- Increase Contrast to **+15**.
- Increase Clarity to **+8**.

▶ **Tip:** Be careful when applying Clarity to a portrait. Too much Clarity emphasizes skin texture and surface characteristics such as freckles and wrinkles.

● **Note:** Your Temperature and Tint values may vary slightly from what is shown in the figure for step 3, because the exact values depend on where you clicked.

4 Press the Shift key, and click Open Object.

The image opens in Photoshop as a Smart Object.

▶ **Tip:** You can try other profiles to see if they work better. For this image, Adobe Color produces a similar result to Adobe Portrait, but other profiles may be too garish or contrasty for skin tones.

A photographer for more than 25 years, Jay Graham began his career designing and building custom homes. Today, Graham has clients in the advertising, architectural, editorial, and travel industries.

See Jay Graham's portfolio on the web at jaygraham.com.

Pro photo workflow

Good habits make all the difference

A sensible workflow and good work habits will keep you enthused about digital photography, help your images shine—and save you from the night terrors of losing work you never backed up. Here's an outline of the basic workflow for digital images from a professional photographer with more than 25 years' experience. To help you get the most from the images you shoot, Jay Graham offers guidelines for setting up your camera, creating a basic color workflow, selecting file formats, organizing images, and showing off your work.

Graham uses Adobe Lightroom® Classic CC to organize thousands of images.

"The biggest complaint from people is they've lost their image. Where is it? What does it look like?" says Graham. "So naming is important."

Start out right by setting up your camera preferences

If your camera has the option, it's generally best to shoot in its camera raw file format, which captures all the image information you need. With one camera raw photo, says Graham, "you can go from daylight to an indoor tungsten image without degradation" when it's reproduced. If it makes more sense to shoot in JPEG for your project, use fine compression and high resolution.

Start with the best material

Get all the data when you capture—at fine compression and high resolution. You can't go back later.

Organize your files

Name and catalogue your images as soon after downloading them as possible. "If the camera names files, eventually it resets and produces multiple files with the same name," says Graham. Use Adobe Lightroom Classic CC to rename, rank, and add metadata to the photos you plan to keep; cull those you don't.

Graham names his files by date (and possibly subject). He would store a series of photos taken October 18, 2017 at Stinson Beach in a folder named "171018_stinson". Within the folder, he names each image incrementally; for example, the first image would be named "171018_stinson_01". This should result in a truly unique filename for each image. "That way, it lines up on the hard drive real easily," he says. Follow Windows naming conventions to keep filenames usable on non-Macintosh platforms (32 characters maximum; only numbers, letters, underscores, and hyphens).

Convert raw images to DNG

It may be best to convert all your camera raw images to the DNG format. Unlike many cameras' proprietary raw formats, the specifications for this format are publicly available so that software developers and device makers can more easily support it.

Keep a master image

Save your master in PSD, TIFF, or DNG format, not JPEG. Each time a JPEG is re-edited and saved, compression is reapplied, and the image quality degrades.

Show off to clients and friends

When you prepare your work for delivery, choose the appropriate color file for the destination. Convert the image to that profile, rather than assigning the profile. sRGB is generally best for viewing electronically or for printing from most online printing services. Adobe 1998 or Colormatch are the best profiles to use for RGB images destined for traditionally printed materials such as brochures. Adobe 1998 or ProPhoto RGB are best for printing with inkjet printers. Use 72 dpi for electronic viewing and 180 dpi or higher for printing.

Back up your images

You've devoted a lot of time and effort to your images: Don't lose them. To protect your photos against a range of potential disasters, it's best to have backups on multiple media such as external storage and a cloud backup service, set to back up automatically. "The question is not if your [internal] hard drive is going to crash," says Graham, reciting a common adage. "It's when."

Adjusting levels

The tonal range of an image represents the amount of contrast, or detail, in the image and is determined by the image's distribution of pixels, ranging from the darkest pixels (black) to the lightest pixels (white). You'll use a Levels adjustment layer to fine-tune the tonal range in this image.

1 In Photoshop, choose File > Save As. Name the file **Model_final.psd**, and click Save. Click OK if you see the Photoshop Format Options dialog box.

2 Click the Levels button in the Adjustments panel.

Photoshop adds a Levels adjustment layer to the Layers panel. The Levels controls and a histogram appear in the Properties panel. The histogram displays the range of dark and light values in the image. The left (black) triangle represents the shadows; the right (white) triangle represents the highlights; and the middle (gray) triangle represents the midtones, or gamma. Unless you're aiming for a special effect, the ideal histogram has its black point at the beginning of the data and its white point at the end of the data, and the middle portion has fairly uniform peaks and valleys, representing adequate pixel data in the midtones.

3 Click the Calculate A More Accurate Histogram button (🔺) on the left side of the histogram. Photoshop replaces the histogram.

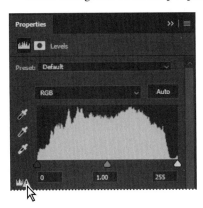

There is a small bump on the far right side of the histogram, representing the current white point, but the bulk of the data ends further to the left. You want to set the white point closer to where most of the data ends.

4 Drag the right (white) triangle toward the left to the point where the histogram indicates that significant highlight tones start to appear.

As you drag, the third Input Levels value (beneath the histogram graph) changes, and so does the image itself.

5 Pull the middle (gray) triangle a little bit to the right to slightly darken the midtones. We moved it to a value of .90.

▶ **Tip:** As you drag the white Input Levels triangle to the left, watch carefully to make sure highlight detail is not lost. Never clip skin tones! If you're wondering which highlights on the image are clipped by the white triangle, hold down the Alt/Option key as you drag it. This tip also works with the black Input Levels triangle.

Editing the saturation in Camera Raw

The Levels adjustments helped significantly, but our bride looks a little sunburned. You'll adjust the saturation in Camera Raw to even out her skin tone.

1 Double-click the 12B_Start layer thumbnail to open the Smart Object in Camera Raw.

▶ **Tip:** Here you're opening Camera Raw in Photoshop, while earlier you opened Camera Raw in Bridge. It's even possible to have Camera Raw open in both Photoshop and Bridge at the same time, working on different raw images in each.

2 Click the HSL Adjustments button (▤) to display that panel.

3 Click the Saturation tab.

4 Move the following sliders to reduce the amount of red in the skin:

   • Reduce Reds to −**2**.

   • Reduce Oranges to −**10**.

   • Reduce Magentas to −**3**.

5 Click OK to return to Photoshop.

Using the healing brush tools to remove blemishes

Now you're ready to give the model's face some focused attention. You'll use the Healing Brush and Spot Healing Brush tools to heal blemishes, smooth the skin, remove red veins from the eyes, and even hide the nose jewelry.

1 In the Layers panel, select the 12B_Start layer. Then, choose Duplicate Layer from the Layers panel menu.

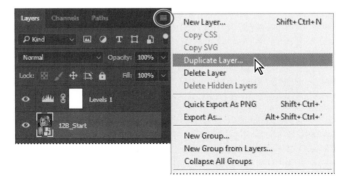

2 Name the new layer **Corrections**, and click OK.

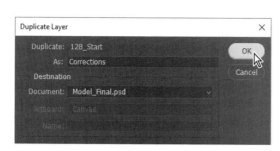 

Working on a duplicate layer preserves the original pixels so you can make changes later. You can't make changes using the healing brush tools on a Smart Object, so first you'll rasterize the layer.

3 Choose Layer > Smart Objects > Rasterize.

4 Zoom in on the model's face so that you can see it clearly.

5 Select the Spot Healing Brush tool (✏️).

6 In the options bar, select the following settings:

- Brush Size: **35** px

- Mode: Normal

- Type: Content-Aware

7 With the Spot Healing Brush tool, brush out the nose jewelry. A single click may be enough.

Because you've selected Content-Aware in the options bar, the Spot Healing Brush tool replaces the nose stud with skin that is similar to that around it.

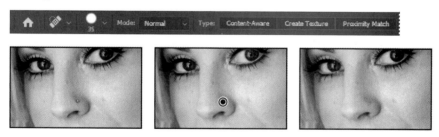

8 Paint over fine lines around the eyes and mouth. You can also brush away freckles and minor blemishes on her face, neck, arms, and chest. Experiment with simply clicking, using very short strokes, and creating longer brush strokes. You can also experiment with different settings. For example, to soften the lines around the mouth, we selected Proximity Match in the options bar and the Lighten blending mode. Remove obtrusive or distracting lines and blemishes, but leave enough that the face retains its character.

The Healing Brush tool may be a better option for larger blemishes. With the Healing Brush tool, you have more control over the pixels Photoshop samples.

9 Select the Healing Brush tool (🖌), hidden under the Spot Healing Brush tool (🩹). Select a brush with a size of **45** pixels and a Hardness of **100%**.

10 Alt-click (Windows) or Option-click (Mac) an area on her cheek to create the sampling source.

11 Brush over the large mole on her cheek to replace it with the color you sampled. You'll smooth out the texture later.

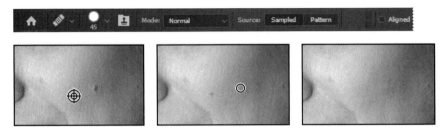

12 Use the Healing Brush tool to heal any larger blemishes that remain.

13 Choose File > Save to save your work so far.

Enhancing an image using the Dodge and Sponge tools

You'll use the Sponge and Dodge tools to brighten the eyes and lips.

1 Select the Sponge tool (🧽), hidden under the Dodge tool (🔎). In the options bar, make sure Vibrance is selected, and then select the following settings:

- Brush Size: **35** px
- Brush Hardness: **0%**
- Mode: Saturate
- Flow: **50%**

2 Drag the Sponge tool over the irises in the eyes to increase their saturation.

3   Change the brush size to **70** px and the flow to **10%**. Then brush the Sponge tool over the lips to saturate them.

You can use the Sponge tool to desaturate color too. You'll reduce the red in the corner of the eye.

4   Change the brush size to **45** px and the flow to **50%**. Then choose Desaturate from the Mode menu in the options bar.

5   Brush over the corner of the eye to reduce the red.

6   Select the Dodge tool (🔍), hidden under the Sponge tool.

7   In the options bar, change the brush size to **60** px and the Exposure to **10%**. Choose Highlights from the Range menu.

8   Brush the Dodge tool over the eyes—the whites and the irises—to brighten them.

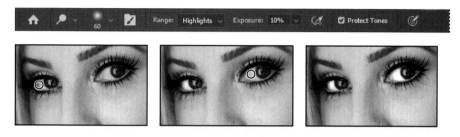

9   With the Dodge tool still selected, select Shadows from the Range menu in the options bar.

10 Use the Dodge tool to lighten the shadow area above the eyes and the areas around the irises to bring out the color.

Adjusting skin tones

In Photoshop, you can select a color range that targets skin tones so that it's easier to adjust the levels and color tone of skin without affecting the entire image. The skin tone color range selects other areas of the image with similar colors, but if you're making slight adjustments, this is usually acceptable.

1 Choose Select > Color Range.

2 In the Color Range dialog box, choose Skin Tones from the Select menu.

The preview shows that much of the image has been selected.

3 Select Detect Faces.

The preview in the selection changes. Now the face, hair highlights, and lighter areas of the dress are selected.

4 Decrease the Fuzziness slider to **10** to refine the selection. Then click OK.

The selection appears on the image itself as animated dotted lines (sometimes called *marching ants)*. You'll apply a Curves adjustment layer to the selection to reduce the overall red in the skin tone of the image.

5 Click the Curves icon in the Adjustments panel.

Photoshop adds a Curves adjustment layer above the Corrections layer.

6 Choose Red from the color channel menu in the Properties panel. Then click in the middle of the graph, and pull the curve down very slightly. The selected areas become less red. Be careful not to pull the curve down too far, or a green cast will appear. You can see the difference you've made by clicking the Toggle Layer Visibility button (the eye icon) in the Properties panel or Layers panel.

Because you selected the skin tones before applying the Curves adjustment layer, the skin color shifts but the background is unchanged. The adjustment affects slightly more of the image than the skin itself, but the effect blends well and is subtle.

 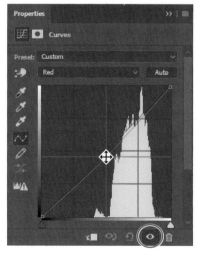 

Applying surface blur

You're almost done with the model. As a finishing touch, you'll apply the Surface Blur filter to give her a smooth appearance.

1   Select the Corrections layer, and choose Layer > Duplicate Layer. Name the layer **Surface Blur**, and click OK in the Duplicate Layer dialog box.

2   With the Surface Blur layer selected, choose Filter > Blur > Surface Blur.

3   In the Surface Blur dialog box, leave the Radius at 5 pixels, and move the Threshold to **10** levels. Then click OK.

The Surface Blur filter has left the model looking a little glassy. You'll reduce its effect by reducing the opacity of the blur.

4   With the Surface Blur layer selected, change the Opacity to **40%** in the Layers panel.

She looks more realistic now, but you can target the surface blur more precisely using the Eraser tool.

5 Select the Eraser tool (✏). In the options bar, select a brush between **10** and **50** pixels, with **10**% Hardness. Set the Opacity to **90**%.

6 Brush over the eyes, eyebrows, the defining lines of the nose, and the detail in the dress. You're erasing part of the blurred layer to let the sharper layer below show through in these areas.

7 Zoom out so you can see the entire image.

8 Save your work.

9 Choose Layer > Flatten Image to flatten the layers and reduce the image size.

10 Save the image again, and then close it.

You've taken advantage of features in both Camera Raw and Photoshop to help this bride look her best. As you've seen, you can move between Photoshop and Camera Raw to perform different tasks as you enhance and improve an image.

About HDR and panoramas in Camera Raw

When you select more than one image in Camera Raw, you can choose Merge to HDR or Merge to Panorama from the Filmstrip menu. HDR (high dynamic range) requires darker and lighter exposures of the same composition, while a panorama requires multiple exposures that make up a larger scene. Photoshop also has HDR or panorama features, but the newer process in Camera Raw is simpler, provides a preview, can process in the background, and produces a DNG file that you can edit in Camera Raw with the flexibility of a raw format image.

Extra credit

Painting with Light: Using Camera Raw as a Filter

In addition to opening files in Camera Raw to start the editing process, you can apply Camera Raw settings as a filter to any file in Photoshop. You'll use Camera Raw as a filter to make adjustments to this still-life image. First, you'll convert the image to a Smart Object so you can use Camera Raw as a Smart Filter, applying changes without affecting the original file.

1   In Photoshop, choose File > Open. Navigate to the Lessons/Lesson12 folder, and double-click the fruit.jpg file to open it.

2   Choose Filter > Convert for Smart Filters. Click OK in the informational dialog box.

3   Choose Filter > Camera Raw Filter. The image opens in Camera Raw.

You converted the image to a Smart Object so you can apply Camera Raw as a Smart Filter. You can also apply Camera Raw as a standard filter, but then you can't return to adjust your settings or hide the adjustments in your image file.

4   Select the Adjustment Brush in the toolbar.

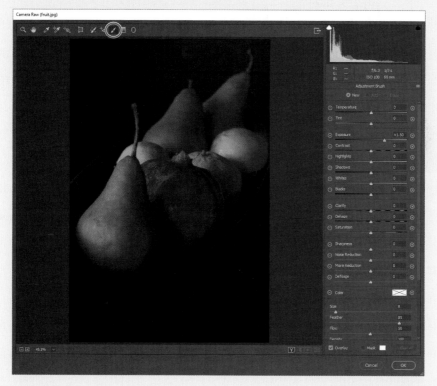

Continues on next page

Extra credit (continued)

With the Adjustment Brush tool in Camera Raw, you can apply Exposure, Brightness, Clarity, and other adjustments to specific areas of a photo by painting them directly onto those areas. The Graduated Filter tool is similar, but it applies the same types of adjustments gradually across a region of the photo that you define.

5 In the Adjustment Brush panel, change Exposure to **+1.50**. Then, at the bottom of the panel, change Size to **8** and Feather to **85**.

6 Brush the fruit where you want to increase the exposure, which reveals more of the color. Continue brushing until the fruit is too bright.

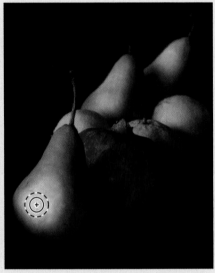

7 Once you've brushed all the fruit, reduce the Exposure setting in the Adjustment Brush panel so the image looks more realistic.

8 To see how your changes have affected the image in Camera Raw, click the Before/After Views button at the bottom of the image window, and choose Before/After Left/Right from the pop-up menu.

9 When you're satisfied with the changes, click OK.

Photoshop displays the image. In the Layers panel, the Camera Raw filter is listed beneath the layer name. You can toggle the visibility icon for the Camera Raw filter to see the image before and after the adjustment. To edit the Camera Raw smart filter adjustment, double-click Camera Raw Filter in the Layers panel.

You might notice that fewer options are available in Camera Raw when it's applied as a filter to a layer. The full range of Camera Raw options is available when it's editing a raw file.

Review questions

1 What happens to camera raw images when you edit them in Camera Raw?

2 What is the advantage of the Adobe Digital Negative (DNG) file format?

3 How can you apply the same settings to multiple images in Camera Raw?

4 How can you apply Camera Raw as a filter?

Review answers

1 A camera raw file contains unprocessed picture data from a digital camera's image sensor. Camera raw files give photographers control over interpreting the image data, rather than letting the camera make the adjustments and conversions. When you edit the image in Camera Raw, it preserves the original raw file data. This way, you can edit the image as you desire, export it, and keep the original intact for future use or other adjustments.

2 The Adobe Digital Negative (DNG) file format contains the raw image data from a digital camera as well as metadata that defines what the image data means. DNG is an industry-wide standard for camera raw image data. DNG can help photographers manage proprietary camera raw file formats, and it provides a compatible archival format that includes edits.

3 To apply the same settings to multiple images in Camera Raw, select the images in the filmstrip, click the Filmstrip menu button, and choose Sync Settings. Then select the settings you want to apply, and click OK.

4 To apply Camera Raw as a filter, choose Filter > Camera Raw Filter in Photoshop. Make the changes you want to make in Camera Raw, and then click OK. If you want to be able to edit the changes later, apply Camera Raw as a Smart Filter.

13 PREPARING FILES FOR THE WEB

Lesson overview

In this lesson, you'll learn how to do the following:

- Use the Frame tool to create a placeholder for a layout.
- Create and stylize a button for a website.
- Use layer groups and artboards.
- Optimize design assets for the web.
- Record an action to automate a series of steps.
- Play an action to affect multiple images.
- Save entire layouts and individual assets using Export As.
- Design for multiple screen sizes with multiple artboards.

This lesson will take about an hour to complete. Please log in to your account on peachpit.com to download the lesson files for this chapter, or go to the Getting Started section at the beginning of this book and follow the instructions under "Accessing the Lesson Files and Web Edition."

As you work on this lesson, you'll preserve the start files. If you need to restore the start files, download them from your Account page.

PROJECT: MUSEUM WEBSITE

It's often necessary to create separate images for buttons or other objects in a website. The Export As workflow makes it easy to save layers, layer groups, and artboards as separate image files.

Getting started

In this lesson, you will build buttons for the home page of an art museum's website, and then generate appropriate graphics files for each button. You'll use layer groups to assemble the buttons, and then create actions to prepare a set of images for use as a second group of buttons. First, you'll view the final web design.

1   Start Photoshop, and then immediately hold down Ctrl+Alt+Shift (Windows) or Command+Option+Shift (Mac) to restore the default preferences. (See "Restoring Default Preferences" on page 5.)

2   When prompted, click Yes to delete the Adobe Photoshop Settings file.

3   Choose File > Browse In Bridge.

● **Note:** If Bridge isn't installed, you'll be prompted to install it when you choose Browse In Bridge. For more information, see page 3.

4   In Bridge, click Lessons in the Favorites panel. Double-click the Lesson13 folder in the Content panel.

5   View the 13End.psd file in Bridge.

There are eight buttons at the bottom of the page, arranged in two rows. You'll transform images into buttons for the top row, and use an action to prepare the buttons for the second row.

6   Double-click the 13Start.psd thumbnail to open the file in Photoshop. Click OK if you see the Missing Profile dialog box.

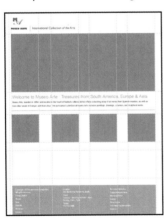
13Start.psd

13End.psd

7   Choose File > Save As, rename the file **13Working.psd**, and click Save. Click OK in the Photoshop Format Options dialog box.

Creating placeholders with the Frame tool

When you lay out objects for a print, web, or mobile device project, it's common to design the layout before you have the final graphics for it. You could add temporary graphics that you plan to replace later with final graphics, but this requires additional file management. You can simplify the design process by creating placeholder shapes, called *frames*, during the early stages of design. As you refine the design and as final graphics become available, it's easy to place graphics directly into a placeholder frame.

You create frames using the Frame tool. A frame can contain an imported graphic, Smart Object, or a pixel layer. When you create a frame, it appears in the Layers panel, because a frame is like a layer group with a vector mask.

The document 13Working.psd contains empty gray boxes. The gray boxes exist only to help you position new frames that you'll create for this lesson. When you create your own designs, you can design using the Frame tool alone.

1   Choose Edit > Preferences > Units & Rulers (Windows) or Photoshop CC > Preferences > Units & Rulers (Mac). In the Units area of the dialog box, choose Pixels from the Rulers menu, and then click OK.

Tip: A quick way to change the unit of measure is to right-click (Windows) or Control-click (Mac) the rulers.

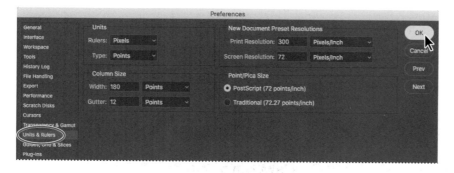

You want to work in pixels because this document is intended to be a web page.

2   Choose Window > Info to open the Info panel.

The Info panel displays information dynamically as you move the pointer or make selections. Which information it displays depends on the tool that is selected. You'll use it to determine the position of the ruler guide (based on the Y coordinate) and the size of an area you select (based on the width and height). It's also very handy for seeing the values of colors under the pointer.

Tip: To customize the Info panel display of the color values under the pointer, click either of the eyedropper icons in the Info panel, and choose the display option you want.

3   If the rulers aren't visible, choose View > Rulers.

Tip: The keyboard shortcut for showing or hiding rulers is Ctrl+R (Windows) or Command+R (Mac).

Adding a frame

Frames are easy to add, because you create them in the same way you'd create a shape such as a rectangle or circle.

▶ **Tip:** You can create an elliptical or circular frame by selecting the Elliptical Frame icon in the options bar for the Frame tool.

1   In the Tools panel, select the Frame tool (⊠).

2   Drag to create a rectangular frame over the large gray rectangle at the top of the document.

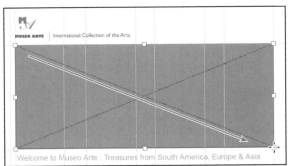

▶ **Tip:** To create a frame of any shape, such as a star, first draw the shape using the Pen tool or a shape tool. Then, with the shape layer selected in the Layers panel, choose Layer > New > Convert to Frame.

The frame appears as a rectangle with an X inside it. The X indicates that it's not just a vector shape, but a placeholder frame. As a placeholder, it's ready to contain a graphic at any time.

Adding a graphic to a frame

When you finalize the images and other graphics that go into a document, you can add them to the placeholder frames you've created.

1   In the Layers panel, make sure the Frame 1 layer is still selected.

2   Choose File > Place Linked.

3   Navigate to the Lesson13/Art folder, select the NorthShore.jpg file, and click Place.

The JPEG image you selected appears inside the selected frame, and is automatically sized to fit the frame.

You can also drag an image from Bridge or the desktop and drop it into a frame in a Photoshop document window; this embeds the image. To link the image, hold down Alt or Option while dragging it into Photoshop.

Editing frame attributes with the Properties panel

When a frame is selected in the Layers panel, you can see and edit frame attributes in the Properties panel. You can take advantage of this to change a frame after you create it.

1 With the Frame tool, draw a rectangle frame between the row of four gray squares and the bottom of the document. The exact size and position isn't important, because you're about to edit it.

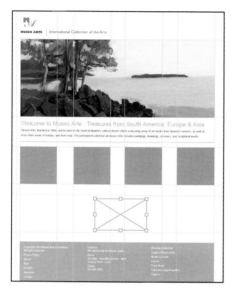

2 With the frame selected, enter the following values in the Properties panel:

- Width: **180**
- Height: **180**
- X: **40**
- Y: **648**

▶ **Tip:** As in the Control panel, you can change the unit of measure in a Properties panel field by right-clicking (Windows) or Control-clicking (Mac) the field. Or you can override a field's unit of measure by typing the unit after the value; for example, **4 in**.

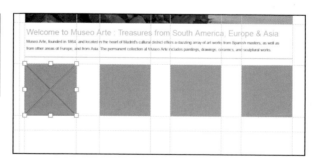

After you apply all of the values, the size and position of the frame should now match the first gray square.

Duplicating frames

The other three squares in the row are the same size, so instead of drawing all four squares manually, you can simply duplicate them. Duplicating a frame is similar to duplicating a layer, because frames appear in the Layers panel.

1   In the Layers panel, drag the Frame 1 layer, and drop it on the Create a New Layer button (⬜). The duplicate layer, Frame 1 Copy, appears in the Layers panel.

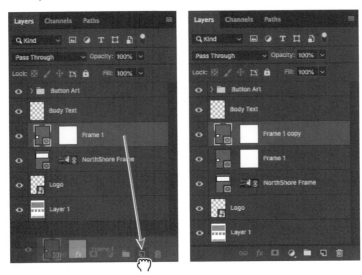

2   With the Frame 1 Copy layer selected, in the Properties panel change the X value to **300**: This makes the duplicate square frame line up with the second gray square.

3   Repeat step 2 to create two more duplicate frames. In the Properties panel, change the X value of the third frame to **550** and the X value of the fourth frame to **800**.

You've created a complete row of four placeholder frames.

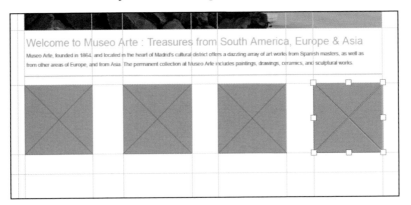

Adding images to frames

When graphics become available to use in the layout, you can quickly add them to each frame. One convenient way is by using the Properties panel.

1   Make sure the first square frame is selected.

2   In the Properties panel, click the Inset Image menu, and choose Place from Local Disk - Linked.

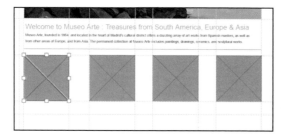

3   Navigate to the Lesson13/Art folder, select the Beach.jpg file, and click Place.

The Beach.jpg file is scaled to fit the frame, the name of the frame changes to Beach Frame, and the folder path to the placed document is displayed in the Properties panel.

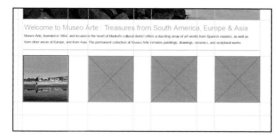

4   Repeat step 3 for the other three square frames, placing the files NorthShore.jpg, DeYoung.jpg, and MaineOne.jpg. Remember that you can also add a linked image to a frame by Alt-dragging (Windows) or Option-dragging (Mac) an image from the desktop and dropping it into a frame.

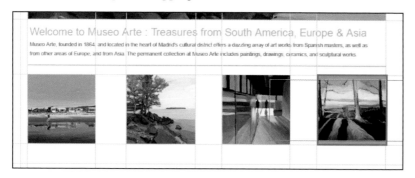

Tip: If you want to select just the frame, click the frame edge with the Move tool. This works best when there aren't nearby objects or guides that might become selected instead.

5   In the Layers panel, click to select the frame layer thumbnail (the right thumbnail with the link icon) of the MainOne Frame layer. This selects just the contents of the frame. (Clicking the left thumbnail would select the frame.)

6   Choose Edit > Free Transform, and as needed, drag the image or its corner handles to improve the composition of the image within the frame.

After adding graphics to frames, it's always a good idea to inspect all of the frames to make sure the graphics are well-composed within them. Feel free to adjust any of the other images within their frames.

● **Note:** If you can't select a frame or its contents with the Move tool, make sure Auto-Select Layer is enabled in the options bar when the Move tool is selected. When Auto-Select Layer is not enabled, you must click the thumbnail of the frame or the contents in the Layers panel.

Using layer groups to create button graphics

Layer groups make it easier to organize and work with layers in complex images, especially when there are sets of layers that work together. You'll use layer groups to assemble the layers that make up each button, and they'll come in handy when you export assets later.

The four frames you created now serve as the basis for buttons. You'll add a label to each, identifying the gallery it represents, and then add a drop shadow and a stroke.

1   Choose Window > Info to open the Info panel, if it isn't already open.

2   Position the pointer over the horizontal ruler, and drag a ruler guide down until the Y value in the Info panel is 795 pixels.

Tip: If you have trouble positioning the horizontal ruler guide precisely, zoom in.

You'll use this guide to draw a band across the bottom of the image for the label.

3 Zoom in on the first square image, of the man on the beach. Then select Beach Frame in the Layers panel.

You'll use this image to design the first button.

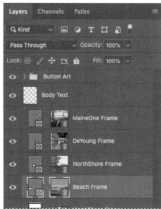

4 Click the New Layer button (⬜) at the bottom of the Layers panel. The new layer is named Layer 2 and appears directly above the Beach Frame layer. Rename it **band**.

5 Select the Rectangular Marquee tool (▭) in the Tools panel. Then, drag a selection across the bottom of the image, as indicated by the guides. The selection should be 180 pixels wide and 33 pixels high. Make sure the selection lines up with the frame along the sides and bottom.

6 Choose Edit > Fill. In the Fill dialog box, choose Color from the Contents menu, and then, in the Color Picker, select a dark blue (R=**25**, G=**72**, B=**121**). Click OK to close the Color Picker, and then click OK to close the Fill dialog box and apply the fill.

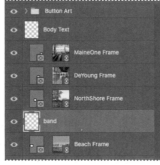

A dark blue band appears at the bottom of the image, where you made your selection. You'll add text to it next.

7 Choose Select > Deselect.

8 Select the Horizontal Type tool, and select the following settings in the options bar:

- Font Family: Myriad Pro
- Font Style: Regular
- Font Size: **18** pt
- Anti-aliasing: Strong
- Alignment: Center
- Color: White

● **Note:** In some versions of Photoshop CC 2019, a new text layer may be created with left alignment even if you specified another alignment before clicking the Horizontal Type tool. You can fix this by applying center alignment after the text layer is created.

9 Click in the center of the blue band, and type **GALLERY ONE**. Use the Move tool to adjust the position of the type layer if necessary.

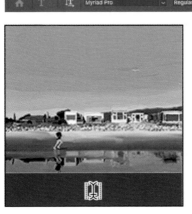 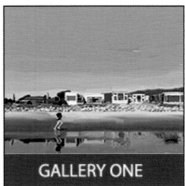

▶ **Tip:** The keyboard shortcut for creating a layer group out of selected layers is Ctrl+G (Windows) or Command+G (Mac).

10 Select the GALLERY ONE and band layers in the Layers panel, and choose Layer > Group Layers.

Photoshop creates a group named Group 1.

11 Double-click the Group 1 layer group, and rename it **Gallery 1**. Then expand the group. The layers you selected are indented, indicating they're part of that group.

12 Drag the Gallery 1 layer group up so that it's above all of the frame layers.

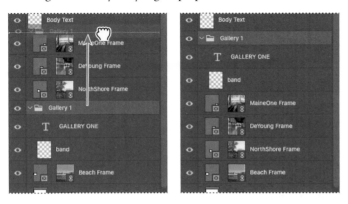

13 Choose File > Save.

Duplicating button bands and text

You've designed the label for one button. You could go through all those steps again to create the band and text for each of the other buttons, but it will be faster to duplicate the layer group you created for the first band and text, and then edit the copies as needed.

1 In the Layers panel, make sure the Gallery 1 layer group is selected.

2 With the Move tool selected, make sure Auto-Select is not selected in the options bar.

3 With the Move tool, hold down the Alt (Windows) or Option (Mac) key as you drag the Gallery One button to the right, and drop it when it snaps into alignment with the second square frame and its guides.

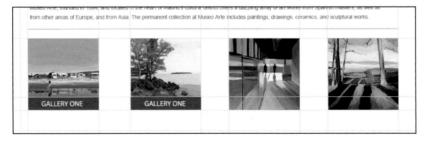

Holding down Alt or Option creates a copy of the selected layer group as you drag it with the Move tool. When you release the mouse button, the copy (Gallery 1 copy) should be selected in the Layers panel.

4   Repeat step 2 by Alt-dragging (Windows) or Option-dragging (Mac) a copy of the second button over the third square frame, and then do it one more time to copy the third button over the fourth square frame, completing the row.

Now edit the text in the three copies to match their images.

5   With the Horizontal Text tool, select the ONE text in the second button, and change ONE so that it now says **GALLERY TWO**.

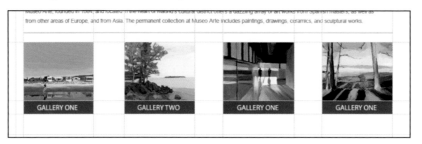

6   Repeat step 5 for the third and fourth buttons so that they say **GALLERY THREE** and **GALLERY FOUR**, respectively.

7   After you finish editing the GALLERY FOUR text, commit the last text edit by selecting the Move tool.

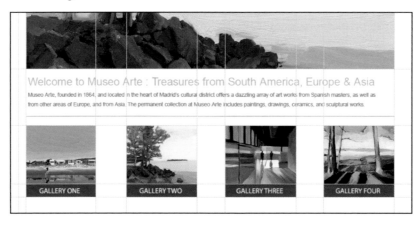

8   In the Layers panel, rename the layer groups to be consistent with their contents:

▶ **Tip:** These steps are easier if you make the Layers panel taller, so that you can see multiple expanded layer groups at once.

- Double-click the name of the "Gallery 1 copy" layer group, and name it **Gallery 2**.

- Double-click the name of the "Gallery 1 copy 2" layer group, and name it **Gallery 3**.

- Double-click the name of the "Gallery 1 copy 3" layer group, and name it **Gallery 4**.

Now move each button image into its layer group.

9   In the Layers panel, do the following:

● **Note:** When dragging layers in step 9, position the pointer over the layer name, not the thumbnails, before dragging.

- Drag the Beach Frame layer into the Gallery 1 layer group, below the GALLERY ONE and band layers.

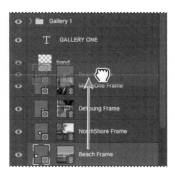

- Drag the upper NorthShore Frame layer into the Gallery 2 layer group, below the GALLERY TWO and band layers.

- Drag the DeYoung Frame layer into the Gallery 3 layer group, below the GALLERY THREE and band layers.

- Drag the MaineOne Frame layer into the Gallery 4 layer group, below the GALLERY FOUR and band layers.

10 Click the arrow next to each of the Gallery layer group icons to collapse them, simplifying the Layers panel display.

Now you'll add a drop shadow and stroke to improve the appearance of the button.

11 Select the Gallery 1 layer group in the Layers panel. Then, click the Add Layer Style button (*fx*) at the bottom of the Layers panel, and choose Drop Shadow.

12 In the Layer Style dialog box, change the following settings in the Structure area:

- Opacity: **27**%

- Distance: **9** px

- Spread: **19**%

- Size: **18** px

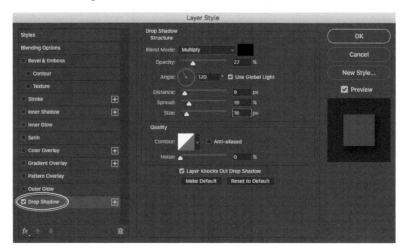

● **Note:** Be sure to click the word Stroke. If you click only the check box, Photoshop applies the layer style with its default settings, but you won't see the options.

13 With the Layer Style dialog box still open, select Stroke on the left, making sure that it's enabled, and apply the following settings:

- Size: **1** px

- Position: Inside

- Color: Click the color swatch to open the Color Picker. Then click the blue band to sample its color, and click OK to select it.

14 Click OK to apply both layer styles.

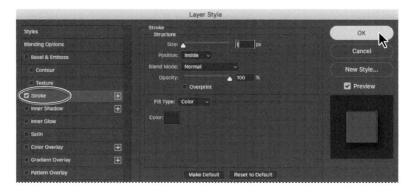

The drop shadow and stroke appear on the button's layer group in the document, and also in the Layers panel.

15 In the Layers panel, position the pointer over the fx icon next to the Gallery 1 layer group. Then hold down the Alt (Windows) or Option (Mac) key as you drag the fx icon and drop it on the Gallery 2 layer group. This is a quick way to copy layer effects to another layer or layer group.

16 Repeat step 15 to copy the layer effects to the Gallery 3 and Gallery 4 layer groups.

17 In the Layers panel, expand the Button Art layer group, and then click the eye icon for the Navigation layer to make it visible. Then collapse the Button Art layer group.

This layer represents the navigation among sections of the museum website.

18 Save the file, and then close it.

Automating a multistep task

▶ **Tip:** You can create conditional actions that change their behavior based on criteria you define.

An *action* is a set of one or more commands that you record and then play back to apply to a single file or a batch of files. In this exercise, you'll create an action to prepare a set of images to serve as buttons for additional galleries on the web page you're designing.

Recording an action

You'll start by recording an action that resizes an image, changes its canvas size, and adds layer styles, so that the additional buttons match the ones you've already created. You use the Actions panel to record, play, edit, and delete individual actions. You also use the Actions panel to save and load action files.

There are four images in the Buttons folder that will serve as the basis for new gallery buttons on your website. The images are large, so the first thing you'll need to do is resize them to match the existing buttons. You'll perform each of the steps on the Gallery5.jpg file as you record the action. You'll then play the action to make the same changes on the other images in the folder automatically.

1 Choose File > Open, and navigate to the Lesson13/Buttons folder. Double-click the Gallery5.jpg file to open it in Photoshop.

2 Choose Window > Actions to open the Actions panel. Close the Default Actions set (folder); you'll create and use your own set for this lesson.

3 Click the Create New Set button (□) at the bottom of the Actions panel. In the New Set dialog box, name the set **Buttons**, and click OK.

Photoshop comes with several prerecorded actions, all in the Default Actions set. You can use action sets to organize your actions so that it's easier to find the one you want.

4 Click the Create New Action button (□) at the bottom of the Actions panel. Name the action **Resizing and Styling Images**, and click Record.

It's a good idea to name actions in a way that makes it clear what the actions do, so you can find them easily later.

At the bottom of the Actions panel, the Begin Recording button turns red to let you know that recording is in progress.

Don't let the fact that you're recording rush you. Take all the time you need to perform the procedure accurately. Actions don't record in real time; they record steps as you complete them, but they play them back as quickly as possible.

You'll start by resizing and sharpening the image.

5 Choose Image > Image Size, and do the following:

- Make sure Resample is selected.

- For Width, choose Pixels from the units menu, and then change the Width to **180**.

- Confirm that the Height has changed to **180** pixels. It should, because original proportions are preserved using the Constrain Aspect Ratio link icon to the left of the Width and Height values, which is selected by default.

6 Click OK.

7 Choose Filter > Sharpen > Smart Sharpen, apply the following settings, and click OK:

- Amount: **100**%

- Radius: **1.0** px

You need to make some additional changes to the image that you can't make as long as the Background layer is locked. You'll convert it to a regular layer.

8 Double-click the Background layer name in the Layers panel. In the New Layer dialog box, name the layer **Button**, and click OK.

▶ **Tip:** If you want to convert a background layer to a regular layer and you don't need to name it, simply click the Background layer's lock icon in the Layers panel.

When you rename a Background layer, you're converting it to a regular layer, so Photoshop displays the New Layer dialog box. But no layers are added; the Background layer becomes the new layer.

Now that you've converted the Background layer, you can change the canvas size and add layer styles.

▶ **Tip:** Use Canvas Size when you want to add area to or remove area from a document; use Image Size when you want to resample, change the physical dimensions, or change the resolution of a document.

9 Choose Image > Canvas Size, and do the following:

- Make sure the unit of measure is set to Pixels.
- Change the Width to **220** pixels and the Height to **220** pixels.
- Click the center square in the anchor area to ensure the canvas is extended evenly on all sides.
- Click OK.

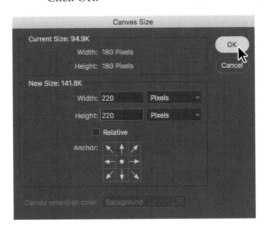 

10 Choose Layer > Layer Style > Drop Shadow.

11 In the Layer Style dialog box, apply the following settings:

- Opacity: **27**%

- Angle: **120**°

- Distance: **9** px

- Spread: **19**%

- Size: **18** px

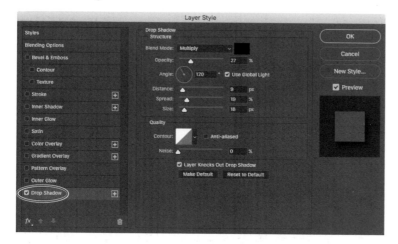

12 With the Layer Style dialog box still open, select Stroke on the left, and apply the following settings:

- Size: **1** px

- Position: Inside

- Color: If the color swatch doesn't already match the other blue band you made, click the color swatch and sample the blue band as you did earlier.

13 Click OK to apply both layer styles.

● **Note:** Be sure to click the word Stroke. If you click only the check box, Photoshop applies the layer style with its default settings, but you won't see the options.

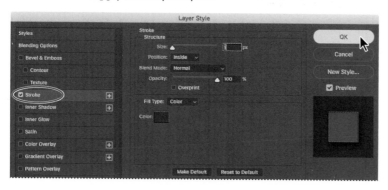

14 Choose File > Save As, choose Photoshop for the Format, and click Save. Click OK if the Photoshop Format Options dialog box appears.

15 Close the file. The Start workspace appears, so click the Back button at the top left corner of the Start workspace (to the left of the Photoshop icon) so that you can see the Actions panel again.

16 Click the Stop Recording button at the bottom of the Actions panel.

▶ **Tip:** As you review an action, you can edit the sequence by dragging steps, edit steps by double-clicking them (if applicable), or remove unneeded steps by deleting them.

The action you just recorded (Resizing and Styling Images) is now saved in the Buttons set in the Actions panel. Click the arrows to expand different sets of steps. You can examine each recorded step and the specific selections you made.

Batch-playing an action

Applying actions is a timesaving process for performing routine tasks on files, but you can streamline your work even further by applying actions to multiple files at once. You'll apply the action you've created to the three remaining images.

1 Choose File > Open, and navigate to the Lesson13/Buttons folder. Ctrl-select (Windows) or Command-select (Mac) the Gallery6.jpg, Gallery7.jpg, and Gallery8.jpg files, and click Open.

2 Choose File > Automate > Batch.

3 In the Batch dialog box, do the following:

- Confirm that Buttons is chosen in the Set menu and Resizing and Styling Images—the action you just created—is chosen in the Action menu.

- Choose Opened Files from the Source menu.

- Make sure None is chosen for the Destination.

- Click OK.

Photoshop plays the action, applying its steps to all the files that are open. You can also apply an action to an entire folder of images without opening them.

Because you saved the file and closed it while you were recording the action, Photoshop saves each of the images as a PSD file in its original folder, and then closes the file. After Photoshop closes the last file, Photoshop displays the Start workspace.

Note: If you get an error when running an action, click Stop. There may be a problem with the action that was recorded, especially if you had to correct a mistake while recording. Try troubleshooting or re-recording the action.

Placing files in Photoshop

The four additional button images are ready to be placed into the design. You probably noticed that each already has a blue band with its gallery name included in the image, so you don't need to perform those steps. They're ready to go.

1 If the file 13Working.psd is in the Recent list in the Start workspace, click its name to reopen it. If not, choose File > Open to open it.

2 In the Layers panel, select a layer group name or the Logo layer. This ensures that the files about to be placed are not added inside any layer groups, because new layers are added above the selected layer.

3 Choose File > Place Embedded.

You'll place these files as embedded Smart Objects. Because they're embedded, the entire image is copied into the Photoshop file.

4 In the Place Embedded dialog box, navigate to the Lesson13/Buttons folder, and double-click the Gallery5.psd file.

Photoshop places the Gallery5.psd file in the center of the 13Working.psd file. But that's not where you want it to go, so you'll move it.

5 Drag the image into position below the Gallery One button. Use the guides to align the image with the one above. When it's in position, commit the change by pressing Enter or Return, or by clicking outside the image.

Note: The bounding box of the placed image is larger than the button, because the bounding box includes the complete extent of the drop shadow.

▶ **Tip:** You can also place embedded files by dragging them into the Photoshop document from the desktop or from other applications. You can drag multiple images to place at once; after you commit one image the next will be placed.

6 Repeat steps 3–5 to place the Gallery6.psd, Gallery7.psd, and Gallery8.psd files so that they line up below the Gallery Two, Gallery Three, and Gallery Four buttons.

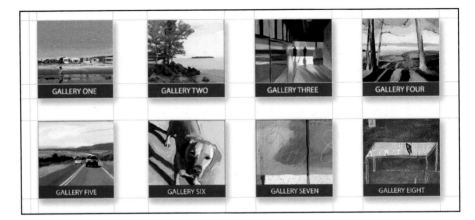

7 Close the file and save your work.

Designing with artboards

▶ **Tip:** If you need advanced control over how layers are exported for web and mobile user interfaces, you may be interested in Adobe Generator. When Adobe Generator is on, Photoshop automatically exports and optimizes layers based on how the layers are named.

When you're designing websites or user interfaces for mobile devices, you may need to create separate image files for buttons and other content. In Photoshop, you can use the Export As feature to export an entire document or individual layers to web- and mobile-friendly formats including PNG, JPEG, GIF, or SVG. In addition to being able to export multiple layers to individual files at once, Export As makes it possible to export to multiple sizes at once if you need to produce sets of images for low- and high-resolution displays.

You may need to coordinate different ideas for a single design, or design variations for different display sizes. This is easier when you use artboards, which are like multiple canvases in a single Photoshop document. You can also use Export As to export entire artboards.

With Export As, you control what gets exported by selecting artboards or layers in the Layers panel.

Duplicating an artboard

▶ **Tip:** You may notice or have been taught to use the older Save for Web command in Photoshop. Although that command is still available under File > Export > Save for Web (Legacy), Save for Web can't export multiple layers, artboards, or resolutions, while Export As can.

You'll use artboards to adapt the design of the museum website for a different screen size. Later, you'll export both designs at once.

1 In the Photoshop Start workspace, click Open. Navigate to the Lesson13 folder, and open the file 13Museo.psd.

2 Choose File > Save As, rename the file **13Museo_Working.psd**, and click Save. Click OK in the Photoshop Format Options dialog box.

This is a web page that's being adapted for a responsive web design so that it will work well on display sizes from desktops to smartphones.

3 Choose Select > All Layers.

4 Choose Layer > New > Artboard From Layers, name the new artboard **Desktop**, and click OK. The artboard name appears above the new artboard, and also on its new artboard group in the Layers panel.

5 Make sure the Artboard tool (⊡) is selected; it's grouped with the Move tool in the Tools panel. Then Alt/Option-click the Add Artboard button to the right of the artboard to duplicate both the Desktop artboard and its contents.

6 In the Layers panel, double-click the name of the Desktop Copy duplicate artboard, and name it **iPhone**.

▶ **Tip:** You can choose artboard presets from the Size menu in the options bar when the Artboard tool is selected.

7 In the Properties panel, click the Set Artboard to Preset menu, and choose **iPhone 6**. That artboard preset applies the pixel dimensions of an iPhone 6, iPhone 7, and iPhone 8 (750 pixels wide by 1334 pixels tall). Now you can develop a design for that iPhone size, using the elements of the Desktop design. It will also be easier to maintain design consistency, since both the desktop and mobile designs are in the same document.

8 Save your work.

Creating a design variation with artboards

You now have different artboards for desktop and smartphone display sizes; the next task is to fit the desktop-sized objects within the width of the smartphone display's pixel dimensions.

1   In the Layers panel, expand the iPhone artboard, and Shift-select the first and last layers in that artboard only. Don't select the artboard name itself.

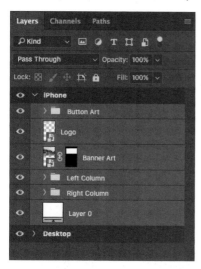

2   Choose Edit > Free Transform.

3   In the options bar, do the following:

- Click the Toggle Reference Point checkbox to select it; this makes the reference point visible in the transformation bounding box, and makes it possible for you to reposition the reference point.

- Select the top left square of the reference point location option. Scaling, rotating, or other transformations will now be performed from the top left corner of the bounding box (instead of the center) until the transformation is committed.

▶ **Tip:** You can position the reference point anywhere inside or outside the transformation bounding box by dragging it.

- Make sure the Maintain Aspect Ratio button (the link icon) is selected, so that the selected layers will scale proportionally.

- Enter **726px** for Width.

4   Press Enter or Return to apply the new settings. (Press Enter or Return only once, to apply the value in the options bar. If you press Enter or Return a second time it will commit the transformation.)

Those settings proportionally scale the selected layers to 726 pixels wide, from the top left corner of the selection, to better fit the artboard.

5 Position the pointer inside the Free Transform bounding box, and then Shift-drag the selected layers down until you can see the entire Museo Arts logo at the top of the page.

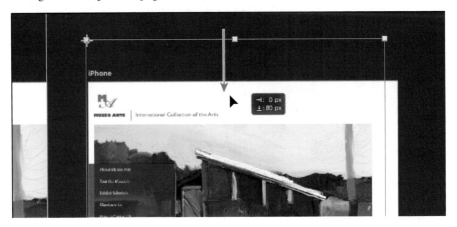

6 Press Enter or Return to exit Free Transform mode, and choose Select > Deselect Layers.

7 In the Layers panel, select the Logo layer, and choose Edit > Free Transform.

8 Drag the bottom right handle on the Free Transform bounding box until the transformation values next to the pointer indicate that the logo is 672 pixels wide, matching the width of the other elements. Then press Enter or Return. This width makes the logo more readable on a smartphone screen.

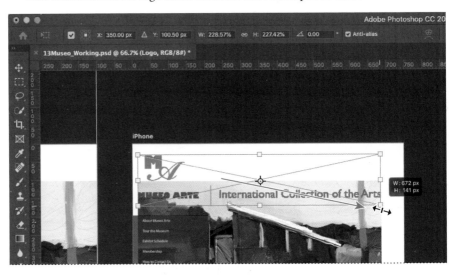

9 In the Layers panel, select the Banner Art, Left Column, and Right Column layers.

10 With the Move tool, Shift-drag the selected layers down until the top is even with the top of the blue button stack on the left.

Now you'll take the two-column layout and make each column fill the width of the artboard. But first you'll need to accommodate them by making the artboard taller.

11 Select the iPhone artboard in the Layers panel, and then, with the Artboard tool, drag the bottom handle of the iPhone artboard until the transformation values next to the pointer indicate that it's 2800 px tall.

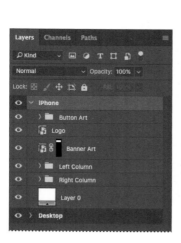

▶ **Tip:** You can also change the height of an artboard by entering a new Height in the Properties panel when an artboard is selected.

● **Note:** Once you start using artboards, resize them only using the Artboard tool. The Image > Image Size and Image > Canvas Size commands work best with a Photoshop document that doesn't use artboards.

12 Select the Right Column layer group in the Layers panel, and then choose Edit > Free Transform.

13 In the options bar, do the following:

- Make sure the Toggle Reference Point checkbox is selected, and then select the top right square of the reference point location option.

- Make sure the Maintain Aspect Ratio (link) button is selected, and enter **672px** for Width.

- Press Enter or Return to apply the new width.

14 Position the pointer inside the Free Transform bounding box, and then Shift-drag the selected layer group down until the transformation values next to the pointer indicate a vertical move of 1200 px (the Y value in the options bar should say about 1680 px when the top right square of the reference point locator is selected). Press Enter or Return to commit and exit the transformation.

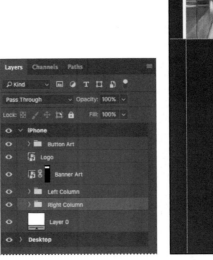

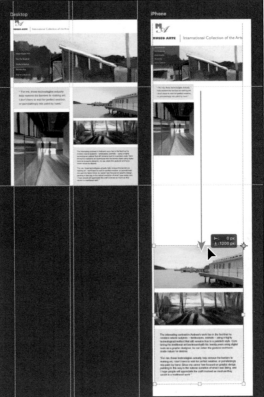

15 Select the Left Column layer group in the Layers panel, and then choose Edit > Free Transform.

16 In the options bar, do the following:

- Make sure the Toggle Reference Point checkbox is selected, and then select the top left square of the reference point location option.

- Make sure the Maintain Aspect Ratio (link) button is selected, and enter **672px** for Width.

- Press Enter or Return to apply the new width.

- Then press Enter or Return to commit and exit the transformation.

Feel free to adjust the positioning and the vertical spacing among the layer groups and layers.

17 Choose View > Fit on Screen to see both artboards at once, and then save your work.

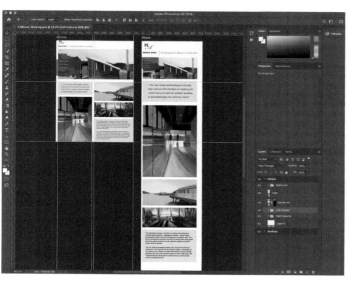

▶ **Tip:** To nudge selected layers or layer groups when the Move tool is active, press the arrow keys. When Free Transform is active, you can also nudge by clicking in a number field and pressing the up arrow or down arrow key.

You've adapted a desktop-sized multi-column web page layout for a single-column smartphone-sized layout, and both layouts exist on two artboards in one Photoshop document.

Exporting artboards with Export As

When it's time to have a client review your designs, you can use the Export As command to easily export any artboard, layer, or layer group into its own file. You'll export the complete desktop and smartphone artboards, and then you'll export the layers of each artboard to their own folder.

1   Choose File > Export > Export As. This command exports each whole artboard, so you see each artboard in the list on the left side of the Export As dialog box.

● **Note:** The Export As dialog box doesn't preview multiple Scale All options. Artboards are previewed at 1x.

You can preview the exported dimensions and file size of each item; the preview is determined by the settings on the right side of the Export As dialog box.

▶ **Tip:** If you frequently use the Export As command with the same settings, choose File > Export > Export Preferences, and specify the settings you use the most. Now you can export to those settings in one step by choosing File > Export > Quick Export As, or choosing Quick Export As from the Layers panel menu.

2   In the list on the left, click the iPhone artboard to select it, and then set the Export As options to the following:

• In the Scale All section, make sure Size is set to 1x and the Suffix field is empty.

• In the File Settings section, choose JPG from the Format menu, and enter **80%** for Quality.

• In the Color Space section, select Convert to sRGB.

• Other settings can be left at defaults.

3   In the list on the left, click the Desktop artboard to select it, and apply the same settings as in step 2.

4   Click Export All, navigate to the Lesson13 folder, double-click the Assets folder, and then click Save or Open.

5   Switch to the desktop or Bridge, and open the Assets folder in the Lesson13 folder to see the Desktop.jpg and iPhone.jpg files representing each artboard. The filenames are based on the artboard names. You can send those files off for client review.

6   Switch back to Photoshop.

Exporting layers as assets with Export As

If the client approves the design, you can then use Export As to create assets for each layer on each artboard, such as images or buttons. Those assets can be used by a web or application developer who executes the design in code.

1   In the Layers panel, Shift-select all layers of the Desktop artboard.

2   In the Layers panel menu, choose Export As. (Do not choose File > Export As.)

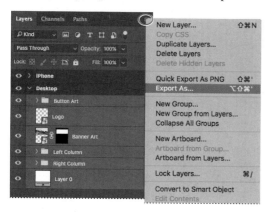

▶ **Tip:** The File > Export > Export As command exports entire artboards. If you want to export specific layers, select them in the Layers panel and choose Export As from the Layers panel menu, not the File menu. Exporting selected layers is useful for updating parts of a design.

Notice that in the Export As dialog box, each layer is listed separately, because they will export separately.

3   In the Export As dialog box, use the same settings as you did in step 2 of the previous section (on page 340).

4   Click Export All, navigate to the Assets_Desktop folder in the Lesson13 folder, and click Select Folder or Save.

You have exported all assets for the Desktop artboard into a single folder.

5   Repeat steps 1–3 for the iPhone artboard.

6   Click Export All, navigate to the Assets_iPhone folder in the Lesson13 folder, and click Export.

▶ **Tip:** If a developer
asks for assets at
multiple scale factors
(for Retina/HiDPI display
resolutions), in the
Export As dialog box
click the plus button
in the Scale All section
to add and specify
additional scale factors
(Size) such as 2x or 3x.
Those will be exported
at the same time. Be
sure to specify the
proper option in the
Suffix field for each
scale factor.

7   In Photoshop, choose File > Browse in Bridge.

8   Navigate to the Assets_Desktop folder in the Lesson13 folder, and inspect the
    images by browsing each folder with the Preview panel open. If you want, you
    can also inspect the assets you exported to the Assets_iPhone folder.

Each layer you exported is in its own file. Just by using the Export As command,
you've created JPG images of complete artboards for two different display sizes, as
well as assets for the individual layers of each artboard.

9   In Photoshop, save your changes, and close the document.

Review questions

1 What is a layer group?

2 What is an action? How do you create one?

3 How can you create assets from layers and layer groups in Photoshop?

Review answers

1 A layer group is a group of layers. Layer groups make it easier to organize and work with layers in complex images, especially when there are sets of layers that work together.

2 An action is a set of one or more commands that you record and then play back to apply to a single file or a batch of files. To create one, click the Create New Action button in the Actions panel, name the action, and click Record. Then perform the tasks you want to include in your action. When you've finished, click the Stop Recording button at the bottom of the Actions panel.

3 Use the Export As command to create assets from layers and layer groups in Photoshop. Create images of each whole artboard by choosing File > Export > Export As, or, to create assets from selected layers and layer groups, choose Export As from the Layers panel menu.

14 PRODUCING AND PRINTING CONSISTENT COLOR

Lesson overview

In this lesson, you'll learn how to do the following:

- Understand how images are prepared for printing on presses.

- Closely examine an image before final output.

- Define RGB, grayscale, and CMYK color spaces for displaying, editing, and printing images.

- Proof an image for printing.

- Prepare an image for printing on a PostScript CMYK printer.

- Save an image as a CMYK EPS file.

- Create and print a four-color separation.

This lesson will take less than an hour to complete. Please log in to your account on peachpit.com to download the lesson files for this chapter, or go to the Getting Started section at the beginning of this book and follow the instructions under "Accessing the Lesson Files and Web Edition."

As you work on this lesson, you'll preserve the start files. If you need to restore the start files, download them from your Account page.

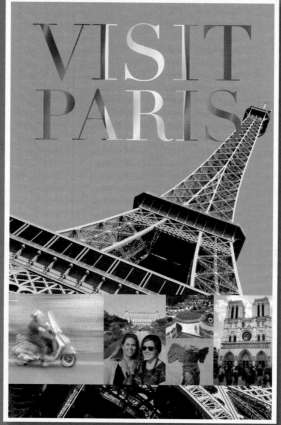

PROJECT: TRAVEL POSTER

To produce consistent color, you define the color space in which to edit and display RGB images, and the color space in which to edit, display, and proof CMYK images. This helps ensure a close match between onscreen and printed colors.

Preparing files for printing

● **Note:** One exercise in this lesson requires that your computer be connected to a printer that supports Adobe PostScript. If you don't have access to one, you can do most, but not all, of the exercises.

After you've edited an image to get the effect you want, you probably want to share or publish it in some way. Ideally, you've been editing with the final output in mind, and you've managed file resolution, colors, file size, and other aspects of the image accordingly. But as you prepare to output the file, you have another opportunity to make sure your image will look its best.

If you plan to print the image—whether you'll print it to your own inkjet printer or send it to a service provider for professional printing—you should perform the following tasks for the best results. (Many of these tasks are described in greater detail later in this lesson.)

- Determine the final destination. Whether you're printing the file yourself or sending it away, identify whether it will be printed to a PostScript desktop printer or platesetter, an inkjet printer, an offset press, or some other device. If you're working with a service provider, ask what format they prefer. In many cases, they may request a file exported to a specific PDF standard or preset.

- Verify that the image resolution is appropriate. For professional printing, 300 ppi is a good starting point. To determine the best print resolution for your project, consult your production team or your printer's user manual, because the optimal resolution can depend on factors such as the halftone screen of a press or the grade of paper.

- Do a "zoom test": Take a close look at the image. Zoom in to check and correct sharpness, color correction, noise, and other issues that can affect the final printed image quality.

- Allow for bleeds if you're sending an image for professional printing: If any color runs to the edge of the image, extend the canvas by ¼ inch on all sides to ensure that the color is properly printed even if the trim line is not exact. Your service provider can help you determine whether you have bleeds and how to prepare your file to ensure it prints correctly.

- Keep the image in its original color space until your service provider instructs you to convert it. Today, many prepress workflows keep content in its original color space throughout editing to preserve color flexibility as long as possible, and convert images and documents to CMYK only at final output time.

- Consider flattening large documents, but always consult with your production team first. Some workflows may depend on other applications, such as Adobe InDesign, which can control Photoshop layers from within their own documents. These workflows may require preserving, not flattening, Photoshop layers.

- Soft-proof the image to simulate how the colors will print.

Getting started

You'll prepare an 11"×17" travel poster for printing on a CMYK press. The Photoshop file is quite large, because it contains several layers and has a resolution of 300 dpi, which is necessary for high-quality printing.

First, start Photoshop, and restore its default preferences.

1   Start Photoshop, and then immediately hold down Ctrl+Alt+Shift (Windows) or Command+Option+Shift (Mac) to restore the default preferences. (See "Restoring Default Preferences" on page 5.)

2   When prompted, click Yes to delete the Adobe Photoshop Settings file.

3   Choose File > Open, navigate to the Lesson14 folder, and double-click the 14Start.psd file. Because the file is large, it may open slowly, depending on your system.

4   Choose File > Save As, navigate to the Lesson14 folder, and save the file as **14Working.psd**. Click OK if the Photoshop Format Options dialog box appears.

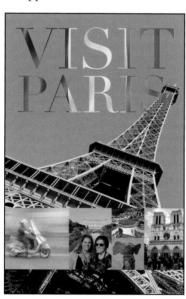

Performing a "zoom test"

▶ **Tip:** If your keyboard has Page Up, Page Down, Home, and End keys, you can use them to inspect a magnified Photoshop document. Home goes to the top left corner, and End goes to the bottom right corner. Add the Ctrl key (Windows) or the Command key (Mac) to make Page Up/Page Down keys navigate horizontally, and add the Shift key to scroll in smaller increments.

It's expensive to redo a big print job, so before you send out an image for final output, take a few minutes to make sure everything is appropriate for your output device and that you haven't overlooked any potentially problematic details. Start with the image resolution.

1   Choose Image > Image Size.

2   Verify that the width and height are the final output size and that the resolution is appropriate. For most printing, 300 ppi produces good results.

This image has a width of 11" and a height of 17", which is the final size of the poster. Its resolution is 300 ppi. The size and resolution are appropriate.

3   Click OK to close the dialog box.

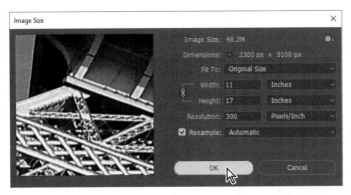

Next, you'll look closely at the image and correct any problems. When you prepare your own images for printing, zoom in and scroll to view the entire image closely.

4   Select the Zoom tool in the Tools panel, and zoom in on the photos in the lower third of the poster.

The photo of tourists is flat and a little muddy-looking.

5   Select the Tourists layer in the Layers panel, and then click the Curves icon
    in the Adjustments panel to add a Curves adjustment layer.

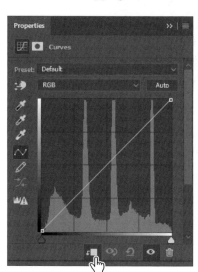

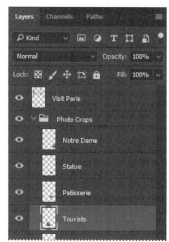

6   Click the Clip To Layer button (⌐□) at the bottom of the Properties panel
    to create a clipping mask.

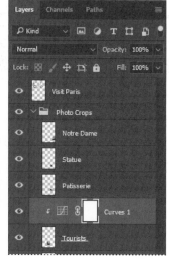

The clipping mask ensures that the adjustment layer affects only the layer directly
below it in the Layers panel.

7   In the Properties panel, select the White Point eyedropper tool, and then click the light area of the building behind the tourists to brighten and correct the color in the image.

The image of tourists looks better. But the image of the statue appears flat and lacks contrast. You'll fix that with a Levels adjustment layer.

8   Select the Statue layer in the Layers panel, and then click the Levels icon in the Adjustments panel to add a Levels adjustment layer.

9   Click the Clip To Layer button at the bottom of the Properties panel to create a clipping mask, so that the adjustment layer affects only the Statue layer.

10 In the Properties panel, click the Calculate A More Accurate Histogram icon (📊) to refresh the histogram display.

Cached histogram data displays more quickly, but is often less accurate. It's a good idea to refresh the histogram before you make edits based on information in it.

11 Move the input level sliders to punch up the image. We used the values 31, 1.60, 235.

 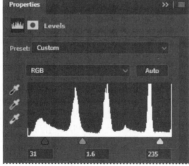

12 Save the file.

About color management

Because the RGB and CMYK color models use different methods to display colors, each reproduces a different color *gamut* (color range). For example, RGB uses light to produce color, so its gamut includes neon colors, such as those you'd see in a neon sign. In contrast, printing inks excel at reproducing certain colors that can lie outside the RGB gamut, such as some pastels and pure black.

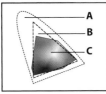

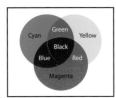

A. *Natural color gamut*
B. *RGB color gamut*
C. *CMYK color gamut*

RGB color model

CMYK color model

But not all RGB and CMYK gamuts are alike. Each monitor and printer model differs, and so each displays a slightly different gamut. For example, one brand of monitor may produce slightly brighter blues than another. The *color space* for a device is defined by the gamut it can reproduce.

The color management system in Photoshop uses International Color Consortium (ICC)-compliant color profiles that work like translators, helping to maintain color appearance when colors are converted from one color space into another. A color profile is a description of a device's color space, such as the CMYK color space of a particular printer. You specify which profiles to use to accurately proof and print your images. Once you've selected the profiles, Photoshop can embed them into your image files, so that Photoshop and other applications can consistently maintain the colors of your images.

● **Note:** Your monitor may have been factory-calibrated, but you may not know how precisely and to what standard. For example, if your print shop recommends that your monitor use the common prepress standard of a D65 white point, how do you know how well your monitor meets that standard? To make sure, calibrate and profile your monitor with D65 set as the target standard.

About calibration and profiling

Calibration means adjusting a device to meet a standard, like making sure a monitor displays neutral gray when neutral gray color values are sent to it. A *profile* describes whether the device meets a standard, and if not, how far off it is so that a color management system can correct for the difference and show image colors accurately.

To get the most out of color management, calibrate and profile your monitor so that you evaluate color on a screen using an accurate display profile. You can use calibration/profiling software that drives a color profiling device. The software uses the device to measure the colors produced by your screen, and corrects for inaccuracies by creating a customized ICC display profile of your monitor. Your system uses this display profile to show colors accurately in any software that is color-managed, such as Photoshop and most other Adobe graphics software.

RGB color model

Much of the visible color spectrum can be represented by mixing red, green, and blue (RGB) colored light in various proportions and intensities. Where the colors overlap, they create cyan, magenta, yellow, and white.

Because the RGB colors combine to create white, they are also called *additive* colors. Adding all colors together creates white—that is, all light is transmitted back to the eye. Additive colors are used for lighting, video, and monitors. For example, an LCD monitor creates color by emitting its backlight through red, green, and blue filters.

CMYK color model

The CMYK model is based on the light-absorbing quality of ink printed on paper. As white light strikes translucent inks, part of the spectrum is absorbed, while other parts are reflected back to your eyes.

In theory, pure cyan (C), magenta (M), and yellow (Y) pigments should combine to absorb all color and produce black. For this reason, these colors are called *subtractive* colors. But because all printing inks contain some impurities, these three inks actually produce a muddy brown, and must be combined with black (K) ink to produce a denser black. (K is used instead of B to avoid confusion with blue.) Combining these inks to reproduce color is called four-color process printing.

Specifying color-management settings

Even if your monitor is calibrated and profiled, accurately previewing colors onscreen also depends on correctly setting up the color-management controls in the Color Settings dialog box in Photoshop.

By default, Photoshop is set up for color gamuts that are more appropriate for an RGB-based digital workflow. If you're preparing artwork for printing on a press, as in the document used in this lesson, you'll want to change the settings to be more appropriate for CMYK-based prepress production rather than screen display.

You'll create customized color settings.

1   Choose Edit > Color Settings to open the Color Settings dialog box.

The bottom of the dialog box interactively describes each option.

2   Without clicking (don't change settings), hover the pointer over each part of the dialog box, including the names of sections (such as Working Spaces), the menu names, and the menu options. As you move the pointer, Photoshop displays information about each item in the Description area.

Now, you'll choose a set of options designed for a print workflow.

3   Choose North America Prepress 2 from the Settings menu. The working spaces and color-management policy options change for a prepress workflow. Then click OK.

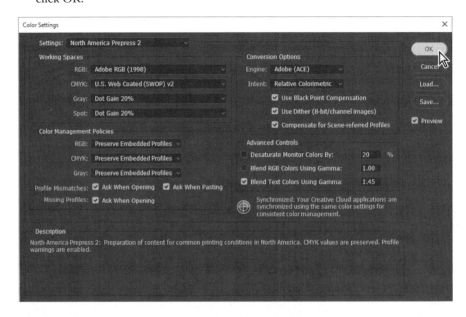

Identifying out-of-gamut colors

Colors on a monitor are displayed using combinations of red, green, and blue light (called RGB), while printed colors are typically created using a combination of four ink colors—cyan, magenta, yellow, and black (called CMYK). These four inks are called *process colors* because they are the standard inks used in the four-color printing process.

Many colors produced by digital cameras and scanners are within the gamut of typical CMYK print colors. But an RGB image may contain some colors, such as colored LED lights or vivid flowers, that are outside a printer's CMYK gamut. Those colors may print with less detail and saturation than expected. Some intense blue colors in RGB can shift toward purple in CMYK.

Before you convert an image from RGB to CMYK, you can preview which RGB color values are outside the gamut of CMYK.

1   Choose View > Fit On Screen.

2   Choose View > Gamut Warning to see out-of-gamut colors. Photoshop builds a color-conversion table, and displays a neutral gray in the image window to indicate where the colors are out of gamut.

The gray gamut warning covers much of the image, especially the blue areas. A typical CMYK press can reproduce a relatively narrow range of blue compared to most RGB gamuts, so it's not unusual for an image to have RGB blue values that are outside a CMYK printing gamut.

Because the gray indicator color can be hard to distinguish in the image, you'll change it to a more visible color.

3   Choose Edit > Preferences > Transparency & Gamut (Windows) or Photoshop CC > Preferences > Transparency & Gamut (Mac).

4   Click the color sample in the Gamut Warning area at the bottom of the dialog box. Select a vivid color, such as purple or bright green, and click OK.

5   Click OK to close the Preferences dialog box.

▶ **Tip:** If your gamut warning area looks different, you may be using different settings in the View > Proof Setup > Custom dialog box (see page 356).

The bright new color you chose appears instead of the neutral gray as the gamut warning color, and it should be much more obvious which areas are out of gamut.

6   Choose View > Gamut Warning to turn off the preview of out-of-gamut colors.

Next, you'll simulate onscreen how the document colors might print, and then you'll bring those colors into the printing gamut.

Proofing document colors on a monitor

You'll select a proof profile so that you can view an onscreen simulation of what document colors will look like when printed. An accurate proof profile lets you proof on the screen (*soft-proof*) for printed output.

A *proof setup* defines the printing conditions, which determines the onscreen simulation. Photoshop provides a variety of settings that can help you proof images for different uses, including for different printers and devices. For this lesson, you'll create a custom proof setup. You can then save the settings for use on other images that will be output the same way.

1   Choose View > Proof Setup > Custom. The Customize Proof Condition dialog
    box opens. Make sure Preview is selected.

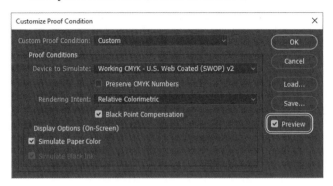

▶ **Tip:** A printer profile
represents not only the
output device, but also
a specific combination
of settings, ink, and
paper. Changing any of
those components can
change the color gamut
being simulated by
the onscreen proof, so
choose a profile that's
as close as possible
to the final printing
conditions.

2   From the Device To Simulate menu, choose a profile that represents the final
    output device, such as that for the printer you'll use to print the image. If you
    don't have a specific printer, use the profile Working CMYK–U.S. Web Coated
    (SWOP) v2, the current default.

3   If you've chosen a different profile, make sure Preserve Numbers
    is *not* selected.

The Preserve Numbers option simulates how colors will appear if they're not converted to the output device color space. This option may be named Preserve CMYK
Numbers when you select a CMYK output profile.

4   Make sure Relative Colorimetric is selected for the Rendering Intent.

A rendering intent determines how the color is converted from one color space
to another. Relative Colorimetric preserves color relationships without sacrificing
color accuracy, and is the standard rendering intent for printing in North America
and Europe.

5   Select Simulate Black Ink if it's available for the profile you chose. Then deselect it
    and select Simulate Paper Color; notice that selecting this option automatically
    selects Simulate Black Ink.

▶ **Tip:** When the
Customize Proof
Condition dialog box
isn't open, you can view
the document with or
without the current
proof settings by
selecting or deselecting
the View > Proof Colors
command.

Notice that the image appears to lose contrast. Paper Color simulates the dingy white
of real paper, according to the proof profile. Black Ink simulates the dark gray that most
printers actually produce, instead of solid black. Not all profiles support these options.

Don't be alarmed by the loss of contrast and saturation that you may see when you turn
on the Display Options. While the image might look worse, the soft-proofing simulation is just being honest about how the image will actually print; paper and ink simply
cannot reproduce white and colors as brightly as a monitor. Choosing higher-quality
paper stock and inks can help a printed image match the screen more closely.

6   Toggle the Preview option to see the difference between the image as it is displayed on screen and as it will print, based on the profile you selected. Then click OK.

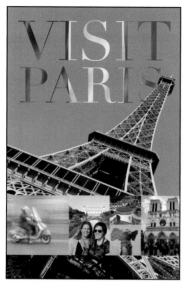

Normal image

Image with Simulate Paper Color and Simulate Black Ink options selected

Bringing colors into the output gamut

The next step in preparing an image for output is to make any necessary color and tonal adjustments. In this exercise, you'll add some tonal and color adjustments to correct an off-color scan of the original poster.

So that you can compare the image before and after making corrections, you'll start by making a copy.

1   Choose Image > Duplicate, and click OK to duplicate the image.

2   Choose Window > Arrange > 2 Up Vertical so you can compare the images as you work.

You'll adjust the hue and saturation of the image to move all colors into gamut.

3   Select 14Working.psd (the original image) to make it active, and then select the Visit Paris layer in the Layers panel.

4   Choose Select > Color Range.

► **Tip:** It isn't always necessary to correct colors that are indicated as out of gamut. The best use of the gamut warning is to know which colors to inspect more closely when you proof document colors. If out-of-gamut colors look acceptable when proofing, they may not need to be changed.

5   In the Color Range dialog box, choose Out of Gamut from the Select menu, and then click OK.

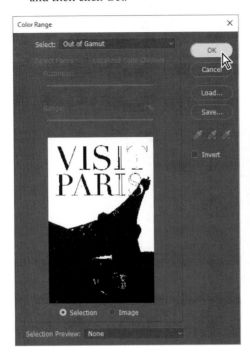 

The areas that were marked as out of gamut earlier are now selected, so you can make changes that affect only those areas.

6   Choose View > Extras to hide the selection while you work with it.

The selection border can be distracting. When you hide extras, you no longer see the selection, but it's still in effect.

7   Click the Hue/Saturation button in the Adjustments panel to create a Hue/Saturation adjustment layer. (Choose Window > Adjustments if the panel isn't open.) The Hue/Saturation adjustment layer includes a layer mask, created from your selection.

8   In the Properties panel, do the following:

   • Leave the Hue setting at the default value.

   • Drag the Saturation slider until the intensity of the colors looks more realistic (we used –14).

   • Drag the Lightness to the left to darken the image (we used –2).

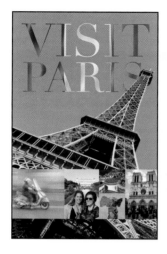

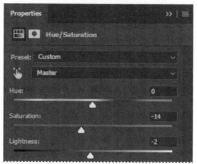

9 Choose View > Gamut Warning. You have shifted most of the out-of-gamut colors so that they're in the target gamut. Choose View > Gamut Warning again to deselect it.

10 Choose View > Extras to enable it, so that selection marquees and other non-printing aids are visible again.

11 Close the duplicate image file (the 14Working copy tab) without saving it.

In this exercise, you shifted out-of-gamut colors into the printing gamut mostly by desaturating them. While this is quick and easy, it's considered a basic technique. Skilled image editors use more advanced techniques to preserve color detail while maintaining as much of the original color saturation as possible. Also, when an out-of-gamut color doesn't contain much detail, as in a flat blue sky, it may be acceptable to leave it unchanged.

▶ **Tip:** You can also make adjustments with Gamut Warning on, so that you know when the colors move into the printing gamut.

Converting an image to CMYK

It's generally a good idea to work in RGB mode as long as possible, so that your edits can take place within the larger color gamut of RGB. Also, converting between modes can cause color value rounding errors that may result in unwanted color changes, especially over multiple conversions.

Once you've made final corrections, you're ready to convert the image to CMYK. If you think you may want to output the image to an inkjet printer or distribute it digitally later, save a copy in RGB mode before converting to CMYK mode.

1 Click the Channels tab to bring the Channels panel to the front.

The image is currently in RGB mode, so there are three channels listed: red, green, and blue. The RGB channel is not actually a channel, but a composite of all three. You also see a channel named Hue/Saturation 1 Mask; this channel contains the mask information for the layer currently selected in the Layers panel.

2   Choose Image > Mode > CMYK Color.

3   Click Merge in the message that warns you that you might lose some adjustment layers. Merging the layers helps preserve the appearance of colors.

Another message appears, saying: "You are about to convert to CMYK using the "U.S. Web Coated (SWOP) v2" profile. This may not be what you intend. To choose a different profile, use Edit > Convert To Profile." This message lets you know that the active CMYK profile is U.S. Web Coated (SWOP) v2, the Photoshop default profile for CMYK color. That profile might not represent the actual prepress specification or proofing standard that will be used. In a real world job, you would ask the print service provider which CMYK profile to use for color conversions; they may be able to provide a custom profile that accurately represents the tonal and color range of their equipment.

4   Click OK in the message about the color profile used in the conversion.

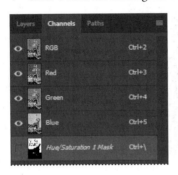 

The Channels panel now displays four channels: cyan, magenta, yellow, and black. Additionally, it lists the CMYK composite. The layers were merged during conversion, so there is only one layer in the Layers panel.

Saving the image as a CMYK EPS file

Some professional printers request that Photoshop images be submitted in EPS format. While this format is used less often in newer prepress workflows, it's still good to know how to convert a document into it. You'll save this image as an EPS file in CMYK mode.

1   Choose File > Save As.

2   In the Save As dialog box, do the following, and then click Save:

   • Choose Photoshop EPS from the Format menu.

   • Under Color, select Use Proof Setup. Don't worry about the warning icon; you'll save a copy.

   • Accept the filename 14Working.eps.

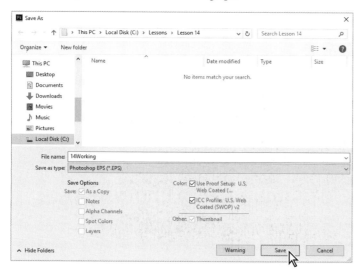

3   Click OK in the EPS Options dialog box that appears.

4   Save and then close the 14Working.psd file.

5   Choose File > Open, navigate to the Lessons/Lesson14 folder, and double-click the 14Working.eps file.

Printing to a desktop inkjet printer

Many color inkjet printers do a good job printing photographs and other image files. The precise settings available vary from printer to printer, and they're different than the best settings for a press. When you're printing images from Photoshop to a desktop inkjet printer, you'll get the best results if you do the following:

- Make sure the appropriate printer driver is installed, and that you've selected it. Leaving the printer driver on a generic setting such as "Any Printer" may result in problems such as incorrect page margins.

- Use the appropriate paper for your intended use. Special photographic and coated papers are a good choice when you're printing photos for framing.

- Select the correct paper source and media setting in the printer settings. The printer varies how it lays down ink on different types of paper. For example, if you're using photo-quality paper, make sure it's selected in the printer settings.

- Select the image quality in the printer settings. Higher print quality is better when viewing is critical, such as for color proofing or framed prints. Lower print quality is useful for speedier printing and for using less ink.

- Don't convert an RGB image to CMYK just to print on a desktop inkjet printer, because most are designed to receive RGB images and convert for their own inks. You might need to convert images to CMYK only for specialized printing, such as simulating separations on a desktop printer equipped with Adobe PostScript.

Printing a CMYK image from Photoshop

▶ **Tip:** Printing color separations on your desktop printer can help verify that colors will appear on the correct plate. But separations from a desktop printer won't match the precision of an actual platesetter. Proofs you create for jobs intended for a press are more accurate on a desktop printer with an Adobe PostScript RIP (raster image processor).

You can proof your image by printing a *color composite*, often called a *color comp*. A color composite is a single print that combines the red, green, and blue channels of an RGB image (or the cyan, magenta, yellow, and black channels of a CMYK image). This indicates what the final printed image will look like.

If you're printing color separations of an image directly from Photoshop, you will typically use the following workflow:

- Set the parameters for the halftone screen. Consult with your print service provider for recommended settings.

- Print test separations to make sure objects appear on the correct separation.

- Print the final separations to plate or film. This is typically performed by your print service provider.

When you print color separations, Photoshop prints a separate sheet, or *plate*, for each ink. For a CMYK image, it prints four plates, one for each process color. In this exercise, you'll print color separations.

1   With the 14Working.eps image open from the previous exercise, choose
    File > Print.

By default, Photoshop prints any document as a composite image. To print this
file as separations, you must set it up accordingly in the Photoshop Print Settings
dialog box.

2   In the Photoshop Print Settings dialog box, do the following:

   •   In the Printer Setup section, make sure the selected Printer is the one you want
       to use.

   •   In the Color Management area, choose Separations from the Color
       Handling menu.

   •   In the Position and Size section, verify that the settings are correct. This
       11"×17" document may be too large for many desktop printers to print at
       actual size; consider selecting Scale to Fit Media for basic proofing.

   •   Click Print. (If you don't actually want to print color separations, click
       Cancel or Done; the difference is that Done saves the current print settings.)

▶ **Tip:** In the
Photoshop Print
Settings dialog box, if
the Separations option
is not available in the
Color Handling menu,
click Done, and make
sure the document is in
CMYK mode (Image >
Mode > CMYK Color).

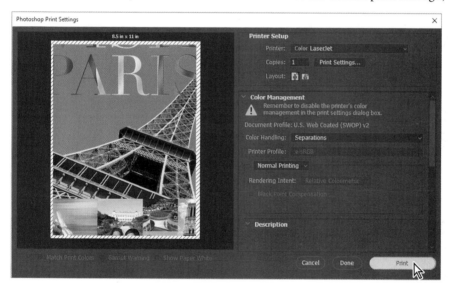

▶ **Tip:** The Position
and Size section of
the Photoshop Print
Settings dialog box is
two sections below the
Color Management
section, so if you can't
see it, scroll down
the right side panel.
Also, you can enlarge
the Photoshop Print
Settings dialog box
by dragging a corner
or edge so that you
can see more options
at once.

This lesson has provided an introduction to printing and producing consistent
color from Photoshop. If you're printing on a desktop printer, you can experiment
with different settings to find the best color and print settings for your system. If
you're preparing images for professional printing, consult with your print service
provider to determine the best settings to use. For more information about color
management, printing options, and color separations, see Photoshop Help.

Extra Credit

Sharing your work on Adobe Portfolio

Integrated into Adobe Creative Cloud is Adobe Portfolio, which you can use to quickly create a well-designed and functional website that showcases your creations, with one-click connections to your social media presence (such as your Instagram, Facebook, and Twitter feeds) and a pre-built contact form that makes it easy for potential clients and customers to get in touch with you. To test it out, you'll first prepare this lesson's image for viewing in a web browser.

1. Open the 14Start.psd file in Photoshop, if it isn't already open. Click OK if the Embedded Profile Mismatch dialog box appears.

   As the original RGB version of the image in this chapter, 14Start.psd contains a wider color gamut than the later version that was converted to CMYK for prepress.

2. Choose File > Export > Export As to prepare the image for display on a website. It's a large, print-resolution image, so it may take a while to display in the Export As dialog box.

3. Choose JPG from the Format menu, and set Quality to **90%**.

4. In the Image Size section, enter **918** for Height. This will proportionally resize the image to 918 pixels high, so that the entire image can be seen at 100% magnification on many displays.

5. In the Color Space section, select Convert to sRGB and Embed Color Profile to help ensure consistent color in Web browsers.

6. Click Export All. Navigate to the Lesson14 folder, and click Export or Save.

Now you can start your online portfolio. The Portfolio user interface you see may vary as Adobe updates the service.

1   In a web browser, go to myportfolio.com, the web address for Adobe Portfolio.

2   At the top of the Adobe Portfolio home page, click Sign In, enter your Adobe ID email address and password, and click Sign In.

3   Click Get Started Free or Edit Your Sites, scroll to preview the layouts you can use, and then choose Try This Layout. We picked Lina. If an "Edit Your Portfolio" button appears, click it.

4   Click the Add Content button, and then click Page. Enter **Visit Paris**, and then click Create Page. If a Continue button appears, click it.

5   Now add your work. Click Files, navigate to the Lesson14 folder, select 14Start.jpg, and then click Choose or Open (the button name depends on the web browser you use). Adobe Portfolio processes the image and adds it to the page.

6   In the Add Content section of the floating remote, click Text, and then type "Poster created for the Visit Paris campaign." Highlight the text to select it, and a formatting bar appears above the text so that you can change text settings if you want.

7   In the preview, click Preview. The buttons at the bottom of the preview show you how the page will look on different device displays and orientations, such as a smartphone held vertically or horizontally.

Continues on next page

Extra credit (continued)

8   In the preview remote, click Back to Edit.

9   As you move the pointer over different page elements, a round edit icon appears in the top left corner of that page element. Click the edit icon to see options for editing that element.

10 Use the floating remote control to add or edit the content on this page, or click the Return to Home button at the top left corner to add and organize more pages on your Adobe Portfolio website.

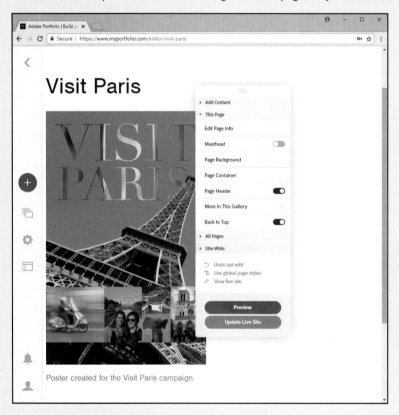

Poster created for the Visit Paris campaign.

You can change many design options for your Adobe Portfolio site, such as the fonts, font sizes, background colors, and spacing. You can also change the overall layout at any time. If you have your own Internet domain name, you can easily connect it to Adobe Portfolio so that your website's address is fully consistent with your brand.

If your site looks good and you want the world to see it, click Publish Site. It's live!

If you published the site but you don't want the world to see it yet, click the Settings (gear) icon, click Unpublish Portfolio, choose options, and click the Unpublish Portfolio button. Alternatively, you can publish the site but set a password in the Password Protection section of the Settings panel.

Review questions

1 What steps should you follow to reproduce color accurately?

2 What is a gamut?

3 What is a color profile?

4 What are color separations?

Review answers

1 To reproduce color accurately, first calibrate and profile your monitor, and then use the Color Settings dialog box to specify which color spaces to use. For example, you can specify which RGB color space to use for online images, and which CMYK color space to use for images that will be printed. You can then proof the image, check for out-of-gamut colors, and adjust colors as needed.

2 A gamut is the range of colors that can be reproduced by a color model or device. For example, the RGB and CMYK color models have different gamuts. Within each color model, various printers, printing standards, and device displays reproduce different gamuts.

3 A color profile is a description of a device's color space, such as the CMYK color space of a particular printer. Applications such as Photoshop can interpret color profiles in an image to maintain consistent color across different applications, platforms, and devices.

4 Color separations are separate plates for each ink used in a document being reproduced on press. Your print service provider will produce color separations of your files for the cyan, magenta, yellow, and black (CMYK) inks.

15 PRINTING 3D FILES

Lesson overview

In this lesson, you'll learn how to do the following:

- Create a simple 3D object using a mesh preset.

- Use 3D tools in Photoshop.

- Manipulate 3D objects.

- Adjust the camera view.

- Prepare 3D files for printing.

- Export a file for remote printing.

 This lesson will take about 30 minutes to complete. Please log in to your account on peachpit.com to download the lesson files for this chapter, or go to the Getting Started section at the beginning of this book and follow the instructions under "Accessing the Lesson Files and Web Edition."

As you work on this lesson, you'll preserve the start files. If you need to restore the start files, download them from your Account page.

PROJECT: 3D LUGGAGE TAG

You can print 3D objects directly from Photoshop. If you have a 3D printer on site, you can print locally. Otherwise, you can export your file for printing by an online vendor.

Getting started

Photoshop has a basic set of 3D capabilities, mostly intended to create simple 3D objects or integrate existing 3D models for use as part of a Photoshop composition. In this lesson, you'll learn how to navigate 3D space, create a simple 3D shape, and print to a 3D printer. You'll do all of this while creating a three-dimensional luggage tag. First, you'll view the finished tag.

1 Start Photoshop, and then immediately hold down Ctrl+Alt+Shift (Windows) or Command+Option+Shift (Mac) to restore the default preferences. (See "Restoring Default Preferences" on page 5.)

2 When prompted, click Yes to delete the Adobe Photoshop Settings file.

3 Choose File > Browse In Bridge to open Adobe Bridge.

4 In Bridge, click Lessons in the Favorites panel. Double-click the Lesson15 folder in the Content panel.

5 View the 15End.psd file in Bridge.

The 15End.psd file contains a 3D rendering of a luggage tag. In this lesson, you'll combine elements to create the luggage tag, and then prepare it for printing. If you want to, you can print it locally to a 3D printer or export it to an online vendor for printing. (You'll see estimated costs before placing the order.)

Before you create the luggage tag, you'll play with the 3D tools to become familiar with the 3D environment.

6 Return to Photoshop.

Understanding the 3D environment

The advantage to working with 3D objects is, obviously, that you can work with them in three dimensions. You can also return to a 3D layer at any time to change its lighting, color, material, or position. Photoshop includes several basic tools that make it easy to rotate, resize, and position 3D objects. 3D tools in the options bar manipulate a 3D object. A Camera widget in the lower left corner of the application window manipulates the camera so you can view a 3D scene from different angles.

You can use the 3D tools whenever a 3D layer is selected in the Layers panel. A 3D layer behaves like any other layer—you can apply layer styles, mask it, and so on. However, a 3D layer can be quite complex.

Unlike a regular layer, a 3D layer contains one or more *meshes*. A mesh defines the 3D object. For example, in the following exercise, the mesh is a cone shape. Each mesh, in turn, includes one or more *materials*—the appearance of a part or all of the mesh. Each material includes one or more *maps*, which are the components of the appearance. There are nine typical maps, and there can be only one of each kind; however, you can also use custom maps. Each map contains one *texture*—the image that defines what the maps and materials look like. The texture may be a simple bitmap graphic or a set of layers. The same texture might be used by many different maps and materials.

In addition to meshes, a 3D layer also includes one or more *lights*, which affect the appearance of 3D objects and remain in a fixed position as you spin or move the object. A 3D layer also includes *cameras*, which are saved views with the objects in a particular position. The *shader* creates the final appearance based on the materials, object properties, and renderer.

That may all sound complicated, but the most important thing to remember is that the 3D tools in the options bar move an object in 3D space and the Camera widget moves a camera that produces your view of the object.

You'll start by creating a simple 3D object from a plain colored layer.

1   In Photoshop, choose File > New. Click Create to accept the default values.

2   Choose Select > All to select the entire background layer.

3   Choose Edit > Fill. In the Fill dialog box, choose Color from the Contents menu, and then select a vivid blue color in the Color Picker. Click OK to close the Color Picker, and click OK again to close the Fill dialog box.

4   Choose Select > Deselect.

5 Choose 3D > New Mesh From Layer > Mesh Preset > Cone. If you see a message asking whether you want to switch to the 3D workspace, click Yes.

▶ **Tip:** If you see an Embedded Profile Mismatch message, click OK.

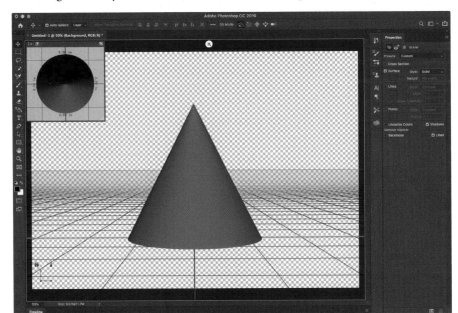

▶ **Tip:** If a window opens describing Adobe Dimension CC, close it. If 3D is an important part of your work, you may want to explore Dimension at a later time. Dimension makes it easy for graphic designers to create high-quality, photo-realistic 3D images. You can composite 2D and 3D assets to build product shots, scene visualizations, and abstract art, and it works with Photoshop. To learn more, go to adobe.com/products/dimension.html.

Your blue layer becomes a blue cone. Photoshop displays a grid, a Secondary View window, a Camera widget, and other 3D resources. Now that you have a 3D object, you can use the 3D tools.

6 In the Tools panel, select the Move tool (✛).

All the 3D capabilities are embedded into the Move tool, which recognizes when a 3D layer is selected and enables the 3D tools.

7 In the options bar, select the Pan the 3D Camera mode (✣).

When no 3D object is selected, the 3D Mode affects how the Move tool changes the camera; when a 3D object is selected, the 3D Mode affects how the Move tool transforms an object.

▶ **Tip:** When using the Move tool in any 3D Camera mode, it's important to drag outside any objects. If you click an object, the object will become selected, so the Move tool will edit the object instead of the camera.

8 Click the edge of the cone or just outside it (but not the cone itself), and drag to move it from side to side or up and down. Return the cone to the center.

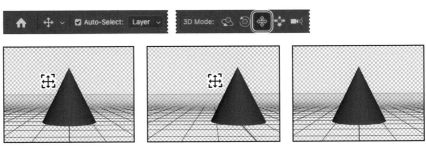

9   Select the Orbit the 3D Camera tool (⟲) in the options bar, and then click and drag the cone to rotate the view. Experiment with the other tools to see how they affect the view of the object.

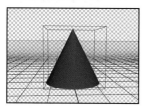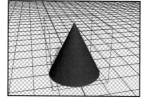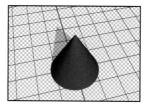

10 With the Move tool, click the cone to select it.

When you select a 3D object, Photoshop displays the 3D Axis widget inside the object. You can use that widget to manipulate a selected 3D object. The three colors of the widget represent different 3D axes: Red represents the x axis, green represents the y axis, and blue represents the z axis. Hover the pointer over different parts of the 3D Axis widget to highlight different controls:

- To scale the selected 3D object uniformly, position the pointer over the gray box at the center of the 3D Axis widget until it turns yellow, and then drag the box.

- To move a selected 3D object along one axis, position the pointer over the arrow at the end of one of the axes on the 3D Axis widget, and drag the arrow.

- To rotate a selected 3D object on one axis, position the pointer over the curved handle just before the arrow at the end of one of the 3D widget axes, and drag the curved handle.

11 Rotate, scale, and move the cone using the widget.

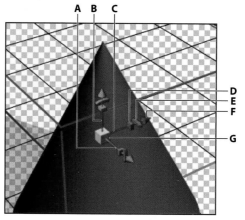

A. Z axis B. Y axis C. X axis D. Scale along X axis
E. Rotate around Y axis F. Move on X axis
G. Scale uniformly

▶ **Tip:** Can't remember which 3D Axis widget color controls which axis? The order of the RGB widget colors corresponds to the order of the XYZ axes: Red controls X, Green controls Y, and Blue controls Z. Also, pay attention to the tool tips that appear as you move the pointer over 3D controls, because they describe what each control does.

▶ **Tip:** Be aware that the 3D Axis moves with an object, so if you can't see the part of the 3D Axis widget that you want to manipulate, it may be at a hard-to-see angle or hidden by part of the widget. Try rotating the 3D view slightly to better see parts of the widget.

12 Right-click (Windows) or Control-click (Mac) the Camera widget in the lower left corner of the application window (it has two axes visible), and choose Top.

 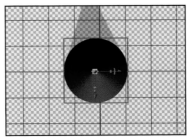

Options in the Camera menu determine the angle from which you see the object. The camera angle changes, but the object itself does not. Don't be fooled by its relationship to the background; the background is not 3D, so it remains in place when Photoshop moves the camera for the 3D object.

13 Choose other camera views to see how they affect the perspective.

14 When you're done experimenting, close the file. You can save your creation if you want to, or close without saving.

Positioning 3D elements

Now that you've gotten a feel for the 3D tools, you'll use them to position the text on a luggage tag.

▶ **Tip:** If you see an Embedded Profile Mismatch message, click OK.

1 Choose File > Open, navigate to the Lesson15 folder, and double-click the 15Start.psd file.

The file contains two 3D elements: the text and the tag itself. Currently, the text is in an awkward position, overlapping the tag. You'll start by centering it.

▶ **Tip:** If you have trouble selecting a 3D object, as you position the Move tool, don't click until the object's 3D bounding box appears around it. A 3D object becomes selected only when you click a solid part of that object, not the spaces around or within it.

2 Make sure the Move tool is selected in the Tools panel.

3 Position the pointer over the "Visit Paris" text, and when its bounding box appears, click to select it and activate its 3D widget.

4 Hover the cursor over the tip of the green arrow until the Move On Y Axis tool tip appears.

5 Click the tip of the green arrow, and drag the type down until it's centered vertically on the red tag.

6 Click the tip of the red arrow, and drag the type to the right so that it's horizontally centered on the red tag.

 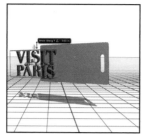 

Your tag is ready to print!

7 Choose File > Save As. Navigate to the Lesson15 folder, and save the file as **15Working.psd**. Click OK in the Photoshop Format Options dialog box.

Printing a 3D file

When you think of printing, you usually think of producing a flat page of two-dimensional text and images. They may be high-quality, amazing images, but you can't see them from different angles, and what you hold in your hand remains a piece of paper or other relatively simple media.

3D printers open up a whole new world of printing opportunities. Instead of printing an image of a thing, you can print the thing itself. The possibilities are endless, including medical uses, prototyping, and creative enterprises such as making jewelry and one-of-a-kind souvenirs.

3D printers were once the province of well-funded labs, but have recently become much more accessible. In many communities, you can use one at a "maker" or do-it-yourself (DIY) space, a shared workshop area where, for a fee, you can use many advanced resources. If you don't have a 3D printer yourself or easy access to one, you can also send your 3D creations to online vendors, who will print them using the material you specify and mail them to you.

You can create 3D objects in Photoshop—or import 3D objects that have been created elsewhere—and print them directly from Photoshop.

Specifying 3D print settings

You don't use the standard Print dialog box to print 3D objects from Photoshop. And before you print, you need to make sure the settings are appropriate.

1   Choose 3D > 3D Print Settings.

The Properties panel displays the 3D print settings, and the image window shows a preview of your 3D object. The preview shows you how it will look when printed, based on the printer you select.

2   Choose Shapeways from the Print To menu in the Properties panel.

Shapeways is an online vendor that prints 3D objects and ships them to you for a fee. There are other online vendors, but Shapeways is easy to use because you can choose its printers directly within Photoshop. If you use another vendor, ask them for instructions for printing from Photoshop.

If you own a 3D printer, choose Local from the Print To menu, and then choose your printer from the Printer menu. If your printer isn't listed in the menu, choose Get Latest Printers from the Print To menu, and then download the profiles for all supported printers.

▶ **Tip:** You can learn more about the materials available through Shapeways, and compare costs of various options, by visiting http://www. shapeways.com/ materials.

When you choose Shapeways from the Print To menu, the Printer menu lists many material options. The material you select affects the appearance and cost of the object you print, and the list of materials depends on which printer you've selected.

3   Choose Plastic - Alumide from the Printer menu. Plastic alumide is a plastic that simulates metal.

The preview of the 3D object changes in the image window to reflect the choices you've made. When you choose Plastic - Alumide, the preview shows a silver-gray tag with extruded text.

4   Make sure Inches is selected in the Printer Units menu to specify how printer volume should be measured.

3D printers have different capacities, and it's important to consider whether your object will fit within the printer's volume. The Printer Volume values are dimmed, because you can't change them; they describe the volume for the printer you've chosen. The Scene Volume values reflect the size of your 3D scene (in this case, a single object). If the Show option is selected, the preview shows a cube outline to represent the printer volume that the scene lies within.

If the scene volume is larger than the printer volume, click Scale To Print Volume in the Properties panel to reduce its size so that your printer can print it. In this case, the scene volume is comfortably smaller than the printer volume.

5   Choose Medium from the Detail Level menu. This option determines how detailed the preview image is.

The Surface Detail options preserve bump maps and other texture and opacity settings when you print. You can leave those options selected, though there are no bump maps or opacity settings in this object.

You're ready to print.

Exporting a 3D object

Printing a 3D object is a little more complicated than printing a two-dimensional image. It's not that much more challenging for the person doing the printing, but Photoshop has to do a lot of behind-the-scenes calculations.

3D printers build objects from the bottom. If you're printing a cube, for example, or another object with a significant base, the printer can create it without further support. However, many 3D objects are irregularly shaped, and the bottom of the object may actually be a set of disconnected surfaces. For example, think of a model of an animal. The bottom of the animal is composed of the four separate feet. In order to print such an object, the printer requires a support structure. That structure typically includes a *raft*, which provides a base to print from, and *scaffolding*, which supports portions of the object so they don't collapse while the rest of the object is being printed.

When you choose 3D Print, Photoshop prepares the object for printing, and calculates any necessary raft and scaffolding as well.

1   Choose 3D > 3D Print, or click the Start Print icon (⊥) at the bottom of the Properties panel.

Photoshop displays a progress bar as it prepares the print job. This may take some time, depending on the speed of your computer.

2   Click OK in the dialog box that informs you that the estimated price may differ from the final purchase price.

3   In the Photoshop 3D Print Settings dialog box, review the estimated price and print size.

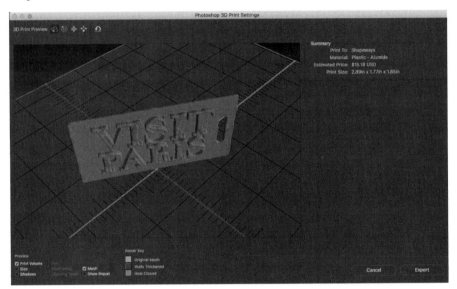

Click options in the Preview area of the dialog box to see the size, shadows, raft, scaffolding, and other aspects of the job. This object requires no raft or scaffolding, so those options are dimmed.

Use the 3D tools at the top of the dialog box to see your object from different angles.

Printing prices vary dramatically depending on the material you choose. You can click Cancel, choose a different printer, and then let Photoshop calculate the price again. You've made no commitments at this point in the process.

4   Click Export.

5   Click Save in the Save dialog box.

Photoshop exports the 3D print file information to the file 15Working.stl.

6   When you're prompted to upload your exported file to the Shapeways website for printing, click Yes to continue to the site, or click No to stop the process.

7   If you continue to the Shapeways site, sign in if you have an account, or create one if you don't. (Creating an account is free.)

8   On the Shapeways website, click Upload. (The Upload button may be hidden in a menu.) Follow the directions for uploading, and if prompted, specify inches as the unit of measure. Choose the file named 15Working.stl.zip, which will be in the Lesson15 folder. Then click Upload.

Shapeways uploads and unzips the file. It displays the object and lists possible materials and their prices, along with a 3D preview you can rotate by dragging.

● **Note:** You are not committed to a purchase until you check out and pay for the object.

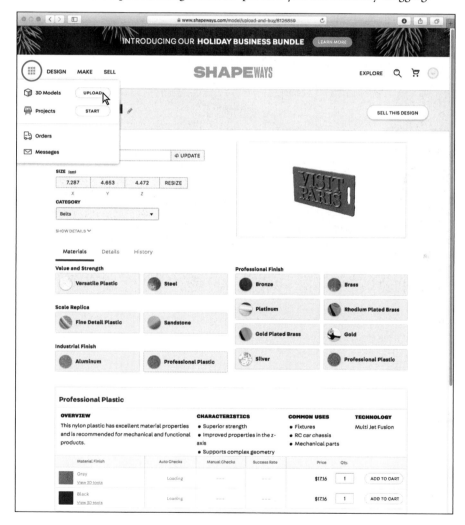

9 If you want to pay to have the object printed, click to apply material options and then click Add To Cart, and then follow the onscreen instructions to place your order. The printed object will be shipped to you.

If you don't want to have Shapeways print the object, you can optionally sign out of the Shapeways site and close the web page.

Review questions

1 How does a 3D layer differ from other layers in Photoshop?

2 How can you change the camera view?

3 Which color represents each axis on the 3D Axis widget?

4 How do you print a 3D object?

Review answers

1 A 3D layer behaves like any other layer—you can apply layer styles, mask it, and so on. However, unlike a regular layer, a 3D layer also contains one or more meshes, which define 3D objects. You can work with meshes and the materials, maps, and textures they contain. You can also adjust the lighting for a 3D layer.

2 To change the camera view, you can move the Camera widget, or right-click (Windows) or Control-click (Mac) the widget to choose a camera view preset.

3 In the 3D Axis widget, the red arrow represents the X axis, the green arrow represents the Y axis, and the blue arrow represents the Z axis.

4 To print a 3D object from Photoshop, first choose 3D > 3D Print Settings, and set up your printer options. Then choose 3D > 3D Print, or click the Start Print icon at the bottom of the Properties panel.

Appendix: Tools panel overview

Photoshop CC 2019 Tools Panel

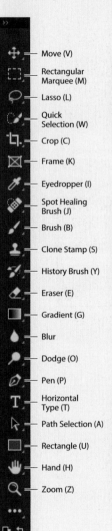

- Move (V)
- Rectangular Marquee (M)
- Lasso (L)
- Quick Selection (W)
- Crop (C)
- Frame (K)
- Eyedropper (I)
- Spot Healing Brush (J)
- Brush (B)
- Clone Stamp (S)
- History Brush (Y)
- Eraser (E)
- Gradient (G)
- Blur
- Dodge (O)
- Pen (P)
- Horizontal Type (T)
- Path Selection (A)
- Rectangle (U)
- Hand (H)
- Zoom (Z)

The Move tool moves selections, layers, and guides.

The Artboard tool moves, resizes, and adds artboards.

The marquee tools make rectangular, elliptical, single row, and single column selections.

The lasso tools make free-hand, polygonal (straight-edged), and magnetic (snap-to) selections.

The Quick Selection tool lets you quickly "paint" a selection using an adjustable round brush tip.

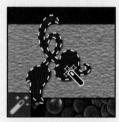

The Magic Wand tool selects similarly colored areas.

The crop tools trim, straighten, and change the perspective of images.

The Frame tool creates placeholder rectangles, so you can design now and drop in final artwork later.

The Slice tool creates slices which can be exported as separate images.

The Slice Select tool selects slices.

The Eyedropper tool samples colors in an image.

The 3D Material Eyedropper tool loads selected material from a 3D object.

The Color Sampler tool samples up to four areas of an image.

The Ruler tool measures distances, locations, and angles.

The Note tool makes notes that can be attached to an image.

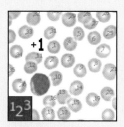

The Count tool counts objects in an image.

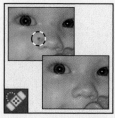

The Spot Healing Brush tool quickly removes blemishes and imperfections from photographs that have a uniform background.

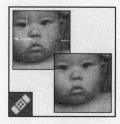

The Healing Brush tool paints with a sample or pattern to repair imperfections in an image.

Continues on next page

Appendix: Tools panel overview (continued)

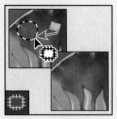

The Patch tool repairs imperfections in a selected area of an image, using a sample or pattern.

The Content-Aware Move tool recomposes and blends pixels to accommodate a moved object.

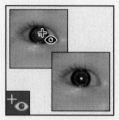

The Red Eye tool removes red eye in flash photos with one click.

The Brush tool paints brush strokes.

The Pencil tool paints hard-edged strokes.

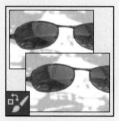

The Color Replacement tool substitutes one color for another.

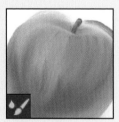

The Mixer Brush tool blends a sampled color with an existing color.

The Clone Stamp tool paints with a sample of an image.

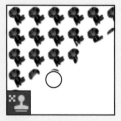

The Pattern Stamp tool paints with a part of an image as a pattern.

The History Brush tool paints a copy of the selected state or snapshot into the current image window.

The Art History Brush tool paints stylized strokes that simulate the look of different paint styles.

The Eraser tool erases pixels and restores parts of an image to a previously saved state.

The Background Eraser tool erases areas to transparency by dragging.

The Magic Eraser tool erases solid-colored areas to transparency in a single click.

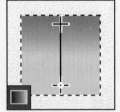

The Gradient tool creates straight-line, radial, angle, reflected, and diamond blends between colors.

The Paint Bucket tool fills similarly colored areas with the foreground color.

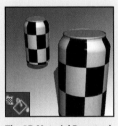

The 3D Material Drop tool drops the material loaded in the 3D Material Eyedropper tool onto the targeted area of a 3D object.

The Blur tool blurs hard edges in an image.

Continues on next page

Appendix: Tools panel overview (continued)

The Sharpen tool sharpens soft edges in an image.

The Smudge tool smudges data in an image.

The Dodge tool lightens areas in an image.

The Burn tool darkens areas in an image.

The Sponge tool changes the color saturation of an area.

The pen tools draw and modify smooth-edged paths.

The type tools create type on an image.

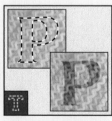

The type mask tools create a selection in the shape of type.

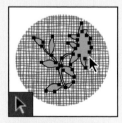

The path selection tools make shape or segment selections showing anchor points, direction lines, and direction points.

The shape tools and Line tool draw shapes and lines in a normal layer or shape layer.

The Custom Shape tool makes customized shapes selected from a custom shape list.

The Hand tool moves an image within its window.

The Rotate View tool turns the canvas for stylus painting and drawing.

The Zoom tool magnifies and reduces the view of an image.

Appendix: Keyboard shortcuts

Learning the shortcuts for tools and commands you use most often can save you time. Want to customize them? Choose Edit > Keyboard Shortcuts. While there, click Summarize to export a list updated with your own shortcuts.

Tools *Each group of tools in the Tools panel shares a shortcut. Press Shift+ the letter key repeatedly to cycle through hidden tools. This list is based on the Essentials workspace; other workspaces may change tool groupings and keyboard shortcuts, so if a shortcut isn't working for you, check which workspace is active.*

Tool	Shortcut	Tool	Shortcut
Move tool	V	Gradient tool	G
Artboard tool	V	Paint Bucket tool	G
Rectangular Marquee tool	M	3D Material Drop tool	G
Elliptical Marquee tool	M	Dodge tool	O
Lasso tool	L	Burn tool	O
Polygonal Lasso tool	L	Sponge tool	O
Magnetic Lasso tool	L	Pen tool	P
Quick Selection tool	W	Freeform Pen tool	P
Magic Wand tool	W	Horizontal Type tool	T
Eyedropper tool	I	Vertical Type tool	T
3D Material Eyedropper tool	I	Horizontal Type Mask tool	T
Color Sampler tool	I	Vertical Type Mask tool	T
Ruler tool	I	Path Selection tool	A
Note tool	I	Direct Selection tool	A
Count tool	I	Rectangle tool	U
Crop tool	C	Rounded Rectangle tool	U
Perspective Crop tool	C	Ellipse tool	U
Slice tool	C	Polygon tool	U
Slice Select tool	C	Line tool	U
Frame tool	K	Custom Shape tool	U
Spot Healing Brush tool	J	Hand tool	H
Healing Brush tool	J	Rotate View tool	R
Patch tool	J	Zoom tool	Z
Content-Aware Move tool	J	Default Foreground/Background Colors	D
Red Eye tool	J	Switch Foreground/Background Colors	X
Brush tool	B	Toggle Standard/Quick Mask Modes	Q
Pencil tool	B	Toggle Screen Modes	F
Color Replacement tool	B	Toggle Lock Transparent Pixels	/
Mixer Brush tool	B	Decrease Brush Size	[
Clone Stamp tool	S	Increase Brush Size	]
Pattern Stamp tool	S	Decrease Brush Hardness	{
History Brush tool	Y	Increase Brush Hardness	}
Art History Brush tool	Y	Previous Brush	,
Eraser tool	E	Next Brush	.
Background Eraser tool	E	First Brush	<
Magic Eraser tool	E	Last Brush	>

Application menus *These shortcuts are for Windows. For Mac, substitute Command for Ctrl and Option for Alt.*

File

New	Ctrl+N
Open	Ctrl+O
Browse in Bridge	Alt+Ctrl+O
Close	Ctrl+W
Close All	Alt+Ctrl+W
Close and Go to Bridge	Shift+Ctrl+W
Save	Ctrl+S
Save As	Shift+Ctrl+S or Alt+Ctrl+S
Export As (entire document)	Alt+Shift+Ctrl+W
Save for Web (Legacy)	Alt+Shift+Ctrl+S
Revert	F12
File Info	Alt+Shift+Ctrl+I
Print	Ctrl+P
Print One Copy	Alt+Shift+Ctrl+P
Exit/Quit	Ctrl+Q

Edit

Undo	Ctrl+Z
Redo	Shift+Ctrl+Z
Toggle Last State (of undo/redo)	Alt+Ctrl+Z
Fade	Shift+Ctrl+F
Cut	Ctrl+X or F2
Copy	Ctrl+C or F3
Copy Merged	Shift+Ctrl+C
Paste	Ctrl+V or F4
Paste Special > Paste in Place	Shift+Ctrl+V
Paste Special > Paste Into	Alt+Shift+Ctrl+V
Search	Ctrl+F
Fill	Shift+F5
Content-Aware Scale	Alt+Shift+Ctrl+C
Free Transform	Ctrl+T
Transform > Again	Shift+Ctrl+T
Color Settings	Shift+Ctrl+K
Keyboard Shortcuts	Alt+Shift+Ctrl+K
Menus	Alt+Shift+Ctrl+M
Preferences > General	Ctrl+K

Image

Adjustments >	
Levels	Ctrl+L
Curves	Ctrl+M
Hue/Saturation	Ctrl+U
Color Balance	Ctrl+B
Black & White	Alt+Shift+Ctrl+B
Invert	Ctrl+I
Desaturate	Shift+Ctrl+U
Auto Tone	Shift+Ctrl+L
Auto Contrast	Alt+Shift+Ctrl+L
Auto Color	Shift+Ctrl+B
Image Size	Alt+Ctrl+I
Canvas Size	Alt+Ctrl+C
Record Measurements	Shift+Ctrl+M

Layer

New > Layer	Shift+Ctrl+N
New > Layer via Copy	Ctrl+J
New > Layer via Cut	Shift+Ctrl+J
Quick Export	Shift+Ctrl+'
Export As (selected layers)	Alt-Shift+Ctrl+'
Create/Release Clipping Mask	Alt+Ctrl+G
Group Layers	Ctrl+G
Ungroup Layers	Shift+Ctrl+G
Hide Layers	Ctrl+,
Arrange >	
Bring to Front	Shift+Ctrl+]
Bring Forward	Ctrl+]
Send Backward	Ctrl+[
Send to Back	Shift+Ctrl+[
Lock Layers	Ctrl+/
Merge Down	Ctrl+E
Merge Visible	Shift+Ctrl+E

Select

All	Ctrl+A
Deselect	Ctrl+D
Reselect	Shift+Ctrl+D
Inverse	Shift+Ctrl+I or Shift+F7
All Layers	Alt+Ctrl+A
Find Layers	Alt+Shift+Ctrl+F
Select and Mask	Alt+Ctrl+R
Modify > Feather	Shift+F6

Filter

Last Filter	Alt+Ctrl+F (Windows), Control+Command+F (Mac)
Adaptive Wide Angle	Alt+Shift+Ctrl+A
Camera Raw Filter	Shift+Ctrl+A
Lens Correction	Shift+Ctrl+R
Liquify	Shift+Ctrl+X
Vanishing Point	Alt+Ctrl+V

3D

Show/Hide Polygons > Within Selection	Alt+Ctrl+X
Show/Hide Polygons > Reveal All	Alt+Shift+Ctrl+X
Render	Alt+Shift+Ctrl+R

View

Proof Colors	Ctrl+Y
Gamut Warning	Shift+Ctrl+Y
Zoom In	Ctrl++ or Ctrl+=
Zoom Out	Ctrl+-
Fit on Screen	Ctrl+0
100%	Ctrl+1 or Alt+Ctrl+0
Extras	Ctrl+H
Show > Target Path	Shift+Ctrl+H
Show > Grid	Ctrl+'
Show > Guides	Ctrl+;
Rulers	Ctrl+R
Snap	Shift+Ctrl+;
Lock Guides	Alt+Ctrl+;

Window

Actions	Alt+F9 or F9
Brush Settings	F5
Color	F6
Info	F8
Layers	F7

Help

Photoshop Help	F1

INDEX

Production Notes

Adobe Photoshop CC Classroom in a Book (2019 release) was created electronically using Adobe InDesign CC. Art was produced using Adobe InDesign, Adobe Illustrator, and Adobe Photoshop. The Myriad Pro and Warnock Pro OpenType families of typefaces were used throughout this book. For information about OpenType and Adobe fonts, visit www.adobe.com/type/opentype/.

References to company names in the lessons are for demonstration purposes only and are not intended to refer to any actual organization or person.

Images

Photographic images and illustrations are intended for use with the tutorials.

Lesson 4 pineapple and flower photography © Image Source, www.imagesource.com; ukulele image from Adobe Stock, stock.adobe.com

Team credits

The following individuals contributed to the development of *Adobe Photoshop CC Classroom in a Book (2019 release)*:

Project Manager: Anne-Marie Praetzel

Writer: Conrad Chavez

Illustrator and Compositor: David Van Ness

Copyeditor and Proofreader: Wendy Katz

Indexer: Conrad Chavez

Technical Reviewer: David Van Ness

Keystroker: Megan Ahearn

Cover design: Eddie Yuen

Interior design: Mimi Heft

Art Director: Andrew Faulkner

Designers: Megan Lee and Sky Yuen

Adobe Press Executive Editor: Laura Norman

Adobe Press Production Editor: Tracey Croom

Contributors

Jay Graham began his career designing and building custom homes. He has been a professional photographer for more than 25 years, with clients in the advertising, architectural, editorial, and travel industries. He contributed the "Pro Photo Workflow" tips in Lesson 5. www.jaygraham.com

Lisa Farrer is a photographer based in Marin County, CA. She contributed photography for Lesson 5.

Gawain Weaver has conserved and restored original works by artists ranging from Eadweard Muybridge to Man Ray, and from Ansel Adams to Cindy Sherman. He contributed to "Real World Photo Restoration" in Lesson 2. www.gawainweaver.com

Special Thanks

We offer our sincere thanks to Joel Baer, Russell Brown, Pete Falco, Rikk Flohr, Steve Guilhamet, Meredith Payne Stotzner, and Jeff Tranberry for their support and help with this project. We couldn't have done it without you!

The fastest, easiest, most comprehensive way to learn
Adobe Creative Cloud

Classroom in a Book®, the best-selling series of hands-on software training books, helps you learn the features of Adobe software quickly and easily.

The **Classroom in a Book** series offers what no other book or training program does—an official training series from Adobe Systems, developed with the support of Adobe product experts.

To see a complete list of our Classroom in a Book titles covering the 2019 release of Adobe Creative Cloud go to:

www.adobepress.com/cc2019

Adobe Photoshop CC Classroom in a Book (2019 release)
ISBN: 9780135261781

Adobe Illustrator CC Classroom in a Book (2019 release)
ISBN: 9780135262160

Adobe InDesign CC Classroom in a Book (2019 release)
ISBN: 9780135262153

Adobe Dreamweaver CC Classroom in a Book (2019 release)
ISBN: 9780135262146

Adobe Premiere Pro CC Classroom in a Book (2019 release)
ISBN: 9780135298893

Adobe Dimension CC Classroom in a Book (2019 release)
ISBN: 9780134863542

Adobe Audition CC Classroom in a Book, Second edition
ISBN: 9780135228326

Adobe After Effects CC Classroom in a Book (2019 release)
ISBN: 9780135298640

Adobe Animate CC Classroom in a Book (2019 release)
ISBN: 9780135298886

Adobe Lightroom CC Classroom in a Book (2019 release)
ISBN: 9780135298657

Adobe Photoshop Elements Classroom in a Book (2019 release)
ISBN: 9780135298657

Adobe**Press**